ULTRABLACK OF MUSIC

VOLUME 2

ULTRABLACK OF MUSIC

VOLUME 2

Achim Szepanski
&
Palais Sinclaire
(Eds.)

London, UK
Washington, DC, USA

First published by Zer0 Books, 2025
Zer0 Books is an imprint of Collective Ink Ltd.,
Unit 11, Shepperton House, 89 Shepperton Road, London, N1 3DF
office@collectiveinkbooks.com
www.collectiveinkbooks.com
www.zero-books.net

For distributor details and how to order, please visit the 'Ordering' section on our website.

Paperback ISBN: 978 1 80341 855 1
eBook ISBN: 978 1 80341 856 8
PCN: 2024942280

A CIP catalogue record for this book is available from the British Library.

Design credit(s): Lapiz Digital

UK: Printed and bound by CPI Group (UK) Ltd, Croydon, CR0 4YY
Printed in North America by CPI GPS partners

CONTENTS

EDITOR'S NOTE

It is with deep regret that Achim never saw the publication of this book. *Ultrablack of Music*, and "ultrablackness" in general, is a term which captures within its limits the discourse produced by Achim and his collaborators, in particular with Lain Iwakura and the cohort populating NON, the editorial project that, in many ways, functioned as the "underside" of Mille Plateaux; though underside is of course a funny term when talking about a möbius strip.

For me, Ultrablackness itself is not something that asks to be defined, nor placed in any discourse; it is simply the circle drawn around a psychotic mind-map of ideas that formed the scaffolding within which Mille Plateaux, the record label, was resurrected after years of hiatus. Due to the nature of Mille Plateaux, and Achim himself, it wasn't going to be enough to simply re-open the label; there had to be a reason to do so; more than a record label, Mille Plateaux, to borrow the language of Guattari, was a weapon against the symbolic, a monstrous war-machine that needs tracks, and tracks need a direction.

During the time that Mille Plateaux shut down, Achim opened NON, and the conversation continued. There was an opportunity in that moment to acknowledge how the game has changed, and how it is still changing. In *Ultrablack Volume 1*, Achim wrote, for example, that the glitch had been swallowed by contemporary art and had been rendered somewhat obsolete; just as with techno music in the period prior, experimental music was no longer, in and of itself, effective. I am not sure what the best language to speak of this in is, but something had been re-coded, something had been territorialized, rendered a part of the thing it was once negating.

In this way, this idea of Ultrablackness is not about saying that "things were better in my day" but rather about recognising that we are dealing with moving targets and that we are bogged down in the indeterminate trenches, fighting a war in which the parameters fluctuate wildly.

It is not just poetic to say that music is a really important and, arguably, fundamental aspect of human life, and I have personally argued in my own writings that many philosophers throughout history position music as a special case. In particular, I used to speak with Achim a lot about this sort of Nietzschean idea that music was the ultimate philosophical black-hole, that music is the ultimate negation (to what we could call hegemony). In that sense, *Ultrablack of Music* is the heart of the entire NON, Force-Inc, Mille Plateaux body.

It is therefore a shame that Achim would not see this book released, because it was his organization and his ideas that brought these people to write together. As the second editor, I did a lot of reading, copyediting, manuscript preparation—this kind of thing—but it was Achim who made this happen, and as I am for everything else he did for me, I am very grateful for his taking me seriously. I believe I speak for everyone in this book when I say that Achim was notorious for taking outsiders seriously, a deeply human gesture reflecting a friend who, while ever casting complex aspersions on the Universe, cared greatly for the world and its inhabitants.

— Palais Sinclaire

0. INTRODUCTION
In and Out of This World

By Jan Heintz

Intro-non-recursions

> "This is the price of seduction. The secret must not be broken, at the risk of the story's falling into banality."[1]

The profound allure of the hole, its gravitational pull, lies precisely in its unburdened existence. Behind its supposed emptiness is an infinite messiness which defies validation, eluding reason's ever so illuminating elaborations, i.e., ultimately escaping cognitive or sonic-fictional territorialisation.[2] These implications can be further

1 s. Baudrillard, Jean & Calle, Sophie (1988): *Suite vénitienne. Please follow me.* Seattle, p. 78–79.

2 This is a reoccurring theme in this anthology: s. Shipley: "I call them brains, but they're not the squishy walnut shapes you'd recognise. More a sticky fluid, one that ultrablackness is prone to smashing." [§1], or Palais Sinclaire: "'Ultrablack', as a way of separating *Black* from "black", is the framework through which music is discussed within this essay,

elucidated in relation to an ultrablack quantum sound/art theory, the way Achim Szepanski's and Jens Schröter's contributions bring to mind and are roughly sketched in this book:

> In quantum field theory, nothingness is by no means empty, but an infinite fullness, a dynamic of iterative opening that cannot be separated from matter. The vacuum is infinitely full of the virtuality of everything that ever was, what is and whatever will be.[3]

Further still, the hole requires no external affirmation. It needs no exhibition or verification, is "self-evident", yet arcane in its own reality.

To measure a hole is to unfold the surround of its devouring force—the very boundaries encircling and belying it: today's catastrophisms of smooth hyper-circulation, reversibility/interchangeability of cancerously proliferating signs without end, nudged by the "structural law of value and equivalence",[4] eminently resulting in the mad-extractive voraciousness of a system imploding and sucking out the last remnants of the forces of the real, to coronate the vulgar corpse of "white pornographic hyperreality" to the total domination of everything.[5]

Given these zombifying dynamics of the global capitalist death machine, its implicit torture wheel of eternal return of the formulaic same, might this allow us to put into perspective

---

and the purpose of discussing music in this way is, by and large, an experiment […] If music is Ultrablack, it is untellable: it's a *Secret*" [§6], or Priest: "reposes fitfully in the crowned anarchy of its own contradiction" [§13].

3 s. §3 (Szepanski, A.) and §4 (Schröter, J.) respectively in this anthology.

4 Baudrillard, J. (1993) *Symbolic Exchange and Death*. London: SAGE, p. 8.

5 s. Szepanski, A. (2024), *In the Delirium Of The Simulation: Baudrillard Revisited.* Nicosia/Berlin: Becoming/NON, p. 97.

Ultrablackness' ultimate in-disposability, in-exchangeability, and refusal-as-activated-negativity, be it in theory, sound, and politics, by gauging anew its potential to grind to a halt and take capital's mad white dynamism off its hinges, to seduce it into its own demise, and pestering it with "scorched-earth strategies … destroying both the logic and logistics of the system"?[6]

Can our nihilarious critterness of ultrablack opacity reside in it, being gifted its abysmal generative force, all while maintaining its enigmatic secrecy, without betraying, selling it out, or depraving it to the insolent horror of bad productivism, in form of a "stupid underground" (Paul de Mann),[7] to become the "next new big thing"—but sharpen fatal strategies against the evermore politically dubious complicity of culture industry *tout court*, against the corporate, and against the teeth-pulling art-world simulacrum?

Non-General-Intellect's Assaults on Digital Non-Music

The debut instalment of Ultrablackness of Music,[8] released four years ago (Szepanski, 2020) by *Mille Plateaux/Force Inc.*, beckoned forth a constellation and network of highly diverse, international contributors, ranging from philosophers, theoreticians, or (sound) artists[9] alike. Back then, it was a coming-to-terms with the question of what French philosopher François Laruelle once coined "irreducible duality", i.e., the question of music/sound/sonic-fictions on

6 s. Sbordoni, A. [§12].
7 s. Mann, Paul (1995): Stupid Undergrounds. Virginia.
8 It is accompanied by a sonic-fictional arsenal as well.
9 Jan Heintz, Frédéric Neyrat, Achim Szepanski, Holger Schulze, Zafer Aracagök, Shintaro Miyazaki, Gerriet K. Sharma, Txgen Meyer, Taylor Adkins & Joseph Weissman, Bernd Herzogenrath, Corry Shores & Melike Başak Yalçin, Algorithmic Committee, Jose Rosales, Stefan Paulus, Marcus Schmickler & Julian Rohrhuber, Thomas Brinkmann, Thomas Köner, Alessio Kolioulis, Benjamin Noys, Lain Iwakura.

the one hand, and theoretisations, conceptualisations of an alien, ultrablack non-frequency-music and its politics on the other hand:

> One is always somehow in the relationship between music and theory. I believe that we must view this relationship as follows: Theorists and musicians do not exchange ideas or reflect upon each other; instead, they lose their distance precisely when they establish a direct sense of the Real (something that is given but simultaneously remains elusive, escapes, or is akin to noise). The theorist who writes sonic fictions is not a mere translator or chronicler of music. In a certain sense, the theorist must become a clone of a suspended or non-mimetic relationship between music and theory. There is no exchange, no reversibility, and no equivalence to be reported between theory and music. Instead, there exists the irreducibility of theory and the sonic. Exchange, correspondence, and trace are avoided. What Kodwo Eshun masterfully demonstrates—theory as music, where one music should correspond to theory—is precisely what is avoided. A strict relationship between theory and music exists only insofar as both elements overlap with each other and are simultaneously irreducible.[10]

Therefore, the anthology marshalled its forces and forged an arsenal and anti-apparatus to critique and assail various targets. It included especially the rampant metastasis of contemporary *Muzak*'s infrastructural nexus with its gratis and free-delivered trash sociality and standard forms of sonic ennui, all the while exploring a wide range of topics in the traversal of the multiplicity of its assaults and viral

10 For a nuanced take on the relationship between sound and theory, s. Szepanski, Achim (2020): "Ultra-Blackness in Music. A Non-Mixology", in: *Ultrablack of Music Vol. 1.* See also: Achim Szepanski and Lain Iwakura in an interview with FAZEmag 113/07.21: https://www.fazemag.de/mille-plateaux-der-zustand-des-ungeformten/ (translated by me).

deployments: inhuman rhythmights, spectral music, drone, post-pop, rhythm, glitch, sonic thanaticism, counter-raving, etc.

In a similar vein, Ultrablack of Music Vol. 2 delves deeper into previously explored themes and issues while also venturing into fairly uncharted territories and generating new ravishing armouries and insights along the way. These include quantum aesthetics/non-music, politics-of-non-movements, the intersection of torture and music, sonic decay and disappearance, disambient sounds, hypergestures, the chaosmotechnical undercommon practices of hallucinogenic ritualised music, chthonic monochords and deep-space sound, sonification (of the non-sonic, e.g., of finance), and hyper- and ultranaturalist sonic epistemologies.

Double Vortexes Internality

Ultrablackness-in-cybernonhumanimality, Cybernonhumanimality-in-Ultrablackness.

> *"Negation, from the very beginning, always a line in the sand. A disintegration, coming apart and to come undone. De-sonance, not resonance.*
>
> A being together in categorial uncanniness, an interplay of the refusal of what has been refused, the undercommon apositionality, a place from which emerges neither self-consciousness nor knowledge of the other but an improvisation that proceeds from somewhere on the other side of an unasked question.
>
> Ultrablackness is a determining force. The outside folding in. Background noise of the thermodynamic disequilibrium. An indifferent un-groundedness, opaque like a heterogeneous mixture or transparent like see-through fluids. Not to be differentiated, but the 0 that defines 1.
>
> Ultrablackness therefore is not to be confused with the void—emptiness—but is intrinsically messy. Black noise, unlike the searing buzz of white noise, is barely audible. Black noise traces the quiver of things we fail to perceive.

> Ultrablack—blacker than black[11]—denotes practices of negation, deconstruction, non-philosophy, pessimism and nihilism, heterogeneity, disintegration, queering, noise, insurrection, etc. It is a kind of disaster studies, (un)learning under the starless sky, an act that breaks down the formal structures of space and time…"[12]

There will never be guarantees, no model to get out of capital's thanaticist stupor and its spiraling vice, just end-games of like-minded conspiracists as fragile-precious real-force.

At first sight, cryptic anomalies camouflage in poetical implausibility, accentuating its queerness and oddity while dooming human superiority to endless mortification. Sonic-fictions paradoxically blending ferality, light-footed bulkiness, and subversive sweetness to adumbrate Ultrablack's non-anticipatable modicum against the genealised terror of the 'over': capital's vampirism but cloned, stolen, cannibalised, re-appropriated.

---

11 s. "Shooting into this deeper and deeper blackness. Until suddenly there was a sense of floating in this liquid blackness. The only way we have to describe it in our language was it was the ultimate blackness, black beyond black. And then I became really aware that somewhere within this ultimate black were these two shiny, slightly pointed, almost insectoid eyes" (Genesis P-Orridge, 2010: 330–340). Maybe P-Orridge mistook the "insectoid eyes" for the tip points of fangs…

12 Lain Iwakura's (organiser) accompanying text to Mille Plateaux's NON-ference in Graz (Austria) in 2023 at Forum Stadtpark and Dom im Berg was a weekend full of lectures, workshops, concerts, screenings, installations, and DJ sets, offering space to unsound practices. Participants included: Achim Szepanski, Cristian Vogel, Marko Ciciliani, John-Robin Bold, Jeronimo Voss, Polymnia, Steroist, Paul Ruben, Automatisme, Tom Lönnqvist, Dmstfctn, Katharina Bévand, Jan Heintz, Becoming.press, Reza Kellner, Martin Stiehl, Lino Leum, Mattin, Uto Pixel, Palais Sinclaire, Paul Wolff, Oto Moto, Andrea Taeggi aka Gondwana, Sukkube, Sun People, Ibrahim Alfa, Marco Simioni, Darko Vukic, Miasma666, cipp0 and many more.

Flashing fangs of resistance by night in form of cruel love—catching, embracing, and unmaking you and the surround into something more hostile and repugnant, feasting on the corpse of our futurelessness.

Injecting imperatives of sweet, true-impoverished life, opaque and uncaptured in captivity-to-end, like hyperpotent acid dripped into your sour daily wretchedness-in-the-making, dissolving you in the abyssal awe glowing in the "still-there" of the "after"—of the most improbable world to come.

Dumped into the terrible wealth of this world and its annihilatory madness, your deafer-than-dead jouissance informs and breeds moonlit No's, x-ed-out, launched bafflements, as spells of your refusal vamped up out of the rubbles of torn humanity's hope.

Ultrablackness is this hole creating an opening in the very heart of things, giving us not something to just *listen to, sonically experiment with or* think *about*—but to non-think this world *through to the end.*

Unsatisfying by standard measures ultrablack sound-fictions, coiling their way out into the darkest night of the universe, launch a delinquent sublimity's laughter which seduces and buries this world from inside out.

References

Baudrillard, J. & Calle, S. (1988) *Suite vénitienne/Please follow me*. Seattle: Bay Press.

Baudrillard, J. (1993) *Symbolic Exchange and Death*. London: SAGE.

P-Orridge, G. (2010) *Thee Psychick Bible: Thee Apocryphal Scriptures ov Genesis Breyer P-Orridge and thee Third Mind ov thee Temple ov Psychick Youth*. Port Townsend.

Szepanski, A. (2020) "Ultra-Blackness in Music. A Non-Mixology", in Szepanski, A. (ed.) *Ultrablack of Music: Volume 1*, Frankfurt: NON.

—. (2024): *In the Delirium Of The Simulation: Baudrillard Revisited.* Nicosia/Berlin: Becoming/NON

Mann, P. (1995) *Stupid Undergrounds*. Virginia: Virginia University Press.

Blasting rays of resistance by night in bursts of cruel love—catching, embracing, and unmaking you and the surround into something more hostile and repugnant; feasting on the corpse of our humanness.

Injecting imperatives of severe, more impoverished life, opaque and unexplained in an inability to end, like hyperpotent acid dropped into your sour daily architectures in the making, dissolving you in a psychical awe glowing in the "still there" of the "after"—of the most improbable world to come.

Dumped into the terrible wealth of this world and its annihilatory madness, your dead-than-dead, immiserable "efforts" and breaths inhabit being's cut-out, launched bafflement, as spells of your ethereal stumped up out of the rubbles of continuum unto its hope.

Ultrablackness is this sole creating an opening in the very heart of things, giving us not something to just *learn or critically reconstruct or think about*—but *to non-think this world enough to free it*.

Unsurviving the standard measure, ultrablack sound-artifices coiling their way out into the darkest night of the universe, launch a delinquent revolutionary laughter which seduces and pulses all world from inside out.

REFERENCES

[illegible] (1988) [illegible]. New York: [illegible].

[illegible] (2013) [illegible]. London: [illegible].

[illegible] (2016) [illegible]. Port Townsend: [illegible].

[illegible]

[illegible] (2020) [illegible]. Berlin: [illegible].

Mann, P. (1999) [illegible] University Press.

I. NIHILARIOUS CREATURES OF THE BLACK TRANSPARENCY

By Gary J. Shipley

How bad can it be if I can't even imagine it?
Worse, much worse.

The windows don't open. A precaution to stop them falling out prevents me falling in. I can hang in this fucking shitstorm of black hail, of black lightning, of black sleet, till my black beard turns grey, turns colourless, till the fucking night has refused to stop.

I bite broken necks through open windows. The same fucking windows that don't open. I'm thin and black and thin again. I swallow glass. I swallow glass vials full of blood. I push my piss inside the bones and cling to scenery. The night smashes us all into white mouths, foul winds, laughter crude like ulcer gunk.

It's forever since, and more of it. The windows never open and the blood is always blacker than what had been blackest to that point. We blow the heads off to get at the kinds of neck we like. The spines are so chewy and white and unclean. The fluids tickle going down. Our teeth as long as fingers drip like the windows of humid rooms lit with warm lights and giant fictions. The news shoots children in the head. All their dreams spurt out. We drink them to feel the overwhelming fucking astonishment.

We clench against each other in the dark. Our vaguely human forms are less than vaguely disgusting, in anything less than blackness. The whitest whites are transparencies, an energetic scribble of veins showing up, the colours, the reds and blues, to us the sound that food makes, nothing more.

Because all this began someplace, we got the urge to kill. We'd do it to ourselves if we could. The origins of humans—larval madness, limbless-like—and now this. We put our hands to work. The nails are black, grown long. We dig through necks.

The ultrablack made sick turns grey. Sick, we become easier to see, easier to shoot. The bullets don't kill, but they make us sicker, and make us easier for more bullets.

We laugh a noise so black it makes nocturnes sound like fucking sunlight.

Our schizophrenia has so many copies it's a stable pattern. The only sanity we have. The meat of what it means for us to think. The fucking stinking meat. Born from a white cunt, like a black bomb.

Morbid fears became morbid ecstasies. Consciousness bloomed like blood in clear water. The more it absorbs, the more we feed from it. Our brains are black holes. We get everywhere. We were the outside we couldn't get outside of. We ravaged paradise and now it comes for us.

We stand upright after feeding and sweat. Sometimes, because it's joyful, we puke. We consume it again as a way of smiling in the direction of some darkest point.

Our teeth, being finger-like, can be articulated. How black we are, cannot, and it's all we ever do.

We are free to do anything. Mortality is no risk, it's not even a thing. We eat from the silly, happy bodies. They know only the excesses of their own limitations. Their brains can be made to look like clouds on sticks. We have forgotten how to cringe.

We spent so long killing ourselves we made it impossible for future generations. If we try now, it's as the punchline to a joke we all share. Our veins don't open anymore. Our heads won't come apart inhaling shotguns.

If I have a soul, it's an oily, over-lubricated indifference.

We time-travel what has become timeless. We can fall forever. There is literally nothing to stop us.

We are terrorists without a cause. All we want is for nothing to have ever happened.

They say they suffer, but how can we believe them? They are tasteless like life never touched them. Their tastelessness is exactly the taste we crave. The absence of flavour is the ultimate delicacy. If we sleep on our backs and dream of feeding, we are prone to drowning on our own saliva. The dreams are more like intersecting swarms of black wasps than dreams. The drowning isn't drowning so much as coming to, breathing someone else's blood.

At least when you're anxious you know you can still lie to yourself. They have no conception of how easy life has been made for them. It's as well we can fuck them and eat them, or else we might be tempted to really do them harm.

Over and over again is our skin reminding us how a sly remark can promise nonexistence.

We make the tiniest particle flinch. Our improbability offends wave functionality, reduces its predictive prowess to a black particulate mist.

I can fuck holes into humans with nothing more than a single unformulated doubt. Their blackness pours free where we can see it. We throw them through windows so we can fuck the breakages. It's so easy it only skirts pleasure. They plead as if they know what pain is, and that there exists some way of making it stop.

Our joy makes a heartfelt wailing sound.

Our drug of choice is every orgasm retracted and boiled slowly into the inverse of all that. Our drug of choice is thus theoretical. Sometimes we make do with mainlining gallbladder secretions from suitably prepared humans into our eyeballs. The high is likened to cancer cancerising, the eating thereof, or to babies decomposing in the womb.

We were criminals, the worst, but the crime went away. Our methods weren't known, our effects splattered all over the fucking show. It's a crime to not care. Apparently, you can desecrate a desecration. Our disguise is no disguise at all. Our perfume is inexplicable to noses everywhere. We didn't kill people so much as hoover up their remains. Our definitions weren't the same. The rank materials for which they still attested love, or so they would have us believe. This phlegm we drink is drawn up from environs outside comprehension, not another universe as such, but the blackest pool you can't imagine.

We gave up before we started. We impersonate needs so we can impersonate the pleasure we might get from so many implosions at once.

Some have said they've seen us: aphids the size of cats in their ornamental gardens. Some have said the words we spoke weren't language, or else language and nothing else. All said, we were so black there was no possible colour we didn't contain, and so we consume—except the colour we were, which was impossible, of course, and nobody believed in it.

When you're this sad you live forever without trying.

When life is devoid of all use, what can death do?

Our lungs are black from breathing all the burning hair. To watch someone's hair burn is fucking mesmerising. It's what we do as sodomites, when the requisite vigour deserts us. There is no requirement that you have a penis; you can use anything. But the effort, the effort to have the desire, already its own echo, ugh: we destroy because inertia can't exist on its own.

We kind of threw a lot of well-dressed white women down large flights of stairs. Some were bleeding from the head when we sodomised them. The little ones put bugs in their mouths to stop them trying to sing. The syntax of our arguments confused how happy they once were.

It's no longer a case of disappointment. Who can even recall enthusiasms and rage? To smirk the way we smirk, like silent music, is unnatural. We'd have to want more from our abstractions than they can offer. The situation doesn't arise.

We got outside despair, all the better to feed off it.

Insatiability is why there are histories. We are neither sated nor insatiable. We are immune to direction. Our bodies are black, our traces transparent.

I threw myself up.

Death is way too concrete for things like us. We imagine a world in order to see death, touch it—a state for creatures that deserve it. Done right, it can remind them they're alive long after it's too late.

We are indiscriminate, honest. Their prayers are all synonyms. We would answer them, but they're not really questions.

What if I told you I've never once lost my way in the dark?

We're from the fucking future, so fucked, so you're yet to even grasp the things we're going to do. Your language doesn't have room for them. Our ingenuities are wasted on you. We are restrained by how rudimentary your pain is. The complexities of a torture cannot outstrip the complexities of its victim—not without squandering the excess.

All humans are ugly to us, even the beautiful ones. We are kind of human too: distant cousins from someplace else. Our respiration: bile songs. They don't so much hear us as get sick.

My black cunt has swallowed entire ecospheres. Babies go in, the whitest bones fall out.

We are so sweet, molasses cute from how we process blood. The sky is an elaborate farce; we see straight through it. Refined agony as music. We take it outside noise. The sound of ourselves makes us cum. The cum is blacker than the inside of a face.

We are beautiful because we never end. Our ugliest thoughts, and they're all ugly, are way too fucking gorgeous for standard human vision. We went wrong somewhere, and we kept on going, refusing to expire.

There's nothing more or less meaningful than when we chew all the flesh off someone's legs and leave the rest. When we remove a face in a series of bites and throw it up and move on. When at dusk injured babies are left at the bottoms of suburban gardens for the foxes to eat.

Just as you can't torture a chicken with the absurdity of its existence, we are similarly limited in the ways we can make humans suffer. Might fuck them with a momentary cognisance that'd smash their brains to bits. A split-second of the kind of terror no human ever had. We descended from the same, the ones that put the pieces back, this new configuration. We the refined models of that panicking to live. We the saddest, most exquisite music. And them fuckers all deaf.

They are like babies teething on pillows all their lives. Never finding the zip. Never suspecting.

Better never to have lived: if only you knew.

We've tried so many times to bring them on, but these gormless shits have not got the aptitude. It's why we gnaw through their necks till the heads come off. I'd say it was frustration if we cared.

Our message is so much more than their diseases.

They have dismissive names for our symphonies like tinnitus.

What does get through manifests itself in physical and mental infirmities that are an insult to their origins. Embarrassing translations of what it is we spend our hours trying to convey. Infections made from only the most filtered versions. Disorders as of a passing blink of the nightmare they could have. Reciting Julius Bahnsen to a bunch of amoebae gives an inkling without coming close. It's pointless, ridiculous, but what else do we live for?

We are lecherous for the purest minds. But babies don't know they're being fucked.

For skinless pitch we sure hold a nice shape. A shapeless shape. Our skin got so thick and deep it wasn't skin anymore.

Our ear-worms were more like snakes, fucking anaconda, swallowed them whole and all they knew was how they suddenly went blind. Got deafer, heard themselves disappear into a darkness they did not own or understand—but by which they were both owned and understood and found less than insignificant (which is a thing, you'd be surprised). Fucking humans, fucking pabulum. The emotions sick-making, and how we love being sick.

If we didn't know how they're all the wrong planet, we'd have suspected we'd ended up there.

We see in the dark, all of it. Not ourselves. We're under lights, burnt up. It's not cannibalism if you don't identify. Is there anything more primitive than a smile that hasn't been processed into something else—a sneer? Our smiles are so processed, it's not possible to ascertain their origins, their intent, their content, their resemblance to anything a mouth might do for the sake of expressing a state that can be thought of as in any way felt.

Your approximations of apanthropy aren't convincing anyone. You retain the idea of an exclusion having taken place. You do not see the basic fucking truth: you invented human company, in order to avoid it. The real feat is to see through it, not to pretend there's something there that you can do without. You cannot begin to imagine what it is to face anything alone: you were formed in crowds and counterfactuals and theoretical juxtapositions of bodies in which the world itself conspires and from which no one is ever totally missing.

They're funny to watch, the way they still believe they can go somewhere.

Their pain became an experiment in sound. Mouths wide open, all those silent afternoons coming out. Endless digressions on the one sigh. Sometimes the children will hum along to us. They don't know they are doing it. To them, it feels like suffering, which to us is the finest pleasure the world can give back. An infant clawing at themselves, exposing blood, is the clearest return on our investment. Their pain—those young enough, susceptible enough—is the only reflection we have.

I was eating the head of the husband when the wife came in. We looked at each other, but she didn't see me. She was wearing beige leggings and she wet herself. I watched the stain spread and tried not to laugh. (Sometimes the noise will enter the room and ruin the effect.) When I bit chunks out of her buttocks, she was still too numb to react in the standard human ways. I liked her. She was fun. I tore her neck out and found little bits of food inside. I stretched the skin from her stomach right up over her head. I was vaguely amused. It wasn't anything much. I'm tired. Always tired, all of us. Cursed though, cursed to overcome it—over and over. The bits of food though, kind of gross.

The woman had a long plait down her back. I cut it off and used it to strangle the dog. That was boring. I think the dog could see me. It wasn't even what I wanted.

It's bad manners to talk using the mouths of real people, but we do it all the time. They are so confused when it happens. They suspect brain tumours. And the things we say…

I call them real people because they are born into this shit. Their reality is flimsy, of course. The suicidal ones are realer, but we tend to leave them alone. We can see their insides are starting to turn black. Their eyes contain a glimmer of some far-off music.

There is something inside of us, blacker even than we are, so black it's like a whole other colour. It has disgusting wings. It flies about inside the areas we seem to occupy. Its gangling legs pulsate and collide and generate the faintest friction-noise of fruit flies fucking in an eardrum.

To be useless is nothing more than embodying life. To be deliberately useless is to make a play for art. To be what we are, unchecked ketone bodies in the blood of the universe, is to corrode all notion of use, and so uselessness. It's no more reliance on the opposing force, or shit set on fire in drums in Vietnam because you wiped the sweat from your face and your face came off and, with it stuck to your hands, it didn't seem decent to go back to your former condescension of waste, or touching yourself like that. Kurtz went too far on the Congo because there was nowhere for him to go, because he couldn't go too far, because he'd reached a limit he could no more accept than transcend.

Did he glimpse us, hear us, try to ingratiate himself via the heads he put on sticks?

The sound you might hear is our enthusiastic snoring.

We are not afraid of light. It's sustenance. It's the fun we have. How can we rescue hippos frolicking in the (poisoned) river? How can we rescue you from the turds out of which you built your paradise? When we try, do we try? Our interventions must seem messy and cruel. Meat drips into tin bowls. When we stand up, our postures are soft. We squeeze an already broken human body to make new words come out. Nobody's around to thank us but the sounds we make. And the sounds we make. The sounds we shake and squeeze and tear from things, because we sometimes call them things, seem a shriek inside, but we are outside and mostly only hear the sweetness we intend.

As it goes, without death, we are pursued by greatness. It's fucking brutal. We succumb to things that, in this language, I cannot explain, and in another you would not understand. It's the constipation of so many generations. The greatness has nothing to do with pleasure, very little does. Foetuses spared life, when we can do that, are sometimes close enough for us to feel an approximate sensation.

They can sometimes hear our voices as growling. They ask each other who is making this noise, and no one is. The places in their rooms without light are black, but we are blacker still—the darkness hidden behind the dark. Imagine a jaguar so black it wasn't there, even when it ripped your throat out. Even as we pull you apart, we are not there. Ours is a cursed nonexistence, in being forced to exist.

We are almost as inscrutable to ourselves as we are to you—more so in some respects; more so because what for you is ignorance is for us an excruciating wonder. But like you we only act because the alternative is the unceasing gibberish of the universe, and more blackness than even we can clench against. To pretend a face when all there is to it is the pretence itself, when what there is besides is facelessness: the apex of sickening predicaments, and powerless to choose otherwise, or to refrain from trying. I would say more but my voice would go wrong.

Your breathing sounds to us like retching.

A ravenous itch to get something out that will never surface and isn't inside.

Because our teeth are so long and so sharp and so like fingers, we get to play with our food. And the food is less food than the play itself. Confronted with so many real people, what else is there to do? The sheerest boredom doesn't come close. If we talk in what sounds to you like squawks and screeches, it's because we've disappeared into a jungle of unbroken darkness, and every noise we make here is poetry. We are at least spared the light we want, until we are not.

You want to know how hideous it is: reality is everywhere—even in our illusions.

Your word 'escape' can only be translated as a snort of bleak amusement.

When we can, we climb up inside the filthiest anuses, the most impacted bowels, and catch our breath. Your painful flatulence is our relief. You have no fucking idea; the ideas are all ours.

There is always one of us around. Hundreds of people go missing every day, thousands every week, and they never come back. Though our impact is not insignificant, we are only responsible for less than half that amount. The ones we process all end up in the same place. I can't tell you. The things done, the why, what would you fucking know? Rest assured they're easy enough to hide. And we keep them alive, sort of. But the sounds we elicit, the fucking sounds, the kind of mercurial music none of you are made for. There's no movement as such, but you could say we dance. We are transported and cannot help ourselves. What might seem ugly is a beauty exceeding human comprehension. The blackest noise. Inside it, we see ourselves. A need we share with you. That much you can get your heads around. And then, of course, the as-yet-unexplored pliability of human heads has something to do with what I'm failing to explain.

In this ultra-fucking-black a brain is smashed to pieces at any time, only to reform again. I call them brains, but they're not the squishy walnut shapes you'd recognise. More a sticky fluid, one that ultrablackness is prone to smashing. We spent our lives and this is what we got in return. As outcasts, we gargle wasps of an infinitely darker stripe, nonpareil songbirds lifted so far from your shitty dreams you'll hear us only in the seconds as you die.

We are nihilarious creatures of the black transparency. We're so fucked our worst nightmares are already real and have deteriorated exponentially in the time it takes to have them. The blackness we're in, and are, is irreversibly tangled. Horror is indistinguishable from just about everything. Any divergence is a glitch we follow in circles that terrorise too perfectly: perpetual motion sickness for the equivalent machine.

However many prostitutes you kill in a row doesn't add up. You're crawling around not killing yourself. You're crawling around killing yourself only in kind. It seems remarkable because extreme pettiness always does. If you could actually fuck things to death that aren't very young girls, or tiny mammals or whatever, maybe then you'd reconcile yourself to this human life of yours.

Madness is somewhere to go. We are all places, no places: we can't go mad—again.

We vindictively esteem the way you can so confidently occupy some sloppy pocket of space and time and yet cannot grok the basic tenets of experiential uncertainty. We love how stupidly you improve through deterioration, and how it never dawns. Evasion produces ghosts; ghosts produce diseases they can die of.

We have lived all your lives and have forgotten nothing. We remember when you were new and no less sallow than you are today. Your perfections hideous, as they always are. Because they are necessarily finished. Because they are lies. Because they induce a browbeaten silence—and/or the flawless sequences of hell.

We are the wrong way round. We were dead before we were alive. Because we are illogical, inconsistent, whatever, we fall to the top, we fart symphonies, we swallow vomit. We progress backwards, exceeding the beginning. We are the realest unrealities. Our belonging is inappropriate, our improprieties proper.

You thought meaninglessness was worse than you could imagine, so you lived it instead.

We're not picky; we can chew you out both ways. We're dead inside for a laugh. The way you would crush a baby's head, for instance, might be thought of as libidinal or perhaps psychotic; whereas for us, that's just a consequence of real-world unease with simple situational dynamics. We both know and don't know what the fuck you're talking about.

If we're greedy, it's not because we want more of anything, or less, but because there is such a thing as pretending too hard, and we want to see where it goes.

Our soft underbelly has rotted out. White mould. Spores the size of grapes. Shit-stained teeth. Smile please! Smile please! Shit-eating grins. Mushing faces into funny new shapes. So fucking pissed on being so almost dead. So flying over our own heads. The indestructible sound of being fatally wounded and never succumbing. The smell of cigarettes extinguished in eyes converted into noise. We take precautions against ever making what you call decisions. We've been caught out before. We're built for pain but we prefer music.

We dress in every camera angle at once: it's exhausting.

It's a windup how we're so full of how desolate we are.

Disappointment's for thumbsuckers. We died from far less. We died because we didn't die. We died because pleasure wouldn't leave us alone. We were haunted by it. We thought better to haunt than be haunted. And then that wasn't what happened. What happened convinced us of a groundlessness we'd never considered. It's been a long time and only all these different things have happened—over and over.

I talk about the destruction and consumption of bodies because I'm still working out how best to convey something, a horror of utter wonderment and profoundly true, that I told myself without knowing what it meant. I'm working with the materials I have, and disgust gets in the way.

In the dark—of it, from it—we send you signs of our enthused indifference. Our standout homogeneity, our glitzy camouflage, becomes this strange acquaintance. A young girl sat choking on a severed foot for several days. The nails were painted a bright pink. Although the sun was out and vivid, the sky was black. There wasn't enough alcohol to stop it. We sent you news, but you laughed at the wrong places.

Don't decry pain if you want a future. We had no such ambitions, and look where we ended up.

I'm sorry to say this, but you too might spring to life at any moment. If you understand me, shake your head. Keep shaking it till your neck breaks, but don't stop. You said you wanted to think again like it meant something. The world can gape without it being an invitation.

To be at peace is to have never lived. The dead do not find peace; they find a hole to crawl into. We found something else, and it crawled into us.

Accept nothing, least of all yourself.

Every house is a madhouse. A construct to compartmentalise a wave, a place to be yourself: delusions one inside the other. There are no houses out here, no madness—only endless black concatenation, protagonist surrender, inverted sameness, a room without walls, floor, or ceiling, merely insinuating space.

Our screams as useless as money: a bonfire of profanities, all heat no light.

We gave you words you can't pronounce to fuck your mouth, to make your tongue fall out. You never noticed because this way of speaking is so common. You regurgitate nothing but bones, perhaps feathers, the flesh all gone. Your tongue has been eaten and supplanted by some other creature. It takes more resolve than any of you possess to relinquish something you never had.

In the dark we appear to merge, but it is only appearance. There is still in place a thing that keeps us apart. Our faceless faces, our withered desires, the slippery non- of this existence: all a kind of taunt. We are not ourselves and we are not each other, but are instead some third thing playing at identity: a counterfactual belonging, an abyss of artificial nerve endings and sunless scatterings.

If we are excretions, then excretions from what? Sources are so precariously averred, they're beneath us. We are not miraculous anymore. We can say that, at least. But then you'd probably envy us our miserabilist ecstasy, and we wonder. For even we are prone to briefly ignoring the expanse we saw but had no part in.

All life inside this ultradark is a kind of insomnia. More so than the world. More so than your basic requirement that all wakefulness be supplemented by its opposite, or else, depending on your disposition, supplanted by it. More than that. What I'm getting at is an insomnia of sleep itself—a contaminated respite, a red-eyed dream of what you imagined sleep would be, and once was.

The misery of memory and the weariness of hope. The chaos of this unwanted focus, this bleary-eyed acuity. You've barely glimpsed it. If you touched it, you'd die from madness. You'd die from madness in an instant. That you cannot grasp this, and so cannot really believe it, is the problem we face, the conversational impasse we're at.

We found ourselves excited by boredom. That's how it started. Luxurious and tortuous, we spun helplessly on the spot. Everything blurring under our focus. We came to appreciate the muddiness of it all, the vitality of despair. The lights went out and we could see in the dark. We saw what was missing, the gaps between things, a sprawling rathole inside the images we'd seen. We might have tried to go backwards, but the performative pressure would have crushed us. The fear and panic destroyed us instead, so we became the hypothetical survivors of such an event.

I imagine our eyes look glassy and black, like thousand-year eggs. I imagine that whatever is reflected in them never escapes. I imagine no difference between what you think of as the apocalypse and us catching sight of ourselves.

Everything we do is impetuous, which is not to say it isn't deliberate. It takes a controlled recklessness to unmake humans like wild animals, when we are neither. Our singing, our music will help tear you to pieces. The sound will snatch your limbs away. You'll think it a crude sublime, but you're less than spiders. If only you knew how insanely ugly you are. If only you knew how all human trauma can be ironic, without ceasing to be painful.

Immortality was one of the biggest lies, but death was by far the greater untruth.

The spectacle of heaven is nowhere to-be-seen. Without these hyphens, what would I be? A writer of lamentations? Worse: a writer of lamentations whose concerns it might be possible to resolve.

Apparently, the world I see is due to age-related scarring in the lenses of my eyes. There's similar scarring too, I'm told, in the canals inside my ears. And yet nobody knows, or if they do, they will not say which one scar represents the cruellest cut, or whether or not it is yet to arrive.

Does anyone still want this to be real? What a sickly question to have to ask, and to receive no answer. I knew there would be long-term effects of that much light: seeing no way round it, and us happening all at once. I had a spy-hole where I'd rest my eyes, and beyond it this darkened room. And though I looked for it I could see it by the way. And there were exorbitant stretches of time before I realised I was looking out again, and I could see others like me in the dark, black shapes against a black background, and how looking for nowhere in particular we'd come to the wrong place.

I used to think this disjuncture between imagination and reality was all that was left of me. Like everyone else, I used my brain the way we think there's always a tomorrow.

The world is a poisoned placenta. It's teargas. Out here, it's this windowpane you're looking through, and it's at least as thick as the entire universe.

An old nurse is talking about all the painfully small preterm babies she's seen. I am listening because no one else is talking and there is nowhere else to sit. Each one she mentions sounds sicklier than the last. Her voice is shrill like someone ought to do something.

Language is excrement. My breath stinks. Everybody's breath stinks. The lagoon I'm in is black and glossy. The water is not deeper than it looks. It's not even water. Sentences conspire to wring necks. I used to talk like the words were coming out.

You sleep, you wake up, and you quickly forget you are not talking to real people. Instead of proclaiming yourself dead, you acclimatised yourself.

We are zombie stars, stripped of light, exploding without dying.

The rain is thick like jam and black. It isn't rain you can hear as it lands. It isn't rain as such. There is nowhere decided upon for it to fall. There is no picture that isn't an impossibility of some sort.

A black dog eats a dead swimmer. It eats her bikini. The crests of foam are black. The sand is black. The sunglasses are decorative. They are all that's left. Every drop of blood is consumed. There is a straight line made up of other straight lines. When it reaches the sea, a cloud falls over.

I cannot express the true horror of the situation that can be generalised across all situations. And while horror and truth are not the same thing, they can only be separated by raw, instinctual whimsies. And though artifice, too, might appear to affect the same result, via angles and reflections and simulative manipulation, the truth of artifice is itself horror, and so the temporary estrangement it provokes never constitutes a clean break.

Our brains fragmented, into swarms like black bees, and we produce the blackest honey. We pollinate a sunless desert, our perfect lattices crammed into the most inhospitable realities. Our muscles flutter and groan with every exertion. Our faithless principles are purely functional. An unspeakable diminishment we resist as if we were alive and it mattered. Conspicuously elaborate and randomised and so removed, in part, at least, from what you'd recognise as those entities classically arranged and mediated by the environments and the biology with which you are familiar.

Though our limbs are noncommittally jointed, and our faces mirrored, the whole a kind of tear-shaped abstraction, a paradox of parts, we appear leisurely mysterious. Our uniform blackness may be antagonistic to solitary pursuits, but having abrogated community through our variegated flatulencies we get to suffer the other as if we are alone, and so simulate difference. Social lassitude produces rotated traumas. The gloop that rises to the surface is a terror you can't imagine, or enjoy. It's with remarkable frequency that we embody all interpretations of our attributes, a decimated show of estimated confluence, a delicious violation experienced as seduction.

Don't ask us about where we came from, or celibate objects, by which we mean our ancestors.

To exist you must be vulnerable to its opposite. To be invulnerable, beyond medicine, is our non- of existence, and more than simple negation. Our anticipations are not constrained by such polarised arrangements. Pounced upon and despised by things we cannot measure, with no imperatives of love or concrete ratios of indifference, we are this frequency outside your range. And so, with your own inferiority acting as your primary prophylaxis, the assassinations we enact are ornamental responses to this discord, this irreversible predicament, and funny for it, always so funny—and so sad, and inevitable—for things like us, who exist only provisionally, only so that existence itself might be undermined.

Omneity is vulgar.

Your huggermugger worldliness is a low bar. The domesticity of human intellect more than hints at your motionless state, your copulative circles. You're imagining a duplex of sorts because your interpretative skills are straining. Have you considered how a life lived biting pillows might be better spent suspended from the neck?

The speed of our eyes in the dark is pure misdirection, as is the articulation of teeth. For fear of saying nothing, I say it wrong. I could mention the curvature of an inferential horizon, the insertion of hands and arms at strategic places, clues smudged into the unmeasurable blackness, same with talk of sacrifices, edificial voids, and whatever else I wilfully mangle. All so many snakes in callipers.

Your dying from pneumonia is a disguise. By which I mean, you might have died any number of ways, and any one of them might be co-opted to hide the fact that nothing of any material significance has occurred.

But we are talking at cross-purposes, because what else is there? Purposelessness is univocal, which is why individuals, in order to survive, feel compelled to reject it.

A body destroyed by fire is beautiful and black and brittle. It will fall apart in your hands. In this powdered state, you will find a kind of disintegrated mayhem, majestically drab. And did you hear the sound it made, that melancholic wolf whistle? Did you hear us dreaming out loud?

All of it stumbled upon. Entangled in the unrewarded effort of it. The discordant harmonics of a lifeless, nasty proof lacquered over with the irreconcilable sludge of undigested genealogies and faster futures to a soundtrack of screeching, excitable noise. What's to miss? Tomorrow's philosophers will know not to bother.

Interconnectedness has a rank odour. The twitching and degenerate fluttering of daft moths.

Appearing confiscated, our nodal deformations, connected perversely, seem this same old disagreeable absorption behind a mask of amative need, our blathered noise dubbed over the already superadded drivel of premeditated speech. A black lucence drools from this vast attempted vagina that has swallowed the fictitious and synthesised hostilities to conjure impersonal, periodically half-human figures, pseudo-quantum predators with an incomplete foothold in any reality. Whenever anything approaching terminology is attempted, the sunken regions proliferate and nothing coherent is said. There is this blackness and the noise of blackness, and we are in it and of it. There's no message and no tune. A clamour that is, but not a clamour enacted by us. A crushing sound and we are crushed. We want for nothing and do not get it. Give up while you can. You only want to solve whatever this is so you can make predictions.

2. DISAMBIENT

By Obsolete Capitalism

4 July 1862:

> *"'Well, I'll eat it,' said Alice, 'and if it makes me grow larger, I can reach the key; and if it makes me grow smaller, I can creep under the door; so either way I'll get into the garden, and I don't care which happens!' [...] She ate a little bit, and said anxiously to herself, 'Which way? Which way?', holding her hand on the top of her head to feel which way it was growing, and she was quite surprised to find that she remained the same size."*
>
> — Lewis Carroll, *Alice in Wonderland*

Alice Wonderland, Alice Ultrablack, Alice Disambient... falling while sounding is like reciting while singing an opera... While trying to find the rhythm in the air, or the limping gait in the fall, with disjointed gestures, in the height or in the precipitation, Alice Wonderland slips into the hole of the ultrablack, where miracles do not avoid the present, but are horrors to escape from. And if they are not horrors, they are nightmares, and what if Alice were to plunge with us into this essay, or this article, or this unintentional list that only makes sense [experimentally] afterwards, into the writing that becomes entangled in language? Well, this Alice Wonderland would suddenly turn into another Alice, Alice Ultrablack. This Alice Ultrablack, who plunges in with us, should do so spontaneously, in our way, with our means and our changes, our rockets above our heads, ultrasonic hisses at infinite speed with imaginative and threatening names.

There is always an Alice in the air in our narrative, for ever since Carroll wrapped her up by disembodying her, she has always reappeared, the eternally «disambiented» maiden, in places from which she emerges from her own variable present to witness the contemporaneity of others. If Carroll-Deleuze's Alice is a history-avoidant child, other authors dismiss her and so she reappears in History. The historicisation of Alice, taken from Wonderland and thrown into contemporary Ultrablack Land, reappears several times in the 20th century. It is a karst and mobile Alice. A historical presence that bears witness to the event, making history and emerging from Childhood. The first Alice we meet is on Kokoschka's bi-dimensional surface of his painting *Anschluss. Alice in Wonderland* (1941/1942). She is naked and full of horror. The event evoked is that of a smaller present: it is the Österreichs Anschluss.

13th March 1938:

"'Alice' and 'Through the Looking-Glass,' involve a category of very special things: events, pure events. When I say 'Alice becomes larger,' I mean that she becomes larger than she was. By the same token, however, she becomes smaller than she is now. Certainly she is not bigger and smaller at the same time. She is larger now, she was smaller before. But it is at the same moment that one becomes larger than one was and smaller than one becomes. This is the simultaneity of becoming whose characteristic is to elude the present."

— Gilles Deleuze, *Logic of Sense*

Alice Ultrablack: "I am naked here, in the midst of the flames. Like Eve, I have only a leaf to cover me. Painted in pink and white, immaculate, I wear a linen wristband with a red cross as a sign of the wound or of a more intimate connection with the wound. Immersed in 19th-century English, I reappear here, among the flames, pointing to you, the observer, the spectator, the reader, the listener. What have you done to avoid this? To avoid the city in flames, to avoid the evil will, to avoid the immoral behaviour of the priest, the soldier, the politician and the bourgeois? I have come here to bear witness to what is happening, to the utter blackness of what exists. The event is reflected in me. You, watching and reading me, are you worthy of the event? '*Do you accept war when it happens, injury and death when they happen?*' Resignation and resentment are the only two images that move you. Now I want to fall again, to plunge into the black hole that belongs to me for some fairytale right. A black, yes, ultrablack fairy tale. Not to be caught. Oskar has painted me in a triangle made of barbed wire. Here, in this event, his Vienna is in flames. I am a prisoner; unfortunately, I could not escape the present. What does it feel like? Millions of us have been there, naked, ragged, behind that barbed wire, frightened, cold as I am, since 1941, when Oskar painted me. What does it feel like? Black hole, deep wells, confined present."

11 March 1977:

> *"It pertains to the essence of becoming to move and to pull in both directions at once: Alice does not grow without shrinking, and vice versa. Good sense affirms that in all things there is a determinable sense or direction: but paradox is the affirmation of both senses or directions at the same time."*
>
> — Gilles Deleuze, *Logic of Sense*

In the ultrablackness of a 1938 Vienna, a more carefree but equally disambiented Alice reappears in Bologna; this time in the pages of the memoir and unconventional notebook of the writer Gianni Celati, who recounts the extraordinary and therefore unrepeatable "Metropolitan Indian" season of 1976/1977. A young academic at the time, he and his students wandered through a city between "the folklore of militant left-wing extremists and that of a miniaturised Budapest". Celati is disambiented, having been expelled from his university classrooms by the militant occupation of the school premises, and so are his wandering students, precariously placed in meeting places, study and accommodation, in a perpetual transhumance between spaces. Disambiented is also Alice, who, in a sort of triple extraction, is taken from Carroll's book to the American underground and psychedelic counterculture of the 1960s, to Gilles Deleuze's book *Logic of Sense*, projected into a symbolic dimension and thus disembodied, in a sort of meta-magical witness of a political, social, existential twilight.

In Celati's pages, Alice is multiplied, a focal point from which dozens and dozens of Alices branch out, literary and non-literary, existential and non-existential, political and non-political. "*Alice is disambiented. The girl who passes alongside the great systems. Especially the central phallic system. The place of the penis in the family. Many have tried to re-ambient Alice, and we don't like it*" (Celati, 2022: 153). And then there is the 'Alice is the devil' of the student collectives, there is the Alice-megaphone or Alice-radio of the political-media countercultural movement, of which Bifo is one of the instigators, and again the uprooted Alice is still floating in Wim Wenders' celluloid circuit (*Alice in the City*, 1974). Celati's Alice is an irreducible figure because of her extension: she floats outside the black hole, represents no one but her own movement of extension and contraction, is everywhere and nowhere, is not a vertical Alice but a horizontal one, one that extends as she contracts. Alice is actually halved. "*Half in one prison (that of adulthood), half in the other (that of childhood)*" (Celati, 2022: 153). As Alice is historicised, she duplicates herself: she is in the book and in the city. She moves back and forth between the thoughts of the writer Celati and the reflections of his students, who are robbed of their innocence by the grim events in the city.

Alice is present at the events of 11 March 1977. Alice walks in the rain, Alice sees the clashes between the police and the students, Alice cries when Francesco Lorusso, a militant of Lotta Continua, is killed by the police. Alice hallucinates dramatically when tanks enter the city, Alice is censored by repression (police closure of Radio Alice on 12 March 1977), Alice is unaccustomed to everyday life, Alice flees, never to return. Alice and the law.

Alice no longer floats. Alice is disambiented. "*Alice as a utopia of non-conflict*" (Celati, 2022: 98). Alice is the paradox of two expressive spaces: ambient and disambient.

13 October 1762:

> *"Without traditions or a compass, the child and the metropolitan inhabitant are equally lost. Deprived of the shelter of 'custom', both must resort to repetition to soften the shocks of the unexpected and to orient themselves as best as they can."*
>
> — Paolo Virno, *Esercizi di esodo*

The opposition of childhood to the rational logic of adults is here the focus of philosophical reflection and the fulcrum of its sonic challenge. Deleuze plays Alice and Carroll to overturn and pervert Platonism, a major topological target of the work *Logic of Sense*, and nonsense is the paradoxical lever used to unhinge the logic of representation. For Deleuze, Alice is the figure of pure becoming, and Alice's disorientation is actually a "horizontal swerving-sliding-slipping, a productive drift of sense, produced in abundance by nonsense" (Palumbo, 2018: 16). To play with language, we need to interweave, intersect and destabilise Celati's disoriented Alice, Deleuze and Kokoschka with the thought of Paolo Virno and Giorgio Agamben.

The political action that pervades all of Paolo Virno's philosophical thought is always filtered through the relationship between life and philosophy. It is therefore not surprising when he states that "*the society of mature capitalism is only 'childish': it is necessary to mobilise against the forces of childhood*" (Virno, 2002: 115). In a memorable page from 'Exercises in Exodus', Virno masterfully frames the relationship between ambient, life and thought.

Virno begins with a careful and committed reading of Giorgio Agamben's *Infancy and History*, the 1978 book that deals with the relationship between experience and language, and whose subtitle is already a political programme: Destruction of Experience and Origin of History. In his book, Giorgio Agamben observes that "*if we were born with a language already perfectly formed, it would have the same function as smell or olfaction in animals. That is to say, it would be the organ of orientation in an ambient*" (Virno, 2002: 116). This 'natural' ambient would be highly inclusive, allowing no distancing or transformation.

Following the line of thought of Giorgio Agamben, Virno says: "*Childhood, the experience of access to language, involves an ongoing rupture between man and any determined ambient*" (ibid.). Here begins the discussion of the fracture between human experience at the level of living in the infantile phase, the elusive Alice who is in all of us, and the chaotic which Deleuze and Guattari call the ambient of all ambients. The gradual transition from glossolalia, the mysterious and imaginary language of childhood, to articulated speech marks a change not only in sense, but also in the ambient. Thanks to the articulation of language, there is a leap from 'nature'. We leap from the ambient to the world. The ambient disappears, the world appears. As Virno notes, the infantile possession of a 'world' certifies one's belonging to that world, but it also certifies its friction and imperfect identification. For Virno, the world is "*a historical world to be modified. Childhood, literally disambienting, opens up the possibility of history*" (ibid.).

This is where the theoretical passage from the Virno–Agamben axis becomes a challenge: disambient would be a positive force that acts with the power of creative childhood in the search for its own language within and against society in order to become the World, that is, History. History begins with disambient, and language is the tool to find one's own voice in the World which is becoming.

The discord and non-compliance that are inherent in the emancipatory disambient are the raw material of reality. The disambient of childhood is productive and disarticulating in the face of contemporary society, which constantly introduces artificiality into the world, reinforcing the idea of an impossibility of political and economic change of the world. To oppose the society of continuous spectacle means "*to reactivate childhood, that is, to dissolve the viscous appearance of a linguistic ambient, to find in the language what disambients and makes a world*" (ibid.: 117)—as if to say that the virtual requires the disambient, and that becoming is created by the childlike sense that plays with the world.

What sounds, then, are there for these Alices who plunge into a well of sound that exists only in the disorientation of sense? Disambient should be the natural soundtrack of this rupture between Childhood and History, Language and Chaos.

References

Carroll, L. (2003) *Alice's Adventures in Wonderland and Through the Looking Glass*. New York: Penguin Books.

Celati, G. (2022) *Alice disambientata*. Florence: Le Lettere.

Deleuze, G. (1993) *The Logic of Sense*, trans. Mark Lester. New York: Columbia University Press.

Palumbo, F. D. (2018) *Alice allo specchio: Deleuze, Carroll e la psicoanalisi*. Salerno: Orthotes.

Virno, P. (2022) *Esercizi di esodo*. Verona: Ombre Corte.

3. ULTRABLACK-QUANTUM-SOUND-THEORY

By Achim Szepanski (ed.)

Muzak

Today, in the main capitalist economies, the circulation of speculative capital is still more intensified in 24/7 modus while the production sector stagnates. If capital has the capacity to set itself as an end in an excessive, growth-oriented, and spiral-shaped movement—the starting point here is, in a certain sense, the end point—then a *sui generis* monetary process of capital dominates the process of production in order to integrate it into the primary monetary circulation and distribution.[1] The actual phase capitalism is more than

1 A strict distinction between circulation and production is questionable. The network of circulation multiplies the interfaces for the occasions of value production. Networked relationships have long since colonised the social field, creating digitality and the social factory and extending the working day to the maximum, to an almost total occupation of life.

ever characterised less by production than by circulation.[2] It is the speculative capitalisation in particular—inextricably linked to the rise of networked computers—that has led to excess as a result of ecstatic movements of growth: too much capital, but also too many images, music, video, and too many signs in general that neutralise any historical meaning and exercise white censorship through excess.

The circulation and production of an *Over* of capital (over-accumulation) is supplemented by an enormous inflation of music, images, and videos of the imaginary itself. We are swimming in a digital flood of image and music without context, of words without meaning and of fake information. Following Baudrillard, we find ourselves in the age of the hyper-circulation of signs, a flood of intensified immanence in all kinds of aesthetics that uncannily

---

Network commodities function as network derivatives and invade the social field so that virtually all social activity is dedicated to maximising the return on capital.

2 Today, everything is absorbed by circulation, and no one may refuse circulation; everything circulates unceasingly, and no one can escape the power of circulation cycles. Circulation is a category that Marx uses to analyse capital more as a process than as a relationship, and his analysis of circulation poses a challenge insofar as we are also dealing with the polysemy of circulation as a concept.
This is what we are dealing with today: pure 24/7 circulation as a condition and as a product of speculative capital (the circulation of spirals and cycles). Cycles of production, cycles of consumption, cycles of exchange and cycles of distribution, all interlinked and overlapping. In the mode of quantum uncertainty, the cycles of circulation combine with the multiple circulation of cycles, and this must be the case because derivatives and capital themselves must constantly be recoded, recombined, replicated and cloned. In circulation, something flows out and comes in again, over and over again—that is, it is a continuum. It is a multiple folded system with relative inner and outer states without absolute exclusions and inclusions; rather, both are folds of the same continuous process. Circulation not only reproduces a stream by means of a network of multiple folds but lets them expand when they come together. Circulation is about size, liquidity, velocity and vectors.

corresponds to contemporary images of oil slicks and water floods (Baudrillard, 1994). According to the logic of over-accumulation and hyper-simulation, even music is nowadays everywhere, but being everywhere is the same thing as being nowhere. The hyper-reality makes no real difference anymore between the real and the unreal. Today's Fuzzy-Fun-Techno cultivates a peculiar form of enjoyment, doom pleasures, emerging from a castrated libidinal economy. Techno, in its essence, is an accomplice of capital, striving to fulfil our desires, despite the evident impossibility of such a task. Presently, there exists a risk that even the ultrablack sound—and theory-fictions—may be recaptured and metamorphose into a mere by-product of hyperreal capitalism.[3]

In the movement of a compulsive and excessive constitution of hyper-reality—with the production and circulation of overabundant digital music and images—all kinds of vital illusions are killed. The Music-Image becomes obscene while everything becomes visible and audible. In general, it is the ubiquity of networked media flows and streams that produce a phatic form of communication, whose purpose is to keep the imaginary lines of communication open for excessive unfolding of dense nodes of knowledge/power. The medium and the real are now vaporised into a single fog whose truth is indecipherable.

The metastasis of musical techniques is the condition *and* the result of an extreme effort to make music always available, an outgrowth that, in the end, blurs even the categorical distinction between background and foreground music. In their ubiquitous phase, music is omnipresent and thus hyper-audible. But like the

3 The stupid underground (Mann, 1995) settles into a strange psychotopography: it is a small zone of the hyper-culture industry, which for Mann is both a pathological movement that produces pathogenic effects, as well as a therapeutic order. The stupid underground presents itself as both a symptom of the disease of capital and an indication of the direction of its cure. But in the stupid underground, the direction of the cure often leads back into the disease; or the cure itself turns out to be nothing more than a symptom (ibid.).

constant drone of a ventilation system, the floods of music become at the same time inaudible (Priest, 2022: 50).

There is an obese system of music and sound. Musical ubiquity, created by all kinds of media—satellite radio, MP3 players, and smartphones—and integrated into daily life, pushes music in an ecstatic way into sound-nihilism, so that its aspiration to be heard is nullified. When music is freed from all noise, we can call it integral music (Baudrillard, 1992b). In the presence of ear-worms (pop music), music becomes truly integral and mutates into a complete delirium in coincidence of perception and thought for Eldritch Priest. Priest shows that it is not only the digital images perceived and recorded, as in a film, that conventionalised mass taste, but also the popular songs in music (Priest, 2022: 5). The looped performance of the ear-worm—the end of which, like capital, is simultaneously its beginning—cannot be exchanged for anything other than itself; the ear-worm includes the presentation of a structure of interchangeability and accelerated circulation. Machine cognition and perception, which orchestrate the sounds and images of billions of successive machine cycles, affirm the ear-worm of an entertainment apparatus that uninterruptedly runs without obstacles.

Music pop-porn, its haunting atmosphere, arises from the ultra-listenability of dead music (the melodic and harmonic pop junk) and makes the affects and sensation of any other music seem superfluous. Take, for example, Baudrillard's arguments about pornography, in particular the so-called *vaginal cyclorama*, through which Japanese workers try to stick their noses up to their eyeballs inside a woman's vagina in order to see better. For Baudrillard, the point here is to remove seduction and distance in order to see the "thing-in-itself" that does not exist. If the obscene is a matter of endless representation and not of sex, then even the interior of the body must still be explored (Baudrillard, 1991). And in the same way, the obscenity of today's garbage music is a matter of endless proliferation. The music-system suffers deliriously and hypertrophically from the ecstasy of the same: more and more of the same of the same circulates (through and with the help of all differences).

This also means that the retro mode has become ubiquitous in music. Although there have been fashionable retro tendencies in pop from the beginning, for a time—until the 1990s, according to Mark Fisher (2014)—it was possible to distinguish "retro" from so-called contemporary music, which captures the moods of an era. Today, all retro styles are sold as contemporary precisely because the real innovation is no longer in the present and there are no truly contemporary alternatives. So, the retro mode has become the standard, which means that retro styles, fashions, and objects are sold as contemporary. When everything is retro, on the one hand, it is meaningless to call certain phenomena retro, and on the other hand, nothing is retro anymore. Time becomes white. Fisher (ibid.) also claims, however, that from a situation in which nothing happens, suddenly everything is possible again. But doesn't it behave rather as Alessandro Sbordoni (2024) writes: "Nothing is possible anymore because nothing is impossible anymore."

Therefore, paraphrasing a Baudrillard quote on elections, one could write: the music industry sprinkles the excited and at the same time exhausted nervous system, makes people listen until they themselves want to listen more and more and more often, and they would actually like to listen to much more. This does not mean that they have a taste or believe in the meaning of music—on the contrary, it expresses a bulimic desire to hear: the music system is voraciously and excrementally devoured and digested. One gets rid of it by excess (not by rejection, but by incorporation)—the whole system is transformed into a huge white musical belly (Baudrillard, 1987). However, Eldritch Priest has interjected here, where there is, in a functional way, only input and output, or if there is everywhere cybernetic feedback as a symptom of fatness, then there is only swallowing and shitting: no memory, no digestion, no gathering of consciousness into a difference that makes a difference (Priest, 2022: 41). The daily repetition of Muzak constructed by the global music-machine orchestrates conditions under which one moment in music seamlessly replaces the next, destroying the force of consciousness that would maybe bring a change to punctual attention into the next moment (ibid.).

The decisive aspect of the 24/7 entertainment machine lies not only in standardisation/differentiation, but in the redundancy of a non-time in which there is no more opportunity not to watch, not to listen, not to shop, not to consume, not to work, or not to retrieve any data. Nevertheless, the 24/7 machine does not hold a uniform time, but unfolds a reduced and polished diachrony in which the differences are reduced to exchangeable and circulating differences—interchangeability is the norm. This is how a shell-like, almost hallucinatory presence is staged—the sequence of smooth and lubricated operations as a special form of timelessness in which pauses, interruptions, and rhythms that make the difference are eliminated (Crary, 2022).

Prosumers consume all content very frequently on their smartphones by constantly looking at the display, browsing, chatting, skipping, listening and watching, deleting, surfing and reading, and always remain immersed in a passivity that online life burdens, while at the same time they are somehow active, i.e., somehow totally involved, a madness of the highest degree. One lives in the ghost worlds of hedonistic digital machines and promiscuous digital contacts. Decisive for the 24/7 clock—which in its ultrafast, narrow-gauge elegance leads to the flexibilisation of everyday life—is no longer the accumulation of things by the subjects, but the expanding and paradoxically differential-uniform flow of employment and consumption of mostly digital offers, which is characterised by the increasing loss of breaks and interruptions and the shrill, short-term nature of activities.

There is a scenario of music, sounds, and noises that one does not necessarily have to listen to, but you still have a kind of perception of it. Perception is not simply a matter of registering what we actually see or listen to, but a way of sensing the eventuality implicit in an encounter between our bodies, brains, and objects. Contemporary listeners hear music in passing through all kinds of environments. Consumers don't immerse themselves into music long enough to be strongly affected by gradual changes in rhythm or sounds. Modulation comes nowadays in discrete packets, in "quanta" (Priest, 2013: 248). Listening in these musical packages organises a kind of automated perception, which also means that the always-fragile attention is constituted by unconscious perception. Although the stream of modulated music might allow for moments of discrete change in the field of perception, music is now based on a naked repetition and so repeated perception: from Muzak in shopping centres to techno club music.

There is an overflow of music and images, which is followed by a certain lack of the symbolic. A glass labyrinth of sounds combines with an overflowing oceanic feeling—the intensity intensifies in the imaginary. There is an accelerated expansion of the colonisation of imagination by the flow of algorithms, which bare the producers of musical streaming. But human perception still consists of some kind of symbolic forms that are abstracted as patterns in the field of experience. In this view, feeling is then to be understood as a continuity between the material forces and the conceptual force. However, there is often a confusion between the symbol and the symbolised. Technologies can produce effects that are so much like feelings that we confuse them with feelings. This then enables a mythology of feelings that can be described as the imaginary (Priest, 2022: 5). Technological transformations and economic hyper-speculation correlate with the floods of music and images that are consumed immersively and produce, on the subjective side, the excess of the egomaniac.

For Baudrillard, already the hi-fi music of the 1970s was associated with a purging of clean and flat sound, and with the liberation from noise, music degenerates into integral music. Flawlessly merging into its own model, music liberates itself from music precisely by restoring the sound to technical perfection. This technical perfection means also that an artificial noise can be added to sound to make it more musical again. (Therein lies even the danger for glitch music, which merely modulates frequencies, exploits errors and corrupts signals; the homogenising indifference of boredom expressed in some serial experimental music must be transformed into a state of minor interest.) For Baudrillard, the stereo effect has already reached the point where hi-fi becomes so uselessly refined that music is lost in the obsession with its fidelity (Baudrillard, 1987). Today, the obsession for that perfect technicality creates a false destiny for music, just as it creates a false destiny for the social—namely, to see its fulfilment simply as a matter of perfect programming, which is already inscribed in the computer.

For Baudrillard, there is a point in the development of electronic music at which the increasing sophistication of programming and playback no longer improves the quality of music but degrades it. By any possible technical definition of musical quality, the standard keeps getting better and better. Baudrillard's critics would rightly accuse him of a certain nostalgia; the quality he laments as lost to stereo never existed in reality. But it is precisely this tautology, this self-definition—the fact that the only criterion for musical quality in relation to stereo is stereo itself—that Baudrillard disputes here. It is not so much an actual quality that he claims has been lost—in which case his critics would be right—but a kind of virtuality that is excluded by any possible definition.

Glitch

Glitch music is usually characterised by a transformation of sound artefacts caused by malfunctions of digital technologies—a malfunction of electrical fuses due to a change in voltage—such as bugs, crashes, system errors, hardware noise, CD skipping, and digital distortion. Acquired because of failure, the glitch sound is essentially the sound of the false in a Deleuzian sense. Glitches refer to the complex algorithms behind the interface and allow different conclusions to be drawn about how they work.[4] In digital systems,

4 "In computing, a glitch denotes a problematic, annoying, or unintended error that, like the definition of error, tends to be negligible, quickly absorbed by the larger, still-functioning system. For example, a website stalls or fails to load, an online video halts or stutters in the middle of

glitches arise from the complexity of algorithms in their interaction, in which certain unforeseen inputs or unanticipated constellations can lead to temporary disruptions. It is possible that the system itself continues to run with the given inappropriate data, but produces surprising results. As a disruption to the conventional flow of information, glitches lead to a momentary absence of the functionality actually expected.

The glitch might be intentionally produced, but usually it is an aleatory event. It might question the functionality of the code, but it does not destroy the code; rather, it arises in aleatory movements of the code itself. With the glitch, it is possible to stop progress because it interrupts the intended flow, while it allows an aleatory flow which might lead to a fragile state of hypertrophy that includes new flows and possibilities. While the glitch draws attention to us and is at the same time intangible, one can imagine the moment when the glitch occurs as a fragile aspect, which will be repeated in different ways. The glitch, which calls into question the logic of music, photo, or video, makes previous events seem contingent. The search for true feedback through the glitch is an impossibility because the glitch only shows conditions, while the event is open for contingent development. A glitch shows a zero level, insofar as a functioning system and its normal operations are interrupted for a short period of time. It follows the same logic as other forms of error: the glitch represents errors in relation to a normatively defined state but can be subjected to a different evaluation when viewed from other perspectives. This possibility of adopting an 'alternative' perspective on the glitch might be decisive for the aesthetic potential of the glitch.

---

a scene, or strange, unexpected colour artefacts splatter across a newly rendered graphics file. When a glitch appears, it indicates a relatively rare moment of unplanned, unprogrammed mediation that, for many glitch artists, provides an opportunity to connect on-screen phenomena with off-screen computational abstractions" (Kane, 2019: 15).

In a post-human way, the glitch shows the turn from the human to the object, in which the human subject now becomes the recipient of the machine; glitch no longer denotes a human activity, but as an accident, it can only be perceived by humans. The acting human operating the machine is displaced from his position as an actor by the glitching technology.

Glitching was developed into a cutting-edge concept in the arts, while at the same time it became codified by capitalist technology and business as a model for improvement and success of all kinds of products, money, and capital. The glitch is not anymore a critical resource against hardcore power structures of capitalism but part of an affirmative relation which continually modulates a kind of form as a constant change to sustain a positive moment which functions as a kind of reconstruction of the system. It will be reproduced again and again and neutralised by the flow of further music or images. When the glitch becomes fashionable or even glamorous, it can be capitalised on all the better.

The glitch refuses now to be a kind of sabotage of the functionality of software; rather, it supports the forms by which digital spaces are organised. The hyperreal world created by the code is exposed now even more as a simulacrum. As a former ghost that interrupts functionality in its opacity to demand silence or noise, the glitch becomes merely weird; it becomes the affirmative horror of capital and power. The media objects that populate technological horror today are not broken; in fact, they work quite well, often perhaps too well.

Dark glitch is instead the non-signal or even non-failure—used not to capitalise the click or the glitch as a quasi-cause of the excess for a successful objective system, but to con-form the non-successful swimming in the black noise of the non-music. It does not give a structure to the formless or make order out of non-sense. Instead, dark glitch includes a polyrhythmic and polyvocal way of interrogating the relationship between formlessness and form. In this way, it opens for a black thought-music, which constitutes the improbability of being written, pinned down, or defined. Gary

J. Shipley writes: "We eat Black Noise and Black Noise eats us, and what's left over is neither us nor Black Noise, but instead an aperture from which some new worm might surface, some new blackness for some new sense" (2021: 191). He continues: "What if ILOVEYOU equates to IEATYOU or IBOREYOUTODEATH or IMONETIZEYOURSOUL or IBURYYOUALIVE?" (*ibid.*, 197). Here each error or glitch, in its specific incorrectness, offers, in the processes of transformation, an insight into the grammatical and even semantic peculiarities of the languages, but also into the functioning of a translation of the algorithm itself, thus indicating the conditions of its creation.

It is the dark simulacra that is meant to hide the absence of truth in a world game. But the absence itself cannot be articulated. The absence is close to the meaning of the game, which lies in the playing itself and at the same time creates the appearance of playing and thus comes close to simulation. The inarticulability defines the boundary between hyperreality and the glitch, a flaw in the code that is irreparable because of its transience. The process of dark glitch is to interrupt—specifically, to interrupt the digital representation in such a way that its simulation of the analog can no longer remain obscured. At the same time, the dark glitch interrupts the code not by undoing digital solipsism, but by highlighting it. The glitch exposes the ecstatics of the simulation as simulation.[5] Dark glitch is not an ordinary malfunction due to an

5 Simulation takes place when a representation precedes the real of which it pretends to be a representation; it produces this real as reality itself instead of modelling a pre-existing reality. The more the simulated reality resembles an existing reality, the less it resembles it. If both realities are the same, the simulated reality is no longer a reality, but a different original. The gap that is necessary to distinguish between copy and original has therefore disappeared. Actually, the representation system can only function on the basis of a gap between representation and reality, but as soon as the gap has closed and the system has lost contact with reality, it has to produce its own reality in order to continue functioning. This real is what Baudrillard calls the hyperreal—which is more real than the real (Szepanski, 2024).

error, but a slippage of the system due to an internal change. It can cause a system to collapse from the inside. On the one hand, the glitch prevents progress because it interrupts the intended development (anti-finality), and on the other hand, it enables an unintended development that leads to new possibilities that disregard the accepted rules of the game.

Ultrablack and Form/Formlessness

Ultrablack sound seems to be the sound of formlessness, while black music might take on a form as a something, but which is also a nothing—to prevent at the end anything from belonging to music. So black is something that is also nothing, as nothing black gets liquid and catastrophic, ultrablack, a nothing that cannot be adequately grasped in the precinct of music. Ultrablack is the nihilistic abyss (can negation take the form of sound?). How, then, is nothingness transformed into black? Or better, how is black transformed into nothingness/ultrablack? Formless to form or form to formless?

First, we have to mention: there is no formlessness per se. The formless and objectless—or if you want to, call it chaos—can only be thought in relation to form; if there is no form at all, then the formless can no longer be any question of thinking, but only of delirium. Even something as immaterial as a feeling or a mood has form, since it expresses a particular composition of effects associated with being a situated organism, situated in daily situations, situated in economy or even in history (Priest, 2013). So, there is also no such thing as "formless music" per se. But be aware that already traditional musical content is a sounding and moving form, not just forms, but forms that are moved in sound. The formal aspect of, for example, an accord is not sufficient to generate content. The form or the formula needs to be moved.

You can't ignore the energetic conditions and entropic processes accompanying any given musical form and expression. Formlessness in musical terms refers then to a lack or absence of the structural order provided by elements of metre, cadence, harmony, theme variation, melody, etc. We can speak at least of *A-forme*, like the ambiguous moment of a non-form or even a formless sound. Eldritch Priest (ibid.: 47) uses Georges Bataille's idea of the *informe* to address how experimental compositions can exploit the deviations of distraction in a way that draws attention to a 'black noise'. In this way, ultrablack sound is unstable—there are always multiple series of events that pass through it.

In opposition to the nostalgic form of music, we must produce non-modulation—a continuous ultra-kinetic motion of form and formless, which fluctuates between the properties of the material and the concrete action. It has to be a non-form, and with Harney and Moten, we can write: "Anti*mater*ial riddimcutting rhythm cutting method—microtonality's overpopulation of measure, *Zaum* preoccupying *Raum* with an extrarational, hyperganjic, dancehallsan skritic, anachorasmiatic, al-Mashic, all mashed up buzz, the alternate groove we in, the devalued and invaluable local insurgency—disobeys our most loving invocation. This gift of spirit gives itself away and zero-one/one-two is left embittered" (Harney and Moten, 2021: 57–58). These are moments in which sequences of sounds have not yet crossed the threshold at which they become a melody. We can think of this suspension as a becoming or an event, which Deleuze describes as that which "eludes the present" and "does not tolerate the separation or distinction of before and after or of past and future" (Deleuze, 1993). The formless begins to build a sound of its own that follows a logic full of paradoxes, a meaning that goes in many directions.

At the end, we must recognise that the attempt to construct pure becoming of the formless can fail, and this failure is also formless. But maybe the movement of non-form must be completed with Simondon's term of information, which presupposes the existence of a system in a state of metastable non-equilibrium that can individuate itself; information, unlike form, is never a unique term, but the signification that springs from a *disparation* and *dissipation*.

Let's try a different path to discover the relationship between form and formless: the non-colour of (Ultra)Black.

Darkness can be gloom, opacity, shadow, or shade. One could speak of dark materials insofar as they are asleep. But there is another kind of darkness. It is no longer simply dark, but it is about a deep and horrible blackness. We do not ask if the world will become dark, but the blackness points to a world without us. Black usually occurs only in alternation with white, just as silence is punctuated by noise. If black is mainly the absence of white, dark the absence of light, then we remain trapped in a world of reflections, dualities, and convertibilities. Only by subtracting from the system of light and colour can one see the generic real of blackness. There is a transition from the colour black, which one can see, to black as a non-colour that one cannot see, and even more, a transition to a nothing-to-see, which in turn one can see.

Ultrablack is a crypto-ontology, a crypto-sound absolutely closed to being. But not only in relation to black as *κρυπτος*, which is closed off from being, we can understand what, for example, François Laruelle understands by the black as a non-colour. According to Laruelle, the idea of black is a cosmological principle (Laruelle, 2018). Separated from the world, of which we form a human, all-too-human image, and from Earth on whose surface we live, there is an indifferent, opaque, black universe. The (ultra)black (as formless or meaningless information) that precedes the light is the condition of the universe: that which fled from the world before the world was born into the world. We are always seduced into thinking of the universe as something that is out there, the factory of the universe that can be seen and felt or seduced of a colour as a purely phenomenological blackness. But blackness is to be thought of as the non-universe, which was not temporally before the universe, nor will it return in a kind of cataclysm. It is always already there, but you cannot see it, even though you can see it. It is a cosmological blackness, the blackness of absolute evil, the blackness of non-being.

Ultrablack differs from black in that it escapes any resemblance with a black that derives its blackness from any dualism of White/

Black, especially in the interaction with light. Ultrablack is close to the blackness of Laruelle's *Universe Black* (ibid.). Ultrablack could also be described as non-black or as *Uchromia*. We look here for the general ultrablack of the abyss, of emptiness and vacuum, the ultrablack of more than silence, of catastrophes and cataclysms. Ultrablack is the basis for a non-music, a new sonic *a-topia* rooted in the generic black universe. Think, for example, of Sun Ra's intergalactic music—broader than interplanetary music—which demonstrates Sun Ra's continual vigilance towards the impossible, the un-thought, the not and the alter.

What if we think of ultrablack as the uncertainty of Calvin Warren's crossed-out black? For Warren, black is also not the colour black, but the index of formlessness, since colour always takes on a form within metaphysics. Despite the indexing of this formlessness, black still takes the form of something or of positivity. The function of this something, which is always also a nothing, is to prevent any something from belonging to the whole/system (Warren, 2018: 58f.).

Both metaphysics and science are obsessed with blackness and nothingness, and the two become synonyms for knowledge and power. Nothingness frightens metaphysics, but metaphysics tries to control it by transforming nothingness/blackness into an object of knowledge, into something that it can be analysed, calculated, and schematised.

The question of nothing and something could now be turned around again: "What is nothing and yet is something?" It is blackness. It is both nothing and something. Similar to black holes and other scientific problems, blackness serves to show the limits of philosophy and science, which cannot be mastered with schematised argumentation and calculation. Black means nothing; nothing means black. Or rather, nothing does not really mean black, because in nothingness, positivity is erased. We must therefore ask ourselves what this positivity inscribed in nothingness is, which transforms nothingness into its shade of black (ibid.: 6).

How does capitalism transform nothingness into something so that it can dominate this nothingness? For Warren, it functions through the 'Negro', who gives form to the formless, but a form that at the same time represents a danger. The 'Negro' is the interstice of capitalist metaphysics, the formless form that fluctuates between man and animal. Warren says that the 'Negro' is black because, in a capitalist world, the 'Negro' must assume the function of nothingness (the formless) (ibid.: 7). However, the racist obsession with functionalising the 'Negro' turns always into hatred, because the nothingness is indestructible.

Black is the excess of form in an anti-black world, but also the interruption of form, the formless. On the one hand, black attempts to move beyond form into non-being (the formless); on the other hand, the supposedly formless, indifferent field of metaphysics is still based on anthropological differences, and this interplay between formlessness and form is what can be called race (ibid.: 33). It is therefore unthinkable to end metaphysics without ending the various systems of anti-blackness in the world. Anti-blackness and its technologies of destruction are designed to erase nothingness: nothingness as formlessness, nothingness as interruption, nothingness as black, nothingness as 'Negro', and finally, nothingness as ultrablack.

Noise and Information

Noise as chaos is the unstable ground on which machines and human existence are based. Order is instead the form of an appearance that permanently massages the turbulent background and is massaged by it. All informational models of order are only approximations to quants, matter, and energy, which is constantly in motion.

Noise is full of distortions, a formless form of dissonance—a complex and high-dimensional concept, it is both internally generated and brought in from outside. Noise dominates two realms: the subjective, constructive one of perception and the objective one of chance in nature (Prado, 2023). The latter is unavoidable, inherent to the kinetic processes in a given world. Objective noise should not simply be understood as an unwanted sound or signal but, with Michel Serres, understood in relation to turbulence, which is order and disorder at the same time—order that dissolves and forms itself through repetition and redundancy, while disorder is generated by new events, madness, uncertainty and the unpredictable. Serres describes the latter as a parasitic relationship, which is productive, regardless of whether it strengthens or weakens sounds or signals (Serres, 2022). For Serres, the physicist of music has to become an anarchist; his domain is background noise, and music is rare. For Serres, the order of a structure is in general an island of rationality in the sea of noise. It manifests itself in the formality of code, which circulates information that must be considered soft because its scale is entropic and preserves discrete quanta only relative to a universally background sea of noise (Serres, 1991).

Beyond the naive reference to unwanted sound, noise is conceptually polymorphous, because it is never about measures of phenomena that qualify noise as a certain kind of disturbance, but about the fragile and kinetic relationship between contingency and control. Even the pure tones we hear have a certain amount of noise, because a mathematically perfect tone would sound strange to our ears. Nature produces irreducible forms of chance in every process and borders on the unpredictable.

Noise has further to be understood as the negative potential, which is not yet capitalised, but as soon as it is integrated into the capitalist-information system, it ceases to be noise and becomes a living corpse. Today, for example, the analysis of computerisation and financial trade shows that material practices of human-machine hybrids use noise to make profits. The problem of speed in High Frequency Trading (HFT) escalates this dramatically, transforming the race for risk-free profits into a race to zero. Noise thus becomes a vital component of the financial system, an unpredictable activity that, paradoxically, can also support the equations that underpin modern financial theory. There is a binary: those who possess information and those who do not, with the latter as noise traders who take advantage of traders who trade on the basis of real information. Financial capital can no longer be discussed without reference to information theory and cyborg science.

Artistic projects translate financial data from financial movements into sound, while projects like *rynb* go one step further and focus on the problem of sonification of resonance and feedback. There is resonance with various strands of noise music and contemporary sonic practices that transform data into sound, including the informational noise in the digital signal itself—a result of the increase in mathematical chaos through HFT. The financial noise is generated by all kinds of cybernetic feedback, kinetics, mimetic forces, and anticipations. *Flash Sonification* by *rynb* aims to show the obscurantism of today's financial processes; the way in which supposedly useless noise is translated into code and information. At the same time, human perception is integrated into the timescales of algorithms. Sonic Noise includes the translation of market data, abstract and material at the same time, into various abstract a-significant semiotics that do not immediately signify anything. Immersing ourselves in sonic noise doesn't guide us towards a logical comprehension of finance. Instead, it instils in us a somewhat ominous anticipation of future financial processes—high-frequency pulses that originated in the rhythm of a heartbeat and have now accelerated to such an extent that they've become indistinguishable from one another. Noise as volatility and fluctuation is an instrument to continuously generate and accumulate profits. On the one hand, noise is a source of volatility, and its elimination, from the perspective of communication theory, a technical matter. On the other hand, Jonathan Beller understands it as a matter of politics and economics, with the elimination of noise corresponding to the suppression of people. In financial terms, volatility is, in turn, an expression of decision-making sequences in price discovery under conditions of uncertainty. It is ironic, Beller argues, that volatility has become an important source of value creation, synthetic finance, and today, sovereigns (Beller, 2021).

The intersection between sonic and informal noise can produce indications such as panic and fear on the one hand, and a dark, ghostly cloud based on the attack of the data on the other. If, instead of attacking Wall Street, people attacked the data centres, they need to understand that the real physical manifestations of finance today are the air-conditioned units and computers of the data centres.

In contrast to music, ultrablack sound must produce a kind of black noise. Eldritch Priest speaks of non-music that keeps its non-form of *informe* from sinking into the mud of mere music. Like noise music, music noise needs to keep its failure, its failure to fail, in ear.

What about the relation between information and noise? Claude Shannon defines information as a measure of entropy, and entropy as a measure of freedom of choice. In contrast to Wiener's definition of information as the negation of entropy, for Shannon, more information leads to greater entropy and uncertainty.[6] A completely predictable message has only one possible outcome and is therefore redundant; it tells us nothing new. By aligning the concept of information with uncertainty, like Shannon, we have the paradoxical conclusion that more information means more uncertainty; maybe then a high entropy of background noise would at the end involve the largest amount of information. Shannon's definition of information entropy thereby at least enables us to think of contingency as belonging to the conditions of possibility of all information processes (Malaspina, 2018).

So, Wiener and Shannon arrive at diametrically opposed ideas about what information is, because Wiener defines information as precisely the opposite of "information entropy", namely as the negation of entropy. While Shannon's concept of information

6 Shannon and Wiener developed different definitions of information and noise, but both thinkers affirmed the second law of thermodynamics, which states that entropy—which measures randomness or uncertainty, terms directly related to noise—tends to increase in isolated systems.

includes the risk of becoming indistinguishable from noise, Wiener's definition runs the risk of producing a conservative form of information that includes nothing new. But neither the maximum state of entropy nor that of structural equilibrium can capture the concept of information in total, because in both cases the concept of information negates potential for transformation and only preserves what exists (ibid.). Metastability, in the sense of Simondon, is instead a dynamic suspension of a system between two forms of equilibrium, between entropic dispersion and structural inertia.

If we go one step further than Shannon and understand information as virtual freedom of choice, then the difference between information and noise loses the aspect of its dualism, which might be characterised by formulas of music and noise, of light and dark, or order and disorder. So, a strict distinction between information and noise is not possible, as, for example, even all capitalist financial markets are permeated by noise to some degree, insofar as transactions in space and time are not without friction. Noise is an aspect of financial trading as part of an embodied, material world. Information includes patterns and order as well as randomness and disorder. Noise and information are not constant and/or unitary concepts, nor are they independent of the frame of reference in which they operate.

Michel Serres conceives his idea of the parasite as the disturbing and noisy third person through abandoning the law of the excluded middle of Boolean logic. Following traditional logic, we must exclude a third possibility between true and false. Serres introduces the parasite into the logic game and deconstructs the logical order that qualifies information over noise. The way in which he uses the parasite in music also negates the scientific misclassifications of noise. The parasite is the processor of any disturbance of logic and brings us close to most general operators on the variables of systems. It makes them fluctuate through their different distances (Serres, 2022). The parasite is a joker that takes on different values depending on its position in a system.

Quantum theory might be helpful to understand what we have written until now and can tell us more about the transformation from noise to sound or from nothingness into something and vice versa. However, because you can't visualise or listen to quants, an arty audiovisual approach to quantum theory can only be made by a wild use. But even quantum physics must produce some kind of visualisations, maybe diagrams or images (sound?). In this sense, even the most unimaginable and unhearable quanta of waves, which are moving far too fast or far too slow for humans to perceive them, leave behind some traces that show up, for example, on images in detectors of a screen (or in ultrablack sound/helium).

Quantum Theory and (non)Music

The universe is initially information. One speaks with quantum theorist Thomas Görnitz of meaningless information or of waves of nothing (Görnitz & Görnitz, 2016). Understanding quantum theory as a new form of holism (micro *and* macroscopic) in physics, to which relations and possibilities can be ascribed as essential characteristics, seems at first glance to be quite absurd. Baudrillard, for example, proposes to accept the microscopic world as it is represented by quantum theory, whereby the strangeness for him lies not in the strangeness of the microscopic world, but in the non-strangeness of the macroscopic world. Baudrillard asks why it is not strange that one readily assumes that the concepts of identity, the excluded middle, the determination of time and space, are effective in the macroscopic world (Baudrillard, 1992a: 29). But has it not long been the case, to argue here with and against Baudrillard, that quantum theory is responsible for physical realities of any size scale—as the physicist Palomaki recently proved, for example, when he showed that a quantum field and a classical oscillator can be entangled, which means nothing other than that classical actual realities of mechanics are entangled with quantum potential realities (Palomaki, 2013). The Nobel Prize winner Anton Zeilinger and his colleagues have succeeded in preparing quantum systems of light with an extension of 100 km, in such a way that measurements could be carried out on them. Such a system originally consists of two photons and forms a unified whole, a diphoton, which expands (Görnitz & Görnitz, 2016: 412).

Quantum phenomena are everywhere. The unsolved problem is therefore not the quantum world, but the world of classical physics. Although it has proven itself in most practical cases, it is ultimately an idealisation that is only approximately correct, and perhaps, in a sense twisted with Baudrillard, only an illusion. We must therefore turn the problem around again. Quantum theory is most general; it applies not only to the microscopic world, but also to the macroscopic world and to cosmology. Peter Mittelstaedt concludes that the previous ontology of classical physics is in question, insofar as it offers idealisations for its world that have proven themselves in practice, but which could prove to be only approximately correct idealisations, i.e., ultimately based on illusions (Mittelstaedt, 2000: 68).

In quantum field theory, the term "vacuum state" is associated with a field of virtual particle-antiparticle pairs that appear and disappear again before the conservation of energy is violated. According to quantum field theory, the vacuum state is a type of energy/matter. It ensures the possibility of finding something even when there is nothing. In quantum field theory, nothingness is by no means empty, but an infinite fullness, a dynamic of iterative opening that cannot be separated from matter. The vacuum is infinitely full of the virtuality of everything that ever was, what is and whatever will be. Deleuze has adopted this idea in his concept of virtuality. He defines the virtual as that which was possible at a given place and at a given time in the past, is possible now or will be possible in the future. The vacuum is a field of pure, unexcited energy and is therefore called a vacuum because it has no recognisable properties or characteristics. Only when the zero-point field of the vacuum is left do things emerge that have properties or characteristics. The quantum vacuum can be imagined as a calm sea that underlies all existing things, which are patterns of dynamic energy written on the quantum vacuum.

As in the *Many Worlds Theory*, Murray Gell-Mann assumes the universal validity of Schrödinger's wave function, which gives rise to the possibility of multiple multiverses, all of which are to be understood as real (Gell-Mann, 1994). Meaningless information or fine-grainedness is to be understood as a kind of pure state of the universe, full of interferences and superpositions: a universe that, with Laruelle, is black; with Serres, is burning;[7] and, with Baudrillard, already contains all the answers to an infinity of questions. For Serres, information lies in form and not in matter. He describes communicative physics as an "intra-material logic", a kind of information-software that works in materiality itself. The universe in all its blackness is completely useless, which is why questions must constantly be asked in a game of error-or-truth and already point to certain solutions and exclude others. It remains questionable whether the error can ever be eradicated, even to some extent, because the observer using one system does not necessarily have to know what other systems (with their observers) provide in terms of alternative descriptions of possible histories of the universe. The paradox now consists in having to think of a multiple but also unified or universal system, without being able to give up difference or a system that is related to environments.

We are and will be inside phenomena. We can never look or listen to the world only from the outside, although the outside is always a part of any phenomenon we create. Essential at this point, when thinking about musical activity (by humans and/or machines) in terms of quantum theory, is that we recognise the importance of the relation between non-locality and location and specificity. For example, making and listening to a piece of music

7 For Michel Serres, white light is the nullity of colours: not because white light is colourless, but because it is so abundant in colour. White light encompasses every colour that could come to the fore as soon as some of the emitting quanta are absorbed. The concept of purity includes for Serres the purity of white light, the quantum matrix of colour and matter. But also, for Serres the universe is not white. It has any colour. It is more black than white, even. But for Serres it always burns.

involves many components, and yet it will always be this special piece of music that we produce or listen to. The production of a piece of music draws on all available resources, perhaps in ways we did not previously realise, and the production process cuts always into the world (and is still contingent).

François Laruelle formulated the term photo-fiction, and maybe there will also be a music-fiction (Laruelle, 2014). Laruelle here takes up an interesting engagement with quantum theory that connects photo-fiction with his own conception of superposition.[8] Photo-fiction produces a fusion as a superposition of the camera on one hand, and philosophical discourse on the other (ibid.). When all the component parts in photo-fiction are that of a photo-moment, a superposition occurs. The camera, the photographer, the discourse, the theoretical oraxioms—all this and more are in superposition, meaning that the outcome of the photographing process is temporarily unknown. With a virtual camera as a mathematical entity, all parameters can be changed, even beyond what is physically possible. Similar superpositions can happen in music, where an instrument is not only related to other instruments, but can also be understood as an approximation of acoustics, harmony, metalworking, and maybe electronics. When used to make music, it is connected to the musician's measuring apparatus and his ability to conduct a range of discourses. Music is the result of a considerable number of material and semiotic

---

8 Non-philosophy has a strong affinity with the two major principles of quantum physics according to Laruelle: firstly, radical immanence (superposition principle), and secondly, one-sided duality (non-commutativity principle). Both principles follow the idempotence (A + A = A), which stands for immanence in its "wave-like" form, i.e., not immanence in the form of a point or a circle, as philosophers often assume (Laruelle 2010b). Idempotence programs the identity of a concept with itself as a result, or, to put it another way, it simulates the identification that makes one concept fall back on another and both see each other on the Möbius strip. It is to be understood as a linear immanence, as a same that has as its first condition the tension of the operation of addition. In short, it is the vectoriality of the same.

practices (in time), and both can be said about musicians and listeners who engage with music.

Let's look at the so-called wave-particle duality. You can observe either momentum or position, but not precisely at the same time. The moment of observation is the event, i.e., the measurement creates facts. A particle can be emitted from a source, behave like a wave on its journey, while at the end it will be recognisable as a particle on the detector screen. This "wave-particle dualism" underlies Baudrillard's assertion that the object today "plays with its own objectivity" and "appears only in the form of fleeting and aleatory traces on the screens of virtualisation" (Baudrillard, 2000: 75). Whereas science once regarded knowledge as a mirror of external reality, computer screens today show that reality is projected rather than reflected.

In quantum theory, there is either a well-defined location or a well-defined speed for the particle, but never both at the same time. This is the core of Heisenberg's indeterminacy relation, which can be expressed in an equation.[9] The fiction of simultaneously existing exact locations and speeds was supplemented in classical physics by the fiction of smallest particles. The essential thing about quanta, however, is not the small, but the exact, which arises when indeterminacy is eliminated in a measurement process and a fact is

9 With Bohr, it is important to differentiate between uncertainty and indeterminacy. Uncertainty becomes the epistemic form of an unavoidable limitation imposed on our epistemic horizon by the simultaneous existence of matter, making it not only uncertain but indeterminate. It is not impossible to know, nor is it uncertain whether we can know. On the contrary, what we know is indeterminate because it is composed as or in itself and carries within it at any moment the simultaneous coexistence of more than one measure, meaning, and place, which makes it impossible to figure out which of these measures, meanings, and places is uniquely responsible for what we know. In this sense, indeterminacy is not the impossibility of determining something. Rather, it describes the awareness that what exists consists of more than one property, quality, or measurement. This completes the paradigm shift from uncertainty to indeterminacy.

achieved. As Heisenberg shows, a quantum particle can be prepared in such a way that it occupies the most precise location possible, or that it is given the most precise momentum possible, so that one of the two quantities remains completely indeterminate. If you want to measure the momentum precisely, you no longer know where the particle is. If the particle is localised, the value of the momentum is undetermined. The localised particle becomes wavy on the one hand, but the wave also becomes discrete on the other.

The wave is a very different kind of phenomenon from the particle. In contrast to particles, waves can overlap at one and the same point in space. If two waves superimpose or overlap, then the amplitude of the resulting wave (which is neither a synthesis of the two waves nor a "new" wave) is a combined amplitude of the first two waves, i.e., the amplitude of the second wave is added to the first wave, and the result is a wave with combined amplitudes, the superposition of the two waves (Barad, 2015: 88f.). The resulting wave is therefore a sum of the effects of each individual component, i.e., it is a combination of the disturbances emanating from each wave individually. This type of combination of effects is called "superposition". The concept of superposition is central to understanding what a wave is (Barad, 2007: 120). In this context, Bohr described the wave function as a mathematical quantity that does not indicate the density of matter spread in space, but the probability of a measurement that shows a particle at a certain location as a whole. Waves are therefore not only waves of matter, but waves of density and probability.

Wave functions can be also used for music theory. Based on the fundamental principles of octave equivalence, scientist and music theorist Guerrino Mazzola (et al., 2016: 196) shows that you can develop different wave functions over an underlying tonal space. Here, Mazzola presents quantum models for static and dynamic tonal attraction and compares them with traditional computational models in musicology. He improves predictions based on symbolic models of music perception between two given tonalities. This involves explicit models of tonalities and of the transition process from one tonality to its successor. Modulation is here viewed as a force interaction between two tonality particles, or as waves which are mediated by a modulation quantum.

So, let's further connect different aspects of quantum theory to music and performance. Mazzola (et al., 2020: 140) gives us the example of a dancer who touches the stage in discrete points, while he is moving continuously. Similarly, in classical musical diagrams, the points are notes, while the continuous curves are waves or gestures.[10] Musicians create gestures while choosing and writing specific symbols on the musical piece (ibid.: 279). Mazzola distinguishes between the symbolic gestures of the curve systems and physical gestures. The surface that transforms symbolic gestures into physical gestures is called a world-sheet (ibid.: 142). The way to obtain these processes (via mathematical-theoretical physical methods), for Mazzola, comes from quantum or string theory.

In the physical theory of waves or strings, elementary objects are not described as points that move in space-time, but as parameterised curves that move through space-time and thereby trace a world-sheet. Strings or waves might correspond to a musical gesture—for example, an up-down movement of a pianist's finger (ibid.: 277). Music can be described not only in terms of points but also in terms of waves, vibrating strings, or (hyper-)gestures. Mazzola calls this world-sheet surface a hyper-gesture (Mazzola et al. 2016: 283). If a gesture is seen as a point itself, the gesture that connects such gesture-points is called a hypergesture. A hyper-gesture is a gesture of gestures, and complex music might be studied in terms of hyper-gestures. The complex of, for example, gestures

10 Gestures are generally not sub-ordinated to semiotics. Mazzola exhibits a dichotomy between wild and tamed gestures, the former being independent of semiotic realms, while the latter are serving semiotic purposes as special types of signs. Conceptual creativity is exhibited in the layer of wild gestures. The communicative characteristic of (wild) gestures stresses their "how-ness" as opposed to their substantial "what-ness."

inside a symphonic orchestra, its instrumental sections, and the performers of each section can be understood as a hyper-gesture. It is also about superposition. Theories of quantum give a new approach to the structures of music. In those quantum systems, a musical note is quantised as a vector in Hilbert space, and the musical score is interpreted as a tuple.[11] Based on Hilbert space, quantum systems allow us to follow the music in a mathematical way. But for Mazzola, it turns out to be too difficult to find a solid solution only in quantum theories. Therefore, Mazzola introduces his theory of hyper-gesture to give a solid answer.

Another way of looking at quantum wave-music is to interpret the relation between rhythm and groove. Mark Abel (2016) writes with the theory of Zuckerkandl about groove and time in relation to rhythm and metrum. For Zuckerkandl, the metrum is not produced from a pattern of strong and weak accents but as permanent oscillation. Series of beats in some pop-music are perceived as 1-2-1-2, etc., where the 2 is not the second beat but kind of away-from-one. Metrum includes a cyclical movement comprising a motion of away and back. So, the metrum might even be able to produce a differentiation of pulses. Metrum can even be dynamic as a wave phenomenon. Metric waves are, then, not about equality but about kinetic impulse, overlapping, and superposition. Zuckerkandl deconstructs the duality between rhythm and metrum, or between intensive and extensive. Metrum can be a *field* and a *wave*, rather than an emptily homogeneous form of measurement. The wave is not an event *in* time, but an event *of* time.

11 The Hilbert space used in a quantum mechanical situation is not a physical space in any conceivable sense, nor is it remotely comparable to the phase space of classical physics. In it, the physical objects are projected into a vector space with many dimensions, and measurands such as position and momentum are traced back to abstract operators. The Hilbert space is therefore an abstract vector space of any dimension, finite or infinite, which has the structure of an inner product with which lengths and angles can be measured.

We will now speak about entanglement. In general terms, entanglement means that the overall state of a composite system cannot be determined by the states of its subsystems. The whole is not the sum of its parts. More specifically, entanglement means that two elements can be directly coupled with each other in such a way that one property of the two parts is no longer determined independently of the other particle. As soon as a property of one element is determined by a measurement, the coupled property becomes apparent in the other. However, entanglement does not only occur when two particles originate from a common source, have interacted directly with each other, or are connected due to a physical law of conservation. Rather, it is sufficient for one of two entangled particle pairs — *A* and *B* / *C* and *D* — to interact with the other under experimental conditions in order for the other two to become entangled with each other. If *A* and *C* are entangled, then *B* and *D* are also entangled, even though the two particles have never met directly. Given this phenomenon, music is not limited to the relationship between a listener and a series of sounds. Rather, the entanglement that constitutes the moment of listening to a piece of music will always consist of several parts in a structure, of which the listener and the music itself are only a moment.[12]

In quantum theory, facts are characterised by real numbers and possibilities by imaginary numbers. The vectorial dimension is introduced by the imaginary numbers, and for Laruelle, this means that the theoretical facts on the complex plane are represented as vectors with a real and an imaginary part. (In quantum physics,

12 A structure is not an object, but rather a way in which objects/relata are set in relation to each other. Quantum theory, however, leaves undetermined whether quanta are objects at all. James Ladyman claims that in the case of state entanglement there are no objects at all, but only relations (structure). Relata would always turn out to be relational structures in a certain relationship. In the physical sense, there is something that exists independently of spacetime distances, i.e., that is not localised in clearly definable spacetime regions.

the vectorial dimension is indexed by the complex imaginary numbers—these are vectors with a real and an imaginary part).

So, let's talk about the *i*, the imaginary number, which embodies the leaps of imagination that allowed numbers to break the shackles of mere magnitude. The imaginary number *i*, the root of minus 1, was of the devil in the Middle Ages and was therefore described by Descartes as imaginary. Today, it is a basic component of the complex number $z = a + ib$. The complex numbers are an expression of the effectiveness of the possible. They are not required for the description of facts. The core of the complex numbers is *i*, the root of -1, i.e., $i^2 = -1$. The number line of the complex numbers *z* can be represented by a two-dimensional plane of real numbers *x* and *y* as $z = x + iy$. However, because $i^2 = -1$, there are additional relationships that do not arise in the real world. As a short formula, it can be noted that facts are characterised by real numbers and that real possibilities can be characterised by imaginary numbers.

For Stephen Hawking, time is a complex number $t + ib$, where *t* is the traditional time value and *ib* is the imaginary component. The classical real space-time is complemented by an imaginary time-space defined by imaginary time (Mazzola et al., 2020: 129). If physicists are entitled to introduce new time dimensions, there is no reason to prevent musicians from doing the same and claiming that experimental sound is hosted in such a time-space that is imaginary to the physical one. This means that, at any classical physical time *t*, we would have an entire time-space defined also by an imaginary time *ib*. There is a transitional processing of past music to future non-music, including the body-instrument-sound interface.

Quantum theory offers us a compelling way to think about music. As an explicitly time-based activity, a piece of music not only has a duration that can be measured against pre-existing time, but it also creates its own time frame. Music creates the time in which it exists, meaning that music temporalises the experience and the world. A composition understood as a time-based sound phenomenon draws on a wide range of available material, and the phenomenon is made up of specific components such as location, technics, sound, environment, time, and listening device, which not only influence the quality of the listening experience but determine the quality of the phenomenon.

References

Abel, M. (2016) *Groove: An Aesthetic of Measured Time.* London: Haymarket Books.

Barad, K. (2007) *Meeting the Universe Halfway: Quantum Physics and the Entanglement of Matter and Meaning.* Durham: Combined Academic.

—. (2012) *Agentieller Realismus. Über die Bedeutung materiell-diskursiver Praktiken.* Berlin: Suhrkamp Verlag.

—. (2015) *Verschränkungen.* Berlin: Merve.

Baudrillard, J. (1976) *Der symbolische Tausch und der Tod.* Munich: Matthes & Seitz.

—. (1987) *Cool Memories. 1980–1985.* Munich: Passagen.

—. (1991) *Die fatalen Strategien.* Munich: Matthes & Seitz.

—. (1992a) *Das perfekte Verbrechen.* Munich: Matthes & Seitz.

—. (1992b) *Transparenz des Bösen. Ein Essay über extreme Phänomene.* Berlin: Merve.

—. (1994) *Simulation and Simulacra.* Michigan: University of Michigan Press.

—. (2000) *The Vital Illusion.* New York: Columbia University Press.

—. (2012) *Von der Verführung.* Munich: Matthes & Seitz.

Beller, J. (2021) *The World Computer. Derivative Conditions of Racial Capitalism.* Durham: Duke University Press.

Crary, J. (2022) *Scorched Earth: Beyond the Digital Age to a Post-Capitalist World.* London: Verso.

Deleuze, G. (1990) *Logic of Sense.* New York: Columbia University Press.

—. (1993) "What is Becoming?" In C. V. Boundas (ed.) *The Deleuze Reader.* 1993: 39–41. New York/Oxford: Columbia University Press.

Fisher, M. (2014) *Ghosts of my Life. Writings on Depression, Hauntology and Lost Futures.* London: Zer0 Books.

Gell-Mann, M. (1994) *Das Quark und der Jaguar.* Munich/Zurich: Piper Publishing.

Görnitz, T., & Görnitz, B. (2016) *Von der Quantenphysik zum Bewusstsein. Kosmos, Geist und Materie*. Heidelberg.

Harney, S., & Moten, F. (2021) *All Incomplete*. New York: Minor Compositions

Kane, C. L. (2019) *High-Tech Trash: Glitch, Noise, and Aesthetic Failure*. Oakland: University of California Press.

Ladyman, J. (1998) "What is Structural Realism?" *Studies in History and Philosophy of Science* 29(3): 409–424.

Laruelle, F. (2010a) *Philosophies of Difference: A Critical Introduction to Non—philosophy*. New York: Bloomsbury.

—. (2010b) *Philosophie non-standard: générique, quantique, philo-fiction*. Paris: Éditions Kime.

—. (2014) *Non-Photografie / Photo-Fiktion*. Berlin: Merve.

—. (2018) *On the Black Universe: In the Human Foundations of Colour*. Ausdruck Books: Online. https://www.abhpp.org/en/publikace/francois-laruelle-on-the-black-universe-2018/

Malaspina, C. (2018) *An Epistemology of Noise*. London: Bloomsbury.

Mann, Paul (1995) *Stupid Undergrounds*. Virginia: University of Virginia Press.

Mazzola, G., Noer, J., Pang, Y., Yao, S., Afrisando, J., Rochetser, C., & Nea, W. (2020) *The Future of Music. Towards a Computational Musical Theory of Everything*. Cham: Springer.

Mazzola, G., Manonne, M., Pang, Y. (2016) *Cool Math for Hot Music. A First Introduction to Mathematics for Music Theorists*. Cham: Springer.

Mittelstaedt, P. (2000) "Universell und inconsistent? Quantenmechanik am Ende des 20. Jahrhunderts." *Physikalische Blätter* 56: 65–68.

Prado Casanova, M. (2023) *The Noise in Noise, Uncertainty, Randomness and Control*. Washington: Rowan & Littlefield.

Priest, E. (2013) *Boring Formless Nonsense: Experimental Music and the Aesthetics of Failure*. New York: Bloomsbury.

—. (2022) *Earworm and Event*. Durham: Duke University Press.

Sbordoni, A. (2024) *Semiotics of the End: Essays on Capitalism and the Apocalypse*. Amsterdam: Institute of Network Cultures.

Shipley, G. J. (2021) *Stratagem of the Corpse: Dying with Baudrillard, a Study of Sickness and Simulacra*. London: Anthem Press.

Serres, M (1991) *Hermes I.* Berlin: Kommunikation.

—. (2022) *Der Parasit.* Berlin: Merve.

Szepanski, A. (2024) *In the Delirium of the Simulation: Baudrillard Revisited.* Nicosia/Berlin: Becoming/NON.

Warren, C. L. (2018) *Ontological Terror: Blackness, Nihilism, and Emancipation.* Durham: Duke University Press.

4. QUANTUM AESTHETICS[1]

by Jens Schröter

Introduction

Historically, the options for formally constructing an artwork and its aesthetics have been expanded and changed by new technologies—even if certain formal options continue to exist (e.g., central perspective). The relationship between aesthetics and technology is therefore complex, as can be seen, for example, in the complicated efforts to determine whether a kind of 'digital aesthetics' can be defined. Quantum theory plays a role on different levels in media history—we can differentiate non-quantum media, quantum media of the first order, and second-level quantum media, i.e., technologies that use quantum effects at the level of information processing itself. The question arises as to whether specific new aesthetics will also emerge here, and in which traditions such aesthetics

1 This is a substantially revised and extended English translation of Schröter (2023).

would be embedded. The text thus poses the historical and systematic question of the possibility of a 'quantum aesthetic'.

In the following section (2), the relationship between quantum theory and media will first be explained. The next section (3) deals with the question of what an aesthetics of technical media or media aesthetics can be. In Section 4, I want to bring Sections 2 and 3 together and discuss what 'quantum aesthetics' may be; I will present several examples of artistic practices that relate to quantum theory in one way or the other (and not necessarily in the way sketched out in Section 3).

Quantum mechanics and media history

The discussion of quantum mechanics and media history would be pointless if it were to denote the obvious fact that media, insofar as they are also material and technological artefacts (alongside institutions, programmes, content, practices, etc.), ultimately consist of the same elementary particles (and forces) as all other material objects. The question rather addresses the role that (the knowledge of) quantum mechanics has played in media history. It is suggested that, in addition to, firstly, media whose creation does not depend on quantum mechanical knowledge (2.1), there are, secondly, first-level quantum media (2.2), and, thirdly, second-level quantum media (2.3).

i. Non-quantum media

Photography is a technology that emerged in the 19th century, long before Planck's first steps towards quantum mechanics, which can nonetheless be described as a non-quantum medium. It did not require any quantum mechanical knowledge for its development and was discovered empirically through experiments with light-sensitive silver halide emulsions (see Schaaf, 2000, for a nice study that traces Talbot's experimental struggle for photography). However, this example is complex: although photochemical effects have long been observed and harnessed in countless photographic experiments, a conclusive theoretical explanation was only achieved with the help of quantum theory in the 20th century (cf. Sponer, 1930, who does not directly discusses photography but other photochemical effects). In other words, photography is ultimately—and this is not really surprising—also based on quantum effects, but no explicit quantum theory was required to make them usable. The same applies to electricity as the basis of all electronic media. Electrical functionality was known relatively early on and could therefore be used practically, even if a consistent explanation for electromagnetic phenomena was only found with quantum electrodynamics in the 20th century (see Feynman, 2006).

ii. First-level quantum media

With the development of quantum mechanics in the 20th century, there was a rapid development of technologies that required this knowledge. In this sense, "it is not digitalisation that is the revolution of the 20th century, but quantum mechanics, which made its technical implementation possible in the first place" (Hagen, 2002: 222, my translation). Or, to put it another way: "By some estimates, 30 percent of the United States' gross national product is said to derive from technologies based on quantum theory. Without the insights provided by quantum mechanics, there would be no cell phones, no CD players, no portable computers. Quantum mechanics is not a branch of physics; it is physics" (quoted in Barad, 2007: 252).

The laser that scans the disc in a CD (or DVD or Blu-Ray, etc.) player is an example of stimulated emission, which was first predicted by Albert Einstein in 1916 using quantum theoretical arguments. The laser was and is also a prerequisite for the production of hologram, which can be found in the simple form of the so-called rainbow hologram as a security feature on numerous banknotes and credit cards (Schröter, 2022). Einstein also provided a quantum-theoretical explanation for the photoelectric effect as early as

1905, which ultimately led to the image sensors found in digital cameras and scanners through the work of Boyle and Smith (Nobel Prize 2009 for Boyle; Einstein got his Nobel Prize 1921 for his explanation of the photoelectric effect).[2] Semiconductor technology, which, in the form of the transistor, is fundamental to modern computer technologies, can be described theoretically using quantum mechanics. However, this example also show that quantum mechanical knowledge is often not directly necessary (more practical concepts from chemistry or solid state physics are often more helpful), or that technologies do not emerge directly from theoretical concepts.[3]

iii. Second-level quantum media

Although the media history of the 20th century was already essentially a history of quantum mechanical knowledge, a "quantum revolution" (Fürnkranz, 2019: 17) is now being proclaimed: the computer becomes the quantum computer, cryptography becomes quantum cryptography and the internet becomes the quantum internet. Has a drastic change taken place? Or is it more a case of sensationalist rhetoric like that which has surrounded the digital for some time (cf. Schröter, 2004a: c)? Although language and money have always been digital codes,[4] and there was already a decidedly digital medium in the 19th century with telegraphy, there is currently a lot of talk about 'digitisation', as if everything had previously been analog.[5] Isn't the much-vaunted digitalisation

---

2 Smartphones tend to use CMOS sensors, which have a different structure but are also based on the photoelectric effect.

3 This would also explain why quantum mechanics is not mentioned at all, or only very marginally, in many media histories (e.g., Winston, 1998).

4 If you understand "digital" in the sense of Nelson Goodman (1968: 159–164) as being based on a discrete and disjunctive code.

5 Nonsensical terms such as 'analog book' (as opposed to e-book, for example) are spreading.

better understood as the spread of microelectronic, and therefore ultimately quantum-based, technologies—in other words, more of a 'quantum mechanisation'?

However, one can justifiably argue that the quantum computer[6] is able to overcome the central principle of so-called digitisation, namely binary coding, as it has been central to computers up to now—at least in the sense that a given *qubit* can now be zero and one at the same time. This means that, although microchips (based on silicon as a semiconductor) are already based on quantum mechanical knowledge, the form of information processing—clearly separated into zero or one—is itself still classical.[7] In quantum computers, the form of information processing itself is realised using quantum effects—the same applies to quantum cryptography. In this sense, insofar as quantum computers and quantum cryptography are methods for the transmission, storage and processing of information and thus media, we can speak of second-order quantum media (in contrast, for example, to 'normal' computers as first-order quantum media, see Dowling & Milburn, 2003; Schröter, Ernst & Warnke, 2022).

In terms of media history, this initially means that the previous binary-digital Von Neumann machines are not the 'end of media history'.[8] New technologies are obviously emerging, and these can be integrated into a media-historical perspective. Kittler describes media history as an escalation: "In a strategic chain of escalations, the telegraph emerged to surpass the speed of messenger posts, the radio to undermine the vulnerability of submarine cables, and the computer to decode radio messages that were as

6 I won't discuss other technologies like quantum cryptography, etc., here.

7 However, the binary principle is historically contingent and only ubiquitous due to its simple circuitry implementation (cf. Schröter, 2004a).

8 At least one passage in Kittler (1999a) can be interpreted in this way: "Before the end, something is coming to an end. The general digitisation of channels and information erases the differences among individual media" (1).

secret as they were interceptable" (1999b: n.p., my translation). Quantum computers would then be the answer to network communication encrypted with PGP (*Pretty Good Privacy*) and related methods—for example, by criminals and terrorists, because this can no longer be deciphered with conventional computers (as it takes too much time). In Winston's sense, this would be a "supervening social necessity" (1998: 6) that drives the development of quantum computers (amongst other things, like the difficulties of quantum simulation or sorting big data, Pandey/Ramesh, 2015). It is no coincidence that one of the first algorithms for the then still hypothetical quantum computers was one for prime factorisation (cf. Shor, 1997)—and many of the encryptions used today are based precisely on the difficulty of such factorisation (cf. Schröter, 2004b: 368f.). However, the home banking of innocent citizens would then no longer be secure either—if those very criminals had quantum computers at their disposal. There are also encryption methods that should be able to withstand quantum computers (cf. Bernstein/Buchmann/Dahmen, 2009), which are more complex, but will then have to be developed preferentially. There are already processes of standardisation of these new algorithms underway.[9]

It is to be assumed that quantum computers will not replace conventional binary-digital computers in the future, but that both technologies will coexist, as they have different strengths and weaknesses in specific areas.[10] For many tasks, conventional computers will continue to be sufficient or even better suited; special computing problems may then be delegated to an integrated quantum chip or via the internet to remote quantum computers.[11] But it is, at the moment, far from clear if there will

9 See https://csrc.nist.gov/projects/post-quantum-cryptography, 11.3.2024.

10 In general, old media do not disappear, but change their function and continue to exist in special niches (a good example of this is the analog record).

11 See https://www.ibm.com/de-de/quantum, 11.3.2024.

be working quantum computers in the near future or even at all (Dyakonov, 2020).

So much for a brief outline of the role of quantum mechanics in the history of technical media. In the following, the question of the aesthetics of technical media, i.e., media aesthetics, will be discussed.

Notes on (digital) media aesthetics

After the Second World War, various forms of abstraction established themselves as the dominant art movement in the USA and, from there, in other Western countries.[12] With explicit recourse to the concept of the medium, art critic Clement Greenberg developed a historical justification for the new forms of abstraction in painting, which found its most compact expression in the two essays 'American-Type Painting' from 1955 and 'Modernist Painting' from 1960 (cf. Greenberg, 1993; 1995). In the latter, he emphasised that, in modernist art, "the unique and proper area of competence of each art coincided with all that was unique in the nature of its medium" (Greenberg, 1995: 86). In order to open up this subject area, artists would have to analyse and explore their medium step by step in order to find out which conventions (e.g., the narrative) are borrowed from other media and are therefore dispensable.[13] In the late 1950s and early 1960s, the first artistic positions emerged that were difficult or even impossible to reconcile with Greenberg's approach (e.g., Pop Art), and which he therefore rejected, but his position initially remained influential.

However, Greenberg's paradigm of media reflection gradually faded away from around the mid-1960s onwards to make way for a 'postmodernism' oriented towards intermediality and quotation

12 Discussing aesthetics is not the same as discussing art—but here I will focus on art and its aesthetic strategies.

13 Obviously, he had to exclude older trends such as Dadaism or Surrealism for his model to work.

or entirely different art forms such as *conceptual art* (3.1), only to reappear in more recent discussions about the artistic potential of digital media (3.2).

i. Crisis of media reflection

Greenberg's programme of a self-analytical reduction of painting and other art forms gradually became entangled in problems at the beginning of the 1960s, because the self-analytical reduction of painting soon threatened to cross the boundary beyond which "a picture stops being a picture and turns into an arbitrary object", and which Greenberg had called for not to be crossed, but "to be observed and indicated" (Greenberg, 1996: 90). The unpainted canvas as a picture moved into the realm of the possible (see Fried, 1967: 23). Ultimately, new developments emerged, such as *Minimal Art*, which shifted the emphasis away from media-specificity. Finally, new technologies appeared on the art scene—first of all video—which, according to Rosalind Krauss, caused the concept of reflection on the medium as the basis of art to disappear because media, such as video, were involved in practices that were too disparate (cf. Krauss, 1999: 30ff.). Thus, in the 1970s and 1980s, forms of art flourished that had broken with any media-reflexive purism and instead worked with multi- and intermedial strategies—often in the form of 'installations'.[14] As a result, Greenberg's role as a critic declined and he became almost the enemy. Even his 'student' Rosalind Krauss proclaimed a 'post-medium condition' (Krauss, 1999).

ii. The comeback of modernism with new media

After the seemingly complete collapse of the Greenberg paradigm, it is somewhat surprising that media reflection is once again playing an important role among newer artists. Theoretician Juliane

14 Which Greenberg of course criticised (cf. Greenberg, 1997: 446ff.)

Rebentisch, for example, notes that in "contemporary art … the knowledgeable reference to the various traditions of the arts and the possibilities of their media … also plays an important role" (Rebentisch, 2013: 105, my translation). Interestingly, just one page earlier, she points out that the "role of technologies and new media in this context should not be underestimated", especially with regard to the "'thematisation' of older means of representation in newer ones (painting in film, for example)". It seems that artists, in particular, who operate in the "medium of digitality" (ibid.: 104), are once again devoting attention to these questions. For example, Thomas Ruff remarks with regard to his digitally processed porn photos from the internet, the *Nudes* (an obvious allusion to a certain tradition of painting): "If I work with a certain medium, then I also want to reflect this medium in the picture" (Ruff, 1999: 75, my translation). In the foreword to his 2001 book *net.art 2.0*, Tilman Baumgärtel explicitly refers to Greenberg in order to legitimise the artistic status of net art through its self-reflexive processes (cf. Baumgärtel, 2001).

Greenberg's argument that illusionism in painting had the effect, if not the purpose, to "dissemble … the medium, using art to conceal art" (Greenberg, 1995: 86) also reappears in Kittler's harsh criticism of user-friendly surfaces and the rapidly spreading 'digital image culture' (Kittler, 1998: 255). One consequence of this media-modernism, therefore, is that computer art would have to continue to dismantle the illusionistic conventions of surfaces in order to finally reflect the technological foundations of its medium. But with computers, it is problematic where exactly the 'surfaces' as merely metaphorical or even disguising representations end and where the 'actual' technological basis begins.[15] So, would artists not

15 "The computer *as a* medium only exists, as it were, by distinguishing itself from itself, in other words: by losing itself in all its *interfaces*, its programmable design methods and user interfaces, i.e., by postponing its 'actual' meaning. The digital medium *eksists* [*sic*] in its multiform metaphoricity" (Tholen, 1999: 21, my translation).

only have to reject standard software, higher programming languages, even assemblers, insofar as these are already conventionalised interfaces, but also reinvent the computer architecture and reject the binary system?[16] That would be like asking painters to found chemical companies in order to synthesise new colours.[17] Or should we demand that artists reflect and exhibit the quantum mechanical knowledge in the technologies? And if so, how?

Quantum aesthetics

The question concerning a possible quantum aesthetics would first have to take into account that quantum physical knowledge is itself only possible on the basis of certain aesthetic processes (in the wider sense). A distinction can be made between at least two levels: first, procedures based on imaging systems of various kinds used in experimental research to record and visualise traces of quantum physical events (cf. Galison, 1997); secondly, there are diagrammatic representations, such as Feynman diagrams, which are important for quantum physics theorising (cf. Stöltzner, 2017). In both cases, visual representations are used to formulate and test quantum theory and its implications.

It seems that artists have a certain fascination for quantum theory and particle physics. An example of the contact between art and quantum physics was the invitation of the famous physicist Anton Zeilinger to *dOCUMENTA 13*. Zeilinger is known for his experiments in quantum information, quantum optics, quantum computing and quantum computation, etc. (although the presentation, at least when I visited it, only included some of Zeilinger's instruments, see *dOCUMENTA 13*, 2012). There was (and is) the

16 The fact that today's computers are binary von Neumann machines is historically contingent and therefore a convention (see Schröter, 2004a1: 1–12).

17 Cf. De Duve (1996: 147), and following on Duchamp's early criticism that (as a rule) painters have to resort to industrially produced colours and that, in this respect, every painting is a kind of *ready-made*.

legendary *Arts at CERN* programme, which offers various types of grants to artists (CERN, 2022a). A very informative report on the programme by its founder Ariane Koek (2017) is titled *In/visible: The Inside Story of the Making of Arts at CERN*. This paper has the tension between the invisible quantum processes and the methods of their visualisation already in the title. However, most of the artistic experiments carried out at CERN refer to the scientific results in a rather metaphorical way.[18] See this example:

> One of the first artworks produced from the art/science 'collision' is *Versuch unter Kreisen* (2012) by German artist Julius von Bismarck. In the exhibition space, four industrial lights hang from the ceiling, rotating in motorised patterns. As viewers enter the space, they automatically try to identify the patterns, but the lights move between order and chaos, between law and disorder. Although there is no overall regular circling of the lights, the mind tries to recognise a law to rationalise them, and this is the most interesting aspect of the piece. There is a pressing need to understand the 'nature' of the lights. The 'enlightening' installation therefore oscillates between an apparent comprehension of the patterns and a lack of comprehension. It ultimately offers a vibrating metaphor for both art and science: the search for nature's disciplined laws and irrational beauty, and the lost and regained understanding of nature as seen through the succession of discoveries and theories.
>
> (Descamous, 2016: 6)

This artwork addresses the process of pattern recognition—that is, finding structures in seemingly random data—and this is also a process that is important for the data analysis at CERN, where patterns in very huge chunks of data are sought; patterns that indicate the appearance of processes predicted by theory. In that

18 See exceptions such as the Semiconductor installation *HALO* by Ruth Jarman and Joe Gerhardt (Semiconductor, 2018).

sense, the artwork exhibits a quantum aesthetic, but on a very general level insofar it thematises a certain process—'pattern recognition'—which is not restricted to the construction of information in particle physics, but can be found nearly everywhere (think of recognising faces in the clouds, etc., otherwise known as pareidolia).

If one wanted to ask about aesthetics in relation to quantum theory or high-energy physics, there is of course the problem that entities such as 'quarks' cannot meaningfully be said to have a visual appearance. Therefore, the question of an aesthetic approach to such entities must always remain metaphorical. But whatever the status of these 'entities', particle physics as an empirical science must (as already mentioned above) produce some kind of visualisations or images (be they diagrams) that can be seen as some kind of evidence.[19] Otherwise, the very expensive and complex accelerators, such as the LHC at CERN, would have no meaning. In this sense, even the most abstract and unimaginable entity has an irreducible perceptible side—namely, in traces that show up on images or in graphs in detectors (cf. as mentioned above: Galison, 1997). It is therefore interesting to look for art that deals, directly or indirectly, with the visualisation strategies used. Since art is (among other things) about experiments with perception, visuality and (re-)presentation, it should come as no surprise that the enormous effort put into visualisation in science is also of interest to artists.

With this in mind, I would like to discuss one artistic position, namely Ryoji Ikeda's multimedia installation *Supersymmetry* (2014). The installation consists of a long series of screens dominated by abstract images, e.g., floating dots and rotating point clouds, which are connected to visualisations via moving lines with cryptic texts or mysterious diagrams.[20]

---

19 See Rheinberger (2021: 67, my translation): "It is certainly not too far-fetched to claim that the visualisation of things that do not reveal themselves to the observer of their own accord, i.e., that are not immediately evident and before our eyes, is part of the basic outline and basic gesture of modern science in general."

20 See a video of the installation here: https://www.ryojiikeda.com/project/supersymmetry/, 11.3.2024.

The screens flicker, sometimes turn blindingly white and then dark again. New images, lines, dots and diagrams appear. All of this is accompanied by a typical Ikedaesque soundtrack consisting of electronic signals and sparse technical noises that are rhythmically adapted to the changes on the screens. The screens are installed in two parallels in the dark, left and right, forming a corridor in which the viewer moves, immersing themselves in the sound and looking at the flickering screens here and there. The installation imitates the aesthetics of scientific visualisation with its curves and diagrams, but defamiliarises it through sheer exaggeration. Nobody can understand what is shown on the screens. This reflects the incomprehensibility of high science (to the layman), especially particle physics and its abstract theories—such as "supersymmetry", a particular extension of the "standard model", which is now a central field of research at CERN (see CERN, 2022b). The appearance of the screens in the dark also alludes to the black boxes of data analysis, which is central to research at CERN. The patterns are constructed by highly complex machine assemblages, but they do not show a 'single event', only complex statistical distributions. The screens and the soundtrack also create a situation of sensory and information overload; it is almost impossible to keep track of the unfolding events. In this way, the installation aestheticises the immense amount of data generated at CERN. The sublime unimaginability of this mass of data and its complexity is translated into a flow of images and sounds that change far too quickly to be perceived, even if they were comprehensible.

However, one might rightly object that Ikeda's installation does not develop any quantum aesthetics, as would have been expected after the explanations in Sections 2 and 3. After all, *Supersymmetry is* a kind of defamiliarising mimesis of the visualisation strategies at CERN and the displays and interfaces used, but does not 'modernistically' reflect the underlying mediality of computers and their interconnectedness with the history of quantum mechanical knowledge.

This reflection is better conceivable with the digital. There is no specificity of the (almost) universal digital medium of the computer, except that of being able to approximately repeat all other specificities mathematically and thereby detach them from their material conditions—which also means that completely new connections and reconfigurations of these transmaterialised specificities would be possible.[21] The detachment of media specificity from its materiality—for example, in the case of a virtual photo camera (cf. Schröter, 2003)—means that, since what is produced is a mathematical entity, all parameters could be changed at will, even beyond what is physically possible. In this sense, an analysis and reflection of the media conditions of photography would be possible in a new and radical way. Consequently, 'media aesthetics' means being able to work with the *transmaterialised* specifics in a completely new way, and this radicalisation of the possibilities for reflecting on the 'media-specific' in the space of the virtual may be one reason why an almost Greenbergian imperative for self-reflection is once again playing such an important role in working with digital media.

But how do we reflect on the quantum mechanical knowledge closely linked to the triumph of digital technologies? One approach to engage with quantum mechanical knowledge would be to address the fundamental discontinuity and 'granularity' of the world. Could a new reading of pointillism make sense? One that does not attribute it primarily to the question of colour perception or new printing techniques in the 19th century (cf. Broude, 1978), but rather as an image of the world as fundamentally granular? After all, the emergence of pointillism coincided (roughly) with the formulation of the quantum hypothesis by Planck (around 1900). This is perhaps too far-fetched (see also Asendorf, 1989). Let's take

---

21 Cf. Noll (1967: 93), who remarked early on about the computer: "This is an active medium with which the artist can interact on a new level, *freed from many of the physical limitations of all other previous media*" (emphasis added, J.S.). New physical limitations arise with regard to the hardware that underlies every computing process and, for example, limits the computer speed due to the 'von Neumann bottleneck', which can play a decisive role in the simulation of highly complex phenomena (see Schröter, 2013).

another example. There is a painting by the African-American painter Jack Whitten, whose mosaic-like structure seems to refer to the fundamental granularity of the world and is called *Quantum Wall (A Gift for Prince)* (2016, acrylic on canvas, with Tivar, 213.4 x 482.6cm. Friedrich Christian Flick Collection).[22] After all, Whitten himself remarks: "The title of the paintings comes from quantum mechanics. It's just something I am very interested in—it gets my imagination going" (in Traps, 2017). And further:

> I'm working with these units of paint, which I call tesserae—originally the word for ancient mosaics. I've studied mosaics for years. I've lived in Greece, on the island of Crete, for the past forty-six years, and I've done a lot of travelling around the Mediterranean basin and Egypt, and there I've seen a lot of mosaics—so it's the mosaic that leads to these paintings. The tesserae, in my mind, is the unit, it's the thing that makes them. I can build anything I want with the tesserae, using all acrylic paint, built layer by layer by layer until I get the thickness that I want.
>
> (ibid.)

Whitten's artistic approach can therefore be understood as building larger structures from fundamental units, a process that is at least similar to the quantum physical description of the world. And in a parallel way, artists who work with digital media today—or better: images—would have to extend the reflection on pixelation to a reflection on the fundamental graininess of the real. However, a reflection on the fundamentally stochastic character of the quantum world would also be conceivable, something that already seems to be hinted at in Ikeda's confusing multiplicity of signals. Perhaps it even necessary to combine the two traits, because otherwise it is not clear why Whitten's strategy is really in any meaningful way related to quantum physics and not just to the history of the mosaic

22 The painting can easily be found by searching for it via Google.

(mentioned by himself). This shows that it is by no means straightforward to attribute to a given artwork a plausible relation to quantum theory or the quantum character of reality.

Furthermore, Whitten makes paintings. His work is not directly related to modern media technologies, except perhaps in the relation of the structure of his paintings to the grains of analog and the grid of digital photography (Shiff, 2017). But although quantum knowledge (the photoelectric effect) is a fundamental base of digital photography (Hagen, 2002), in what sense is this quantum aspect reflected in his paintings? The argument to relate his painting, just because it is called 'Quantum Wall', to quantum theory, is perhaps overstretched.

Another important artistic project is *Black Quantum Futurism.*[23] The collective participated in *DOCUMENTA 15*:

> Based in Philadelphia, USA, Black Quantum Futurism (BQF) is the collective practice of Camae Ayewa and Rasheedah Phillips. Their work sets forth new connections of time and space, thereby becoming liberated from the constraints of linear time. Their writing, films, and performances draw on sources such as alternative futurities, Afro-diasporan temporalities, quantum physics, housing futures, and speculative fiction as frameworks through which to reconnect to the past and create new futures.[24]

In this project, it is especially important that "in quantum mechanics the traditional Eurocentric notions of causality, based on the linear, sequential meta-assumptions ... must be suspended" (Imani, 2015: 40). Quantum theory is used here as a resource for post-colonial and critical strategies that criticise, amongst other things, certain models of time. Moreover, quantum theory is compared to ancient African knowledge to expose again the limits of hegemonial *white* forms of knowledge (see Phillips, 2015). Quantum the-

---

23 https://www.blackquantumfuturism.com, 11.3.2024.

24 https://documenta-fifteen.de/en/lumbung-members-artists/black-quantum-futurism/, 11.3.2024.

ory's disruption of classical physics is therefore analogised with the (potentially) disruptive effects of African forms of knowledge for hegemonial Eurocentric knowledge. *Black Quantum Futurism* won in 2021, similar to Ikeda, the *Collide Residency Award* at CERN with a proposal entitled "CPT Symmetry and Violations"[25]:

> 'The project seeks to understand the ways in which quantum physics can influence how people think about, experience and measure time in everyday reality, exploring the possibilities that quantum physics offers beyond the limitations of traditional, linear notions of time,' explain the artists. 'Through the project we will connect with scientists based at CERN to learn more about their investigations of time in physics—specifically through studying experiments being done on CPT symmetry, CERN scientists' investigations into quantum theories of gravity, and other phenomena of quantum physics as it concerns inquiries into time.'[26]

There are many more artistic initiatives operating in a more or less convincing way with quantum theory.[27]

Coming back to the description of first order quantum media, let's take as an example the laser, which is a widespread technology operating in several media technologies like CD or BluRay players, laser printers, and is a condition for holographic (and kinegrammatic) technologies, which are important for security technologies on credit cards, etc. (Schröter, 2022). Can we, speculatively, imagine an artistic practice that reflects on this quantum technology? Could certain kinds of music that are based on wilfully damaged CDs—like some early music by Oval[28]—be understood as

25 The title alludes to basic symmetries and their violations

26 https://home.cern/news/news/knowledge-sharing/black-quantum-futurism-wins-years-collide-residency-award, 11.3.2024

27 https://www.iamaq.org/what-is-quantum-art, 11.3.2024.

28 See https://en.wikipedia.org/wiki/Oval_(musical_project), 11.3.2024: "Disdaining the use of synthesizers, Oval instead deliberately mutilated

reflecting on the process of reading the CD with a laser, and therefore be understood as reflecting on the operations of CD players as being based on the quantum technology of the laser? But Oval's music could also be read as reflecting on the problems of algorithmic error correction in CD players to cope with the messed-up signals. Would these two aspects together be enough to count as a genuine 'quantum-modernist' aesthetic of media reflection?

Another approach may be found in the holographic artworks by Dieter Jung. His *Light Mill* (1986)[29] is a complex installation that uses (multiplex) holography, a pictorial medium based on lasers (see Schröter, 2014: §9). Only rotating and intersecting planes of colour, moving with the movements of the observer, are visible. Could we say that, by showing only light, Jung reflects in a Greenbergian sense on the coherent light of the laser? Or is this too vague an analogy, since the light we see in the installation is not coherent?

There are several other examples from the field of music, in which compositional strategies are related to quantum theory. *Quantum Music* was a research project funded by "Creative Europe" (a funding scheme from the European Union):

> This highly original and innovative project managed to push boundaries and bring together the distant worlds of music and quantum physics. The main outcome of the pilot project was an interactive multimedia show Quantum Music, featuring new, specially designed hybrid keyboard instruments, new library of quantum sounds developed from the experiments and formulas of quantum physics and new compositions written specially for this show.[30]

CDs by writing on them with felt pens, then processed samples of fragmented sounds to create a very rhythmic electronic style."

29 See https://isea-archives.siggraph.org/art-events/dieter-jung-light-mill/, 11.3.2024.

30 See http://quantummusic.org, 11.3.2024.

Several papers were published in the context of the project, which discuss interesting questions like "Can we hear the sound of quantum superpositions?" (Vedral, 2018) In another paper, it is asked what it means to compose using quantum information, and therefore what the notion of "quantum music" exactly means. Thereby, the history of (Western) music is divided into a "classical" part (using the analogy between "classical"—that is, pre-quantum—physics and the established notion of "classical music") and a "post-classical" part, which is associated with quantum theory:

> John Cage's music and Merce Cunningham's choreography broke the classical way of composing and explored randomness and silence [...], which can now be seen from a new perspective through the knowledge of the quantum vacuum; and in György Ligeti's "Poème symphonique" (1962), John Cage's "4' 33"" (1952) and Steve Reich's "Pendulum Music" (1968) we actually have some famous modern classics that include the important quantum phenomenon of probabilities (even though this was not the expressed intention of the composer).
>
> (Helweg, 2018: 63)

Moreover, certain highly experimental approaches are suggested:

> As a quantum listener you might like to listen to Richard Wagner's opera backwards (as anti-particles). Or the complete Rolling Stones records compressed to the duration of one second (as it would be "heard" from the outer universe). Or Giuseppe Verdi's Requiem as a 100-years-long performance (as if the atoms could listen to the music from our world). Or try to program a "probability button" on your computer that can select unexpected excerpts from different music – not to forget a journey into a Musical Hilbert Space (where we have all the existing music in the world together with all the not yet existing music).
>
> (Ibid.: 64)

After this, the author discusses systematically different approaches of using quantum theory for musical composition, e.g., "quantum narratives", where only the title of a work is inspired by quantum theory, or "sonification", in which the auditory display of quantum experiments is used—similar to the approach of Ikeda (discussed above). Many more possible strategies and concrete works are presented.

There are further experimental initiatives for experimenting with music and quantum effects. The *Danish Cultural Institute* houses an initiative called "Quantum Aesthetics":

> 100 years ago, the Danish scientist Niels Bohr received the Nobel prize for his revolutionary discoveries in quantum physics. His way of thinking still influences diverse spheres of our society today. Within the framework of our project 'Quantum Aesthetic' three sound artworks have been created by the three artists—Jacob Kirkegaard from Denmark, Tie Yann from China, and Anna Fišere from Latvia, who work with sound as their primary medium. The works are incredible examples of how scientific concepts and theory can inspire art and lead to new ways of thinking about the world. The art pieces show us that art and science may not be as dissimilar as we may think.[31]

It is obvious that there are many artistic approaches that take recourse to quantum theory in one way or the other—most often not in the form of a (neo-)modernist reflection on the media used

31 https://www.dki.lv/quantum-aesthetics-2/, 11.3.2024. I want to mention here a further project: in 2003, former lead singer of (post-)punk band *Killing Joke,* Jaz Coleman, was commissioned by the Institute for Complex Adaptive Matter (ICAM) to compose a three-part concerto *Music of the Quantum,* expressing the ideas of the quantum and emergence in musical form, which he co-produced with his brother, Piers Coleman, who is a condensed matter physicist at Rutgers University (https://en.wikipedia.org/wiki/Jaz_Coleman, 11.3.2024.). There are other initiatives that have "quantum" in their name, but do not seem to be relate not at all to quantum theory; see https://quantum-musical.de, 11.3.2024.

and their quantum materiality (Schröter, 2022). The plurality of approaches shows that it is an open question of how the knowledge of quantum theory can be used in artistic strategies. But obviously, a need is felt to develop aesthetic approaches in relation to quantum theory—perhaps its strangeness and abstractness mandates this type of translation?

It is even more speculative what aesthetic potentials will be possible with the upcoming second-level quantum media.[32] The high computing speed of quantum computers could make new forms of presentation realisable—for example, in the field of holographic display technologies, which have so far also suffered from the problem of too large and too complex data volumes (cf. Winston, 1998: 341). The acceleration of fundamental processes in the field of artificial intelligence (cf. Lloyd/Mohseni/Rebentrost, 2013) could also lead to new forms of interactive art or image/text generation. But only the future can tell—in any case, interesting unknown areas of quantum aesthetics are opening up here.

References

Asendorf, C. (1989) *Ströme und Strahlen. Das langsame Verschwinden der Materie um 1900*. Giessen: Anabas.

Barad, K. (2007) *Meeting the Universe Halfway: Quantum Physics and the Entanglement of Matter and Meaning*. Durham and London: Duke University Press.

Baumgärtel, T. (2001) *[net.art 2.0] Neue Materialien zur Netzkunst*. Nuremberg: Verlag für moderne Kunst.

Bernstein, D., Buchmann, J., & Dahmen, E. (2009) *Post-quantum Cryptography*. Berlin and Heidelberg: Springer.

32 If we exclude, for a moment, the slightly grotesque staging of the quantum computing systems itself, especially in the case of the IBM-Q, see https://en.wikipedia.org/wiki/IBM_Q_System_One#/media/File:IBM_Q_system_(Fraunhofer_2).jpg, 11.3.2024.

Broude, N. (1978) "New Light on Seurat's 'Dot': Its Relation to Photo-Mechanical Color Printing in France in the 1880s". In *Seurat in Perspective*: 163–175. Englewood Cliffs, N.J.: Prentice-Hall.

CERN (2022a) "Arts at Cern." Last access 11.03.2024. https://arts.cern

CERN (2022b) "Supersymmetry." Last access 11.03.2024. https://home.cern/science/physics/supersymmetry

De Duve, T. (1996). *Kant after Duchamp*. Cambridge/MA and London: MIT Press.

Descamous, G. (2016) "When Art and Science Collide: Arts at CERN." *Afterimage* 44(3): 6–7.

dOCUMENTA 13 (2012) *Anton Zeilinger*. Vol. 76 von dOCUMENTA (13): 100 Notes – 100 Thoughts, 100 Notizen – 100 Gedanken. Ostfildern: Hatje Cantz.

Dowling, J. P., & Milburn, G. J. (2003) "Quantum Technology: The Second Quantum Revolution." *Philosophical Transactions: Mathematical, Physical and Engineering Sciences* (361) 1809: 1655–1674.

Dyakonov, M. I. (2020) *Will We Ever Have a Quantum Computer?* Cham: Springer.

Einstein, A. (1905) "Über einen die Erzeugung und Verwandlung des Lichtes betreffenden heuristischen Gesichtspunkt." *Annalen der Physik* 322(6): 132–148.

Einstein, A. (1916) "Zur Quantentheorie der Strahlung." *Mitteilungen der Physikalischen Gesellschaft Zürich* 18: 47–62.

Feynman, R. (2006) *QED: The Strange Theory of Light and Matter*. Princeton and Oxford: Princeton UP.

Fried, M. (1967) "Art and Objecthood." *Artforum* 5(10): 12–23.

Fürnkranz, G. (2019) *Vision Quanten-Internet: Ultraschnell und hackersicher*. Berlin and Heidelberg: Springer.

Galison, P. (1997) *Image and Logic: A Material Culture of Microphysics*. Chicago and London: Chicago UP.

Goodman, N. (1968). Languages of Art. An Approach to a Theory of Symbols. Indianapolis: Bobbs-Merrill.

Greenberg, C. (1993) "'American-Type' Painting." In *The Collected Essays and Criticism. Vol. 3: Affirmations and Refusals*, 1950–1956. Edited by John O'Brian. Chicago and London: University of Chicago Press, pp. 217–235. First published 1960.

Greenberg, C. (1995). "Modernist Painting." In *The Collected Essays and Criticism. Vol. 4: Modernism with a Vengeance*, 1957–1969. Edited by John O'Brian. Chicago and London: University of Chicago Press, pp. 85–93. First published 1960.

Hagen, W (2002) "Die Entropie der Fotografie: Skizzen zu einer Genealogie der digital-elektronischen Bildaufzeichnung." In *Paradigma Fotografie: Fotokritik am Ende des fotografischen Zeitalters. Band 1*, ed. by Herta Wolf, 195–235. Frankfurt: Suhrkamp.

Helweg, K. (2018) "Composing with Quantum Information. Aspects of Quantum Music in Theory and Practice." *Muzikologija* 24: 61–77 doi: 0.2298/MUZ1824061H

Imani, N. O. (2015). "The Implications of Africa-Centred Conceptions of Time & Space for Quantitative Theorising: Limitations of Paradigmatically-Bound Philosophical Meta-Assumptions." In *Black Quantum Futurism. Theory and Practice. Vol. 1*, ed. by Rasheedah Phillips, 31–48. Philadelphia: Afrofuturist Affair.

Kittler, F. (1998) "Gleichschaltungen. Über Normen und Standards der elektronischen Kommunikation". In *Geschichte der Medien*, ed. by Manfred Faßler und Wulf Halbach, 255–268. Munich: Fink.

Kittler, F. (1999a) *Gramophone, Film, Typewriter*. Stanford: Stanford University Press.

Kittler, F. (1999b) "Von der Implementierung des Wissens: Versuch einer Theorie der Hardware" Last access 03.03.2022. https://nettime.org/Lists-Archives/nettime-l-9902/msg00015.html

Koek, A. (2017) "In/visible: the Inside Story of the Making of Arts at CERN." *Interdisciplinary Science Review* 42(4): 345–358.

Krauss, R. (1999) *"A Voyage on the North Sea". Art in the Age of the Post-Medium Condition*. New York: Thames and Hudson.

Lloyd, S., Mohseni, M., & Rebentrost, P. (2013). "Quantum Algorithms for Supervised and Unsupervised Machine Learning." Last access 11.03.2024. https://arxiv.org/pdf/1307.0411.pdf.

Noll, M. (1967) "The Digital Computer as a Creative Medium." *IEEE Spectrum* 4(10): 89–95.

Pandey, A., & Ramesh, V. (2015) "Quantum Computing for Big Data Analysis." *Indian Journal of Science* 14(43): 98–104.

Phillips, R. (2015) "BQF Correspondence Chart." In *Black Quantum Futurism. Theory and Practice. Vol. 1*, ed. by Rasheedah Phillips, 76–77. Philadelphia: Afrofuturist Affair.

Rebentisch, J. (2013) Theorien der Gegenwartskunst zur Einfü*hrung*. Hamburg: Junius Verlag.

Rheinberger, H. (2021) *Spalt und Fuge. Eine Phänomenologie des Experiments*. Berlin: Suhrkamp.

Ruff, T. (1999) "Suchmaschinen. Ein Interview von Susanne Leeb." *Texte zur Kunst* 36: 71–75.

Schaaf, L. (2000) *The Photographic Art of Henry Fox Talbot*. Princeton: Princeton University Press.

Schröter, J. (2003) "Virtuelle Kamera. Zum Fortbestand fotografischer Medien in computergenerierten Bildern." *Fotogeschichte* 23(88): 3–16.

Schröter, J. (2004a) "Analog / Digital – Opposition oder Kontinuum?" In *Analog / Digital – Opposition oder Kontinuum? Zur Theorie und Geschichte einer Unterscheidung*, ed. by Jens Schröter and Alexander Böhnke, 7–30. Bielefeld: transcript.

Schröter, J. (2004b) "Technik und Krieg. Fragen und Überlegungen zur militärischen Herkunft von Computertechnologien am Beispiel des Internets." In *Die Medien und ihre Technik: Theorien – Modelle – Geschichte*, ed. by Harro Segeberg, 356–370. Marburg: Schüren.

Schröter, J. (2004c) "Das Ende der Welt. Analoge und Digitale Bilder – mehr oder weniger Realität?" In *Analog/Digital – Opposition oder Kontinuum? Beiträge zu Theorie und Geschichte einer Unterscheidung*, ed. by Jens Schröter and Alexander Böhnke, 335–354. Bielefeld: transcript.

Schröter, J. (2013) "Medienästhetik, Simulation und, Neue Medien'." *Zeitschrift für Medienwissenschaft* 8(1): 88–100.

Schröter, J. (2014) *3D: History, Theory and Aesthetics of the Technical-transplane Image*. New York et al.: Bloomsbury.

Schröter, J. (2022) "The Laser: On the Quantum Materiality of Media in the Twentieth Century." *Necsus Journal*, Autumn 2022, https://necsus-ejms.org/the-laser-on-the-quantum-materiality-of-media-in-the-twentieth-century/

Schröter, J. (2023) "Was ist Quantenästhetik?" In *Kunst, Design und die "Technisierte Ästhetik"*, edited by Lars C. Grabbe, Tobias Held, Christiane Wagner, 216–231. Marburg: Büchner.

Schröter, J., Ernst, C., & Warnke, M. (2022) "Quantum Computing and the Analog/Digital Distinction." *Grey Room* 86: 28–49.

Semiconductor (2018) "HALO." Last access 11.03.2024. https://semiconductorfilms.com/art/halo/.

Shiff, R. (2017) "Image that comes out of Matter". In *More Dimensions that you know. Jack Whitten Paintings 1979–1989*, ed. by Richard Shiff, 7–31. Zürich: Hauser & Wirth.

Shor, P. W. (1997) "Polynomial-Time Algorithms for Prime Factorisation and Discrete Logarithms on a Quantum Computer." *SIAM Journal on Computing* 26(5): 1484–1509. Last Access 11.043.2024. doi: 10.1137/S0097539795293172.

Sponer, H. (1930) "Der photochemische Primärprozeß." *Zeitschrift für angewandte Chemie* 43: 823–830.

Stöltzner, M. (2017) "Feynman Diagrams as Models." *The Mathematical Intelligencer* 39(2): 46–54.

Tholen, G. C. (1999) "Überschneidungen. Konturen einer Theorie der Medialität." In *Konfigurationen / Zwischen Kunst und Medien*, ed. by Georg Christoph Tholen and Sigrid Schade und Heiko Idensen, 15–34. Munich: W. Fink.

Traps, Y. (2017) "Quantum Wall: An Interview with Jack Whitten." Last access 22.02.2022. https://www.theparisreview.org/blog/2017/03/01/quantum-wall-an-interview-with-jack-whitten/.

Vedral, V. (2018) "Can We Hear the Sounds of Quantum Superpositions?" *Muzikologija* 24: 15–19 doi: 10.2298/MUZ1824015V

Winston, B. (1998) *Media Technology and Society: A History from the Telegraph to the Internet*. London and New York: Routledge.

5. ACOUSTICS OF RESISTANCE FOR AN ULTRABLACK WOMB

(NON)Poetic Confessions of a Philosopher-Juggalo

By Giorgi Vachnadze

> *"The fact that we live in a world where John Lennon was murdered, yet Barry Manilow continues to put out fuckin' albums… goddammit. If you're gonna kill somebody, have some fuckin' taste. I'll drive you to Kenny Rogers' house, alright? Get in the car, I know where Wham lives!"*
>
> — Bill Hicks (1990)

The mobilisation of tastelessness as a guerrilla strategy against algorithmic mall-music, with the aim to deactivate neoliberal noise through an acoustics of Ultrablack resistance, is what the current paper plans to accomplish. A weaponised viral deployment and fatal strategy against the corporate simulacrum. A tactics of contamination. Put poison in their data! Better yet, let's put expensive musical equipment in the hands of psychopaths, criminals and degenerates. Jacked-up losers in sweatpants with hardly even a basic sense of rhythm. This is what the contemporary music scene deserves. Let's amplify violence, create a dark and filthy womb of pure noise. Let us regress into the womb of a different species. As Merleau-Ponty would have it, if the world is *enfleshed*, why not literally? Why not in violence? Why not in obscenity with Baudrillard?

What if George Bataille was an octagon fighter? But he kept losing? But then, after successive concussive assimilations of blunt force trauma to the head (and progressive CTE), he decided to start a metal band? This is the kind of rupture we're looking for: a fatality, not just in the Nietzschean sense, but in the sense of *Mortal Kombat*. Give brain damage to the listener. A Wittgensteinian gapless series of profanity and degradation, a recursivity of pure *showing* without telling. Pure logical rigour, absolute castration for the listener and a formidable encounter with the jouissance of symbolic disintegration and death. Manifest the syntax of madness inside the recording studio. "Liberate my madness," because "I can't be a part of a system such as this" (Slipknot, 1999). We need to make Foucault's first pages of *Discipline and Punish* look like a walk in the park, or a picnic. To give it an update at least. Make the listener feel like Damiens (the regicide), consider it a rite of passage and initiation. A bastard child of their entrepreneurial spirit: their secure, productive and healthy zooified pathetic biopolitical excuse for a life. Quad Erat Demonstrandum.

> *"I'd rather be dead than be a fuckin' prisoner in your matrix of fucking consumer bullshit! Go ahead, spend your money on some stupid fucking trend. Some shit that's gonna be gone by next year!"*
>
> Jared Gomes from (Hed) PE (2007)

We need to upgrade the planet by drowning it in entropy. An Ultra-Blackout (2004) for a planetary evolution (PE). "*Blow out they speakers!*" The key is to let the rhythm drown in noise, a violent assemblage of post-structuralist syncopations. The rhythm emerges from time to time, here and there, through the "polyphony" of noise; the cacophony of heterogenous acoustic relations—everyone's a drummer, even the vocalist! It operates as a lure, a decoy to keep the listener hooked by the flesh of her eardrums. Create music that subjectivises the "consumer" into masochism. An overflowing event, the acoustic object must dominate completely, dispersing and fragmenting the subject. No more interpretations, no artists, no authors. The headphones are an apparatus of desubjectification—untraining, contamination, viral contagion, capture and perfect crimes. Put the corporate idiots in *our* pockets; invest in this! Make a big venue. Turn blood into gold, trash into candy, enter the Sandmine ((Hed) PE, 2021), transcend through violent noise.

Noise can induce a dream-like state; the direct counterpart of complete silence. If the latter is inaccessible, you can always revert to the former. One can meditate under noise, given there's enough noise—as in, *too much* noise. The death drive is full of vitality, and Ultrablack Music, granted a very particular variety, can help you build an entropic womb. An Ultrablack Womb, not unlike Lao Tzu's (2021) Womb of light and silence, can give you some space for yourself, for contemplation. You can dwell there, at the limit; a dark Stoic's act of resistance. "Tao presents as empty, dark, and complete potential, the inexhaustible womb of everything. How very deep is its emptiness. How ancestral" (Lao Tzu, 2021). Teenagers know this all too well: "Visibility is a trap" (Foucault, 2020). The Ultrablack Womb is a black-box inside the panopticonic algorithms of governmentality: it has a stacking effect, and over time, it creates gaps and blind-spots in the electronic eye (Lyon, 1994). Surveillance may be all-encompassing, but so is darkness, so is blackness, so is resistance, so is the Tao.

> Forget the idea, that the copyright is meant to protect the right of the author, the copyright is meant, eventually, to protect the right of the publisher. Not to protect the author, but

> to be able to ascribe responsibility to the author ... [to enable] the possibility to judge and condemn [the author].
>
> (Agamben, 2010)

As a case study for an acoustics of resistance for an Ultrablack Womb take Nullset... in math? No, more like Nullset *on meth.* A new *methematics* of music and radical anti-copyright politics offered by Nullset, aka Gangsta Bitch Barbie—an underground post-metal band from Boston that (for completely understandable reasons) "did not make it big". Take a look at "their" song called *Sympathy from the Devil...* Yes, they did name their song after the Rolling Stones' hit *Sympathy for the Devil*—not as a tribute either, but as an act of thievery. These lyrical marauders have proudly deployed an anti-apparatus, where every line in their song—virtually every sentence of the verse—is a stolen lyric or title from all the iconic bands and musicians considered (mostly) as modern-day classics. From Ozzy's "Suicide Solution", *Ride the Lightning* and *Puppet Master* by Metallica to "Free Bird" and "Stairway to Heaven", Van Halen's "Running with the Devil", Led Zeppelin's "Hey, Hey What Can I Do", to Alice in Chains' "Man in the Box", The Ramones, The Who's "Baba O'Riley" ("Teenage Wasteland"), *Back in Black* (AC/DC), to Simon Harris's Public Enemy's and Limp Bizkit's "Bass" ("How Low Can You Go"), i.e., "Bring the Noise", the entire song sounds like a generic commercial rock radio station gone schizo-haywire. The song ends with a "...get your lawyer, these lyrics are mine" scream-smug affirmation—an emotion one wouldn't think possible—followed by an arguably pretty decent guitar solo. Should we join Nullset? Let's kill *other* authors! Q.E.D.

Borrowing from Lyotard, we need an Auditory Ultrablack Libidinal Economy of music. A sound that escapes the great Zero of consumer nihilism, producing incommensurable intensities of incalculable audibles on the surface of the audiophiliac ephemeral skin. Deploy a multiplicity of ineffables (Cleveland, 2022), NON-monetisable, NON-binary acoustic singularities; blasting unsayables, distortions and malfunctions. Indeed, "there is no need to begin with transgression, we must go immediately to the very limits of..." (Lyotard, 2020). What can be heard, what is allowed to be heard, what we cannot avoid hearing and what it makes sense to hear. If it cannot be counted, it cannot be commodified. Acoustic libidinal-bar algorithms must be replaced with loud intensities. Unexpected revelations of the unnameable, the Tao and the Lacanian Real in the unlikeliest of places. Can the Tao of the Yin manifest in the underground metal scenes of New York; Boston; Richmond, Virginia; and Huntington Beach, California? Before we answer the question, we should first learn to recognise the face of the enemy.

To take a line of flight from the metronome-beat style, AI-generated, functional mall-music dispositif, let us look at Jones & Schumacher's (1992) paper on *Muzak*. In *Muzak: On Functional Music and Power,* Jones & Schumacher perform a Foucauldian analysis of background music, i.e., elevator music or functional music, in order to expose the discursive power-mechanisms that motivated their vast distribution and consumption since the early 20th century. Jones & Schumacher analyse Muzak as a disciplinary technology, which aims to subjectivise the listener at different locations (sites) of consumption and production and analyse its various objectives. From the workplace to the shopping centre, while travelling, paying bills, or waiting for a customer service rep on the phone, an acoustics of normalisation operates discreetly. The biopolitical strategies around functional music have been growing since the beginning of the 20th century, starting with workplace governance during the times of Taylorism and Fordism. At this point, there is a wealth of scientific knowledge about the effect music has on human behaviour and physiology. Jones & Schumacher (1992) cite *Wyatt & Langdon* (1937) from *Husch* (1984): "*In 1937, two British industrial psychologists published a report for the British Industrial Health Research Board entitled 'Fatigue and Boredom in Repetitive Work', which suggested that music in the workplace had the potential to reduce absenteeism and early departures and enhance productivity in short-cycle, highly repetitive jobs.*" A shorthand description for

Muzak could therefore be: "the musical conveyor-belt." Nothing less than a tool for Pavlovian training.

Muzak inaugurated the beginning of musico-social engineering through psychology, social sciences and management studies. "Muzak's marketing ideology is founded on claims to be able to motivate employees and increase productivity through scientifically proven physiological and psychological effects" (Jones & Schumacher, 1992). The notion of "stimulus progression" played a central role in Muzak's acoustic eugenics. Stimulus progression involves the application of scientific methodology to the composition of songs and their ordering into playlists. "Muzak's programmers invented an 'objective' method of arranging and categorising individual tunes by means of tempo, rhythm, instrumentation, and orchestra size" (Jones & Schumacher, 1992). Each melody was coded according to a *stimulus* value on a numerical scale from 1 to 5, where 1 signified slow tempo and relaxation, while 5 stood for "bright and upbeat arrangements". Various combinations of songs and playlists that catered to various goals of training and subjectivising consumers and the labour-force were then stored in Muzak databases for convenient retrieval, distribution and selling. Q.E.D.

In this sense precisely, refusing the dispositif of the consumer-metronome, another one of Nullset's "masterpieces," the song *H Bone* from the 2008 album *Nullset*, addresses the ills of commercialised music directly: "*It's just another business, in the end lookin' for duckets. The DJ plays the single, you say 'fuck it'. Splashin' your cash down, because it sounds fat, the other ten tracks are whack, and you've been had.* [Parodying in a mocking voice:] *'But the video was gonna go platinum, with the images that represent my album.'*" What can be more symptomatic of the music industry under capitalism than the artist dedicating the very content of their song to the problematic of exploitation and the appropriation (or complete disfigurement) of their work?

Another exemplary case: *Gears* by Lamb of God (2020) lays down a formidable critique of coded desire, consumerism, corporate governance and the banality of entrepreneurialism. The opening verse—"You suffer from a manufactured sickness and envy by design, pre-calculated status and patterns of desire, accumulation and adoration, built to feed your ostentation, perpetually unsatisfied, but you never question why"—describes the jouissance of consumption, the artificiality of symbolic positioning (status), endless accumulation and hoarding, as well as the vanity of narcissistic exhibitionism, all inherent to the consumer society. Later in the song: "Empty actions to fill the time, commercial gods keep you in line, industry and empire thrive, while you're dying for always more" (Lamb of God, 2020)—the artist develops a post-colonial critique of globalised capitalism, describing its direct effects on the individual. The neoliberal subject suffers from an *anomie* (Durkheim, 2015), a sense of purposelessness and alienation imposed by a system that aims to hide an imperialistic agenda through the "neutrality" of economic interest. "Your endless hunger automated, industry defined" (Lamb of God, 2020)—automated desire is arguably one of the loftiest catchalls to define the link between automation and subjectivity under capitalism.

A similar sentiment drives the work of Lynn Straight, a New York-born artist and vocalist for the band Snot. The songs "Unplugged" and "Mr. Brett" from the album *Get Some* (1997) express the same sense of disillusionment and anger with the capitalist mode of production, class inequalities and devaluation of art, especially as they apply to the music industry and the punk-rock scene: "*There ain't no room for us in your alternative nation. Seems you've had control for much too long. Your greed and your dishonesty only add to my frustration. Can't you see the powers that be, they don't give a fuck about you and me. Somebody better say this 'cause there ain't nobody tryin' to save us; just enslave us, leave us hangin' by the rope that they just gave us, Victim of your mistrust… Liar!*" Later in the same song, "Unplugged": "*You, your dance, your stupid cash advance. No, I'm not a victim of circumstance, not gonna leave my life to chance*", and later still: "*You rape the hearts of us, the artist, you reap the benefits. Your pockets they get fat as our souls bleed. Oh, your gettin' away with murder, 'Son you failed to read the fine print.'*

Label whores like festering sores; don't you know they've got a deal for you!" The second song, "Mr. Brett", is addressed to "the" Mr. Brett or Brett Gurewitz, the guitarist and songwriter for the punk-rock band Bad Religion. His current net worth is around $12 million. The song is a direct assault on Gurewitz and a creative attempt to expose the hypocrisy and inconsistency behind someone's being a "rich punk-rock artist": "*Mr. Brett, we won't pay that fee to keep you livin' in luxury. Some say genius, some say mistake. But you've become, what you used to hate!*" And the last part of the verse that follows the chorus: "*Punk rock life's been good to you, now corporate punk's the thing to do, obnoxiously, you raised your fee you'll see to it we'll all get screwed.*" Q.E.D.

Snot, (hed) P.E. and Nullset present us with the underground of the underground, so to speak; a group of bands that belong to the undifferentiated mass of a subculture that refused to become a "subculture", i.e., a false and artificial organised transgression offered by commercialised rock music, censored radio hits and pop-punk. The collection of strings that ties all of this obscenity together is a multiplicity of acoustic techniques of resistance as we see them deployed throughout various mediums. The artists mentioned above construct an Ultrablack Womb of fluctuations, turbulence and noise, which allows one to shelter oneself from different subjectivising technologies of the self, Muzak being a prime example. These musicians deploy poetic critiques of exploitation and legal appropriation of creative work under capitalism. Unlike philosophers, they *show* their frustration, they transfer their affective states directly to the listener. Tastelessness is a very important weapon within the struggle (be it class struggle or other). Taste is dictated through market trends, and the market operates as a governmental paradigm. Creating tasteless music allows for a direct dissent and refusal of self-commodification. It allows for an encounter with the Other. Tasteless music can be used as a desubjectivising technique, as well as an unmediated source of empathy with those who suffer. Tastelessness is the means through which one enters the entropic womb of acoustic resistance.

Discography

Hicks, B. (1990) *Dangerous*. Invasion Records. [album]

(hed) P.E. (2007) *Insomnia*. Suburban Noize Records. [album]

—. (2004) *Blackout*. Jive Records. [album]

—. (2021) *Sandmine*. Regime Music Group. [album]

Lamb of God (2020) *Lamb of God*. Epic & Nuclear Blast Records. [album]

Nullset (2012). *I Call Zeus*. Kunaki, LLC. [album]

—. (2008). *Nullset*. Grand Royal. [album]

Slipknot (1999). *Slipknot*. Roadrunner Records.

Snot (1997). *Get Some*. Geffen Records.

References

Agamben, G. (2017) *The Omnibus: Homo Sacer*. Berkeley: Stanford University Press.

Baudrillard, J. (2008) *Fatal strategies*. Translation by J. Fleming. Los Angeles: Semiotext(e).

—. (2017) *Symbolic Exchange and Death* (Revised). Translation by I. H. Grant. London: SAGE Publications.

—. (2020) *Simulacra and Simulation* (31st ed.). Translation by S. F. Glaser. Chicago: University of Michigan Press.

Cleveland, T. (2022) *Beyond Words: Philosophy, Fiction, and the Unsayable*. Washington, DC: Rowman & Littlefield.

Durkheim, E. (2005) *Suicide: A Study in Sociology*. New York: Routledge.

European Graduate School (27 April 2010) Giorgio Agamben. *The Process of the Subject in Michel Foucault*. [Video] www.youtube.com/watch?v=ybkjlMDDmJo

Foucault, M. (2020) *Discipline and Punish: the Birth of the Prison*. Translation by A. Sheridan. Penguin Books.

Husch, J. (1984) *Music of the Work Place: A Study of Muzak Culture*. Unpublished doctoral dissertation. Amherst: University of Massachusetts.

Jones, S. C., & Schumacher, T. G. (1992) "Muzak: On functional music and power." *Critical Studies in Media Communication* 9(2): 156–169.

Lao Tzu (2021) *Tao Te Ching: Power for the Peaceful*. Translation by M. S. Mullinax. Minneapolis: Fortress Press

Lin, P. (21 November 2023) *Can this data poisoning tool help artists protect their work from AI scraping?* Center for Art Law: Online. https://itsartlaw.org/2023/11/21/can-this-data-poisoning-tool-help-artists-protect-their-work-from-ai-scraping/

Lyotard, J. F. (2020) *Libidinal Economy*. New York/London: Bloomsbury Publishing.

Lyon, D. (1994) *The Electronic Eye: The Rise of Surveillance Society*. Minneapolis: University of Minnesota Press.

Merleau-Ponty, M. (1962) *Phenomenology of Perception*. London: Routledge.

Nietzsche, F. (2009) *Ecce Homo: How to Become What You Are*. Oxford: Oxford University Press.

Shipley, G. J., & Pawlett, W. (2020) *Stratagem of the Corpse: Dying with Baudrillard a Study of Sickness and Simulacra*. London: Anthem Press.

Wittgenstein, L. (1958) *The Blue and Brown Books* (Vol. 34). Oxford: Blackwell.

—. (2021) *Tractatus Logico-Philosophicus*. Centenary Edition. L. Bazzocchi & P. M. S. Hacker. London: Anthem Press.

—. (2010). *Philosophical investigations* (4th cd.). Translation by P. M. S. Hacker & J. Schulte. Hoboken: John Wiley & Sons.

Wyatt, S., Langdon, J. N., and Stock F. G. L., Medical Research Council (Great Britain) & Industrial Health Research Board (Great Britain). (1951) *Fatigue and boredom in repetitive work*. His Majesty's Stationery Office.

6. GHETTOGOTHIC (GHE20G0TH1K)

by Alessandro Sbordoni

"Every code of music is rooted in the ideologies and technologies of its age, and at the same time produces them."

— Jacques Attali (1985: 18)

From 2009 to 2019, Venus X and Shayne Oliver hijacked New York's club music with the sound of GHE20G0TH1K rave parties. Gunshots and the noise of helicopters are sampled and drop-mixed with rap, grime, footwork, jungle, reggaeton, dancehall, ballroom, and industrial music. MP3 audio files are played on the sound system by Black, Latinx, and queer DJs. To deconstruct the dance floor, first of all deconstruct the loudspeaker.

When MP3s are played on a sound system, the texture is rather grimy. Released during the second-wave loudness wars in the 1990s, the MP3 encoder is a trade-off between bit size and audio fidelity (or, why the songs on your MP3 player sound like shit). Twenty years later, the same audio format was reformatted by GHE20G0TH1K as a sonic weapon against the music industry. It is a guerrilla mix tactic against the high-fidelity audio of electronic music.[1]

The sonic warfare of the 21st and 22nd century is about the violence of the sound frequencies, psycho-audiological operations, and sonic branding (Goodman, 2010). But it is also about the fight for the control of codes and sonic equipment. Combat vehicles, artillery, and war tactics return as sound systems, audio formats, and recording standards.

The MP3 audio format was captured in the late 1990s. As a result, music piracy over the internet is reproduced. Temporary autonomous audiozones are created soon after. Later, when the MP3 audio file is sound-engineered by non-white, non-male, and queer musicians in New York, it is because the dance floor itself is under siege.

*

Jean Baudrillard writes in *The Illusion of the End*, first published in 1992, one year after the release of the MP3 audio format:

> We are all obsessed with high fidelity, with the quality of musical 'reproduction'. At the consoles of our stereos, armed with our tuners, amplifiers and speakers, we mix, adjust settings, multiply tracks in pursuit of a flawless sound. Is this still music? Where is the high-fidelity threshold beyond which music disappears as such? It does not disappear for lack of music but because it passed this limit point; it disappears into the perfection of its materiality, into its own special effect.
>
> (Baudrillard, 1994: 5–6)

The sound engineer takes precedence over the musician. The music that was directly lived recedes into a representation. Sound tech-

1 For more guerrilla mix tactics, see Monacelli., E. (2023) *The Great Psychic Outdoors: Lo-Fi Music and Escaping Capitalism.*

nology feeds back into itself. The sound of recorded music is much more real than the musical performance.

There is no more difference between the original and the copy. The aura of the work of art is replaced by the aurality of the technological device.

*

No recordings, please. In 2009, the sound of GHE20G0TH1K rave parties is always less than its own reproduction. The MP3 encoder is such that the original signals are no longer retrievable. To update Walter Benjamin's terminology, there is a negative aura around these underground parties. Music is no longer about repetition but its absence from space and time. Music is not about representation anymore.

The bootleg recordings of GHE20G0TH1K resident DJs—such as Total Freedom, NGUZUNGUZU, and Kingdom—sound disruptive because they are. The MP3 encoder jams the sound system with another kind of noise. Black, Latinx, and queer people reverse-engineer audio into politics. The CDJs used by Venus X and Shayne Oliver are not audio devices but sonic weapons of disruption. The conceptechnics of dance music is disassembled into its machine parts.[2]

*

In 2019, Simon Reynolds introduced the term 'conceptronica' to define a trend in electronic music where conceptualism takes the place of sound. In a deleted section of the article, the British music critic cites Achim Szepanski's label Mille Plateaux as a pioneer of the new genre. GHE20G0TH1K's deconstructed club music is cited as another example in the original article, alongside a number of

---

2 For more about conceptechnics, see Eshun, K. (1998) *More Brilliant Than the Sun.*

artists associated with the New York dance party: Jam City, Chino Amobi, Lotic, Amnesia Scanner, SOPHIE, and Arca.[3]

Simon Reynolds interviewed Mille Plateaux's electronic group Oval in the late 1990s. He writes with contempt: "They [Oval] talk of not wanting to produce a merely 'predictable outcome' of the hardware and software, of wishing to 'offensively suggest' the existence of sound worlds 'from "outside" the digital domain', of having invented a 'completely new music-paradigm'" (Reynolds, 2017: 45–46). Then, music does not play from within but from without.

Cut the crap. GHE20G0TH1K is not a concept but the destruction of concepts. It is not about music but the reproduction of its own nothingness. Achim Szepanski (2019) writes: "If one cannot theorise this type of music in toto, it is not because one cannot hear this music, but because it remains the unheard in the audible."

Back to sound engineering 101. Designed by the Moving Picture Experts Group (MPEG), MP3 is not an audio format but a coding procedure. With a sampling frequency of 44.1 kHz, the MP3 encoder eliminates information about sound above 22.05 kHz. It deletes and approximates the data about sound above the level of the audible. The MP3 encoder then exploits the auditory system to return noise to the level of the inaudible, consuming the bandwidth with a louder audio signal. Negation, then, takes the place of noise itself. The buzz of the machine takes the place of any concept as such.

3 Music was already conceptual when, a quarter of a century ago, Kodwo Eshun wrote: "Far from needing theory's help, music today [in 1998] is already more conceptual than at any point this century, pregnant with thoughtprobes waiting to be activated, switched on, misused" (Eshun, 1998: 3). Likewise, as the book's incipit reads: "Respect due. Good music speaks for itself. No Sleevenotes required. Just enjoy it. Cut the crap. Back to basics. What else is there to add? All these troglodytic homilies are Great British cretinism masquerading as vectors into the Trad Sublime" (Eshun, 1998: 7). However, as Matt Colquhoun also remarked, what is different in the 21st century is that more and more popular music is conceptual and political.

Noise is no longer the disruption of the message; instead, the message itself is the destruction of noise.

*

The logo of GHE20G0TH1K designed by Venus X is a biochemical hazard symbol.

The sonic radiation of GHE20G0TH1K intoxicates the music biz. The white, male, cis-gender club culture is contaminated. It reproduces the metastasis of the code. Acid rains into the dance floor. The sound-reproduction technology generates another relationship with the music that is cancerous and malignant. There is no model of the same any longer but the reproduction of an aberrant signal: NO.[4] Negation takes the form of sound. Then, the code reproduces itself until the destruction of the world "as we know and sonically experience it" (Heintz, 2020: 8).

*

After the global financial crisis of 2007–2008, GHE20G0TH1K is the crash of the political economy of dance music. As GHE20G0TH1K founder Venus X stated in 2019: "Something happened where everyone thought the world was going to end. We capitalised on that fantasy and the fear of what it would feel like on the last night of Earth. It started in 2009 so you had three years of apocalyptic behaviour before you realise it's not happening. Then you just continue and make it a lifestyle."[5] The MP3 audio format is as much a machine part as it is the

4 Compare with Schulze, H. 2020. *Sonic Fiction*, §6 "NON: Ultrablack Resistance". "The one message, the one action, the one intervention of ultrablackness is taking an axe and ramming it into the fake common ground or shared table and saying: NO" (Schulze, 2020: 128).

5 Layla Halabian, Venus X on the Origins of GHE20G0TH1K, a Club Night that Shaped the 2010s.

currency of the sound-banks and the club-goers. But there is no codec standard between sound and music anymore. Music is no longer distributed by the system of reproduction but goes further into its own ravage.

*

Jacques Attali writes in his magnum opus, *Noise: The Political Economy of Music* (1985: 11):

> Music is prophecy. Its styles and economic organisation are ahead of the rest of society because it explores, much faster than material reality can, the entire range of possibilities in a given code. It makes audible the new world that will gradually become visible, that will impose itself and regulate the order of things; it is not only the image of things, but the transcending of the everyday, the herald of the future.

The mass production of music records and music sheets herald the society of the spectacle by one hundred years in the same way as the classical music of Ludwig van Beethoven sets the scene for the middle-class society of the 19th century. In contrast, the music of GHE20G0TH1K is not the sign of another society. The MP3 encoder is not the sound of the society of the 22nd century. It is the herald of the destruction of the world.

If you cannot hear it, it is because it is not audible with 20th century sound technology.

*

In the golden age of high-fidelity reproduction, Jacques Attali listens to the audible in the inaudible. When the French musicologist and economist turns on the volume, he listens to the sign of repetition: for example, in the night club where “it is increasingly the same music that is heard, and same dances danced."(Attali, 1985: 119–120). Then, the song ends and it does not finish ending.

Turn the volume up. Set the sampling rate low. Play the MP3 audio file on the sound system. From the point of hearing of the loudspeaker,[6] the world is already over. Again and again, zeros after ones.

"For the code to undergo a mutation," writes Jacques Attali, "a certain catastrophe must occur" (Attali, 1985: 34). Etymologically, the meaning of the word catastrophe, from the Ancient Greek *katastrephein*, is "to overturn". It is when the knobs are turned to the limit that the system of sound is reverted. From the perfection of the sound system to its imperfection, again "the only strategy is catastrophic [...]. Things must be pushed to the limit, where quite naturally they collapse and are inverted" (Baudrillard, 2004: 4).

Crank it up so it is no longer audible as music. GHE20G0TH1K makes inaudible the destruction of the world that will become invisible.

It is the catastrophe of audibility.

*

Where is the no-fidelity limit below which music disappears as such?

When the sound of deconstructed club music is played through a music-recognition application like Shazam, the software sometimes does not return a matching result. Likewise, speech-recognition system such as Apple's *Siri*, the Android Assistant, or Microsoft's *Cortana* fail to translate the recording of screams into text (Fuller, 2019).

The technology that re-encodes deconstructed club music is the medium for another channel of miscommunication. It is a semio-blitz to the reproduction of the code.

---

6 Another phrase sampled and edited from *More Brilliant Than the Sun* (Eshun, 1998).

*

The music genres are short-circuited. It is not possible to distinguish between ghetto, goth, and noise music anymore. Something inaudible is introduced between one signal and another. Ray Brassier turns the volume up: "the term 'noise' oscillates between that of a proper name and that of a concept; it equivocates between nominal anomaly and conceptual interference" (Brassier, 2009: 62).

The deconstructed club music of GHE20G0TH1K is not a sub-genre of noise music. Rather, the format of such music negates the concept of noise itself. Nothing is so trite as the frustration of music critics to define it as yet another "music genre".

When deconstructed club music exits GHE20G0TH1K, the afterparty takes place on Soundcloud. For example, listen to Swaggot Trilltape, the first mixtape produced by Arca and mixed by Shayne Oliver, featuring songs such as Kanye West's "Diamonds from Sierra Leone", The Beach Boys' "I Get Around", The Prodigy's "Firestarter", Beyonce's "Green Light", Aphex Twin's "Diamonds Are Forever/Avril 14", Jim Jones's "Gettin' to the Money", but the sounds are so mashed-up, edited, pitched, and distorted that it is hard to call it a "mixtape" anymore (instead, it is a "trilltape"). As the description of *Swaggot Trilltape* reads: "THIS AINT MUSIC, ITS THE SOUNDS YOU REMEMBER AFTER YOU EXIT THE CLUB ON YOUR WAY HOME". The signal is not there anymore. The ghettogoths already remix it.

*

GHE20G0TH1K is more a decoding procedure than a rave party in New York. It is a dance culture jamming.

Since 2009, Venus X and Shayne Oliver decode the late-capitalist format of club music. "Decoding," writes Mark Fisher (while cross-fading from Jean Baudrillard to D&G), "is not so much a matter of translating—or understanding, comprehending—code, as dismantling it" (Fisher, 2018: 112). The output is deconstructed club music.

*

Deconstructed club music is an instruction manual to disassemble the CDJ. "Many times, rather than beat-matching two songs, they'd [Venus X and Shayne Oliver] use the cue buttons on their CDJs like samplers, switching between cue points to loop and layer phrases manually. They'd mix in wild, discordant sound effects as inflection points in their sets, often bringing packed dance floors to a screeching halt in a frenzy of confusion and chaos" (Pearl, 2017). The songs are not mixed but played at the same time altogether with the sounds of gunshots and screams on playback. The conceptechnics is re-engineered with only a USB drive plugged into a CDJ. The sound archive stored in the USB drive is not reproduced through the loudspeaker. Its function is not to record information but to reset its relationship with the hardware back to zero.

The use of technology is given tactical priority over any musical structure. The CDJ tool is liberated from the whiteness of its automatism.

The beats are abstracted (no more four-on-the-floor). The tracks are skipped. The sounds are live-sampled. The BPMs are now higher, now lower. The algorithm returns as an algorhythm. It is not, to remix the words of Franco "Bifo" Berardi (2018: §8), the rhythm of the machine versus the rhythm of the music player. There is, in fact, no more difference between the rhythmics of dance, music, and technics. The algorhythm is the rhythm of DJing itself.

Sound technology feeds forward into itself. The machine deprograms the dance floor. It is not part of the RAM but the rave of the machinery.

*

The rave simulates another space and time, which is not the space and time of capitalism. Technology is the medium (and drugs are a kind of technology, too).

The bootleg recordings of GHE20G0TH1K are the sign of a negative space and time. The aura of the sound returns as the negative aura of the destruction produced by the barbarity to end this world (Culp, 2016; Szepanski, 2020). It is a scorched-earth strategy that destroys the logic and logistics of the system.

After the end of the world, GHE20G0TH1K throws another dance party. GHE20G0TH1K blackens the aura of the end with the soundtrack of the apocalypse. The ultrasound of destruction consumes all the bandwidth. The aurality of music is made inaudible by its own techno-logic. The seven trumpets are decoded and return as a septet of zeros.

There is then no more music as such, because the sound itself is already nothing more and nothing less than the blackness of this world.

The negativity of such music is already another relationship with the technology and ideology that produced it. It is the catastrophe of sound and the sound of the catastrophe.

*

The deconstruction of the club gives way to deconstructed club music. GHE20G0TH1K makes inaudible the end of the world that will become invisible tomorrow.

Dance, twerk, shuffle, and mosh to the ultrablackness of sound.

Works cited

2010: "GHE20 G0TH1K – The Official Mixtape" by Venus X (DISmagazine)

2011: "The Claw" by NGUZUNGUZU, Total Freedom & Kingdom (Fade To Mind)

2012: "Classical Curves" by Jam City (Night Slugs)

2013: "Incinerator" by Dreamcrusher (This Ain't Heaven Recording Concern)

2014: "That's Harakiri" by Sd Laika (Tri Angle)

2015: "Mutant" by Arca (Mute)

2016: "PHOENIXXX" by WWWINGS (Planet Mu)

2017: "PARADISO" by Chino Amobi (*NON*)
2018: "Power" by Lotic (*Tri Angle*)
2019: "Sentient" by Lila Tirando a Violeta (*New Motion*)
2020: "Tearless" by Amnesia Scanner (*PAN*)
2021: "Assembler" by Yen Tech (*SVBKVLT*)
2022: "Lost Cuts" by KAVARI (n.a.)
2023: "Black Armor" by twofold (n.a.)

References

$hayne (2012) *Swaggot Trilltape.* Soundcloud. https://soundcloud.com/amethystxxxxxxxx/hba-swaggot-trilltape.

Attali, J. (1985) *Noise: The Political Economy of Music* (trans. B. Massumi). Theory and History of Literature, Volume 16. University of Minnesota Press: Minneapolis, London. (Original work published 1977).

Benjamin, W. (2008) The Work of Art in the Age of Mechanical Reproduction (trans. J. A. Underwood). London: Penguin (Original work published 1938).

Baudrillard, J. (1994) The Illusion of the End (trans. C. Turner). Cambridge: Polity Press. (Original work published 1992).

Baudrillard, J. (2004) Symbolic Exchange and Death (trans. by I. H. Grant). Sage: London. (Original work published 1976).

Berardi, F. "Bifo". (2018) Breathing. Semiotext(e): New York.

Brassier, R. (2009) "Genre Is Obsolete". In Iles, A. (ed.), *Noise & Capitalism:* 60–71. Arteleku Audiolab: Navarra.

Colquhoun, M. (1 November 2019) Thieves of Fire: Conceptronica and Cultural Capital. *Xenogothic*: Online. https://xenogothic.com/2019/11/01/thieves-of-fire-conceptronica-and-the-theft-of-cultural-capital/.

Culp, A. (2016) Dark Deleuze. University of Minnesota Press: Minneapolis.

Eshun, K. (1998) More Brilliant Than the Sun. Quartet Books: London.

Fisher, M. (2018) Flatline Constructs: Gothic Materialism and Cybernetic Theory-Fiction. Exmilitary Press: New York.

Fuller, M. (2019) Screaming. In Goodman, S., Heys, T., & Ikoniadou, E. (eds), *AUDINT—Unsound:Undead*: 43–46. Urbanomic: Falmouth.

Goodman, S. (2010) Sonic Warfare: Sound, Affect, and the Ecology of Fear. The MIT Press: Cambridge, London.

Halabian, L (2019) Venus X on the Origins of GHE20G0TH1K, a Club Night that Shaped the 2010s. *Wired*: Online. https://www.dazeddigital.com/music/article/47192/1/venus-x-on-the-origins-of-ghe20g0th1k-a-club-night-that-changed-the-world.

Heintz, J. (2020) Foreword — Dark Precursions: Technocultures, Inhuman Rhythmights and the Ultra-Black of Non-Music. In Szepanski, A. (ed.) (2020), *Ultrablack of Music*: 7–8. NON/Mille Plateaux: Frankfurt am Main.

Monacelli, E. (2023). The Great Psychic Outdoors: Lo-Fi Music and Escaping Capitalism. London: Repeater.

Pearl, M. (2017). The Art of DJing: Venus X. *Resident Advisor*: Online. https://ra.co/features/2966.

Reynolds, S. (2017). Low End Theory. In Reynolds, S., & Diefenback, K. (eds) (2017) *Techno-Deleuze and Mille Plateaux*: 31–46. Rizosfera: Reggio Emilia. (Original work published 1996).

—. (10 October 2019). The Rise of Conceptronica. *Pitchfork*: Online. https://pitchfork.com/features/article/2010s-rise-of-conceptronica-electronic-music/.

—. (3 November 2019) Conceptronica - Further Thoughts + Deleted Scenes. *blissblog*: Online. http://blissout.blogspot.com/2019/11/conceptronica-further-thoughts-deleted.html.

Schulze, H. (2020). Sonic Fiction. Bloomsbury: New York, London.

Szepanski, A. (9 June 2019) Deleuze/Guattari and the Schizo-Attractor (Ultrablack of Music). *NON*: Online. https://non.copyriot.com/deleuze-guattari-and-the-schizo-attractor-ultrablack-of-music/.

—. (ed.) (2020). Ultrablack of Music. NON/Mille Plateaux: Frankfurt am Main.

7. ON THE REFRAIN OF PAIN AND IMAGINING[1]

By Eldritch Priest

We all know the story of Cage's visit to the anechoic chamber. He came in wondering what silence sounds like and left believing that sound would never leave him. But Cage left the anechoic chamber. He walked away and left the corporeal cacophony of his body safely behind. "There will be sounds until I die", he said. Sure. But he always had the prerogative to decide how those sounds will be heard. Sound is everywhere. How wonderful! But what if the technician who assisted Cage had locked Cage in that echoless room? What if those two sounds, "one high and one low", couldn't be turned down or shut off? How wonderful would sound be then?

This is something that composer Karen Eliot[2] asked herself after learning in 2004 from Afghanistan war veterans (whom she met

1 First published in Priest, E. (2013) *Boring Formless Nonsense: Experimental Music and the Aesthetics of Failure.* London/New York: Bloomsbury.

2 "Karen Eliot" is a multiple-use name. Multiple-use names are what art critic Stewart Home defines as "'tags' that the avant-garde of the seventies and eighties proposed for serial use" (http://www.stewarthomesoci-

while working as a lab assistant at the Alan Edwards Centre for Research on Pain at McGill University) that the American military had been using sound and music in their interrogation of detainees, particularly at a prison located at Bagram Air Base. These veterans, whose phantom limb pain was being studied at the centre, spoke about the use of acoustic weapons, such as the LRAD,[3] on the battlefield, and about interrogations in which prisoners were placed in small cells and submitted to a constant stream of loud and shrill music (mostly rap and metal music). It was this image of the prisoner, confined to a nearly featureless room and forced to endure a condition that Cage himself raised to the level of art, that took hold of Eliot's imagination and led her to ask how the sense of this constant exposure to sound/music might be expressed differently than it was by Cage's comfortable reassurance.

But Eliot took up this question in a peculiar way. Rather than conducting her test in the controlled environment of a laboratory, Eliot locked herself in a practice room in McGill's music department where she spent nine hours subjecting herself to a recording of John Cage's *Freeman Etudes* (1977–90), played at a nearly steady volume of just over 120 decibels. In a journal entry, on the first night of her sound test, Eliot wrote:

> It's always struck me as slightly curious why the US army has never thought to use experimental music, that is, "art" music like the kind that I am listening to right now, as a torture device. I understand how the aggressiveness of rock or metal music, or the obnoxious exhortations of *Barney's Theme*, might affect a detained listener by virtue of their sheer volume and/or asinine refrains, but I can't help wondering whether the glacial pace of a piece like Leif Inge's 9 Beet Stretch (2002), or the restiveness of Michael Finnissy's five-hour *The History of Photography*

ety.org/sp/multi.htm). Ideally, anyone can adopt a multiple-use name for some artistic and/or subversive purpose.

3 Long Range Acoustic Device.

in Sound (2001), or perhaps the skull-rattling buzz of Phil Niblock's *Five More String Quartets* (1993) would be an even more effective form of torture. In an article I read the other day, US Army Psychological Operations Company Sergeant Mark Hadsell, cites "unfamiliarity" as an essential factor in how heavy metal negatively affects detainees, by which he almost certainly means "Muslims". But by that reasoning, experimental composition should be even more effective than metal.[4]

My thoughts about this "oversight" are that most PsyOp officers, or more likely, the combat soldiers who are directly involved in applying music as a torture device, are themselves so wholly unfamiliar with experimental music that if they did happen to somehow encounter such a music, say, during a summer leave at the now defunct US army garrison Darmstadt, where it's not inconceivable that they could stumble upon a concert given as part the Darmstadt Summer Music Workshop, they would find themselves on the other end of the proverbial waterboard, and thus disinclined to make experimental music a weapon of their own for fear of punishing themselves in its application. Of course I'm stretching things and playing fast and loose with Sgt Hadsell's musicological perspicuity, for, as any military personnel will tell you, who has received training by SERE (Survival, Evasion, Resistance, and Escape) on how to resist various coercive techniques by subjecting oneself to those same techniques, knowing what it's like to be drowned, I mean, to be "drowned for pretend," gives one a certain insight and thus a certain "familiarity" with the experience, which, so it's said, ought to make one, if not immune, then less susceptible to persuasion through pain. Again, I'm being somewhat facetious here, but even though we're talking about music and not things like bamboo shoots or thumbscrews, it's curious to think about how the same musical object can have different

4 See "Sesame Street breaks Iraqi POWs," BBC News, 20 May 2003, http://news.bbc.co.uk/2/hi/middle_east/3042907.stm

effects on different people, such that in one case its affect is pleasurable while in another it's torturous.

While Eliot doesn't disclose what exactly she experienced during the nine hours of her self-interrogation, after this experiment her own music began to exhibit a certain sensibility, or appetite rather, for particular kinds of psychological effects that arise when the body is put under duress, especially the kind of duress that characterises contemporary forms of so-called "enhanced interrogation techniques", techniques that isolate and amplify the body's capacity to distress itself by continually feeding variations of its corporeal competence back into its form.

For example, a lot of the music that Eliot has written in the past few years explores the kind of repetition that Gilles Deleuze & Félix Guattari characterise as one of "intensive variation". Basically, intensive variation refers to a type of repetition in which the iterations of a gesture or a phrase don't refer to one another as particulars to a universal—our familiar theme to variations—but instead serialise the connections between their singular expressions, as echoes in a chamber or waves on the ocean do. Applied to language, Deleuze & Guattari (cf. 1987) suggest that the fixed idea of a word or a proper name derives not from a pre-existing ideal category of "life" or, let's say, "Music", but rather from the continual act of enunciating or doing it. Music is an idea remaindered—expressed—from the intensive variations of its being done over and over again, forming between each gesture, movement, work, oeuvre, an immanent "line of continuous variation". Each iteration of a song, or a word, or an idiom, or more locally, a melodic phrase or an ornament, swerves indeterminately along a virtual continuum that expresses the sense of its musical activity, and this continuum itself swerves along a continuum of what we might call a style or genre. Thus, the sense of Music, or of speech for that matter, is an effect, an expression of certain differential relations—i.e., pitch, phonemes, amplitude, rhythm—articulated in sound that, following Deleuze & Guattari's notion of the refrain as a pattern of intensities that form alliances with other intensive periodicities, is perpetually modifying, adjusting, and disciplining its continuous variation (ibid.: 310).

In Eliot's work, one can hear an attempt to fabricate intensive variations through a process that ramifies the tendencies of what, musicologically speaking, we might loosely call a melodic style. Eliot struggles to do this by isolating a melodic idea and exaggerating its connotative lineaments to abstract and intensify its characteristic refrain. That is, she manipulates the drifts that are already at play in the idea of a melodic style by over-stressing its sensible and conceptual regularities.

This approach to melody was developed in an earlier chamber piece of hers titled *pleasure drenching…* (2003–4).[5] In this work, Eliot follows a three-fold procedure to create what she describes as a "melodic theatre," a type of lyric drama in which the same character is played in different ways by multiple actors. At first, Eliot generates pitch material using Per Nørgård's "infinity series",[6] which she then

5 Listen to a recording of *pleasure drenching…* here: http://strangemonk.com/audio/pleasure%20drenching.MP3
The score is here: http://www.strangemonk.com/wp-content/uploads/2014/04/pleasure-drenching-scoresmall.pdf

6 The infinity series is a procedure for generating pitch material (as well as harmonic and rhythmic material) developed by the Danish composer Per Nørgård in the late 1960s. Its simplest expression derives from "mirroring an initial interval symmetrically downwards and upwards", which generates the pitch material (Christensen, 2004: 107). While this series can be generated using only two notes, things really get interesting when the procedure is applied to a set of pitches with a characteristic flavour or mood. The significance of this serial technique, as opposed to many others, is that the original set of pitches, along with facets of its mood, continually reappears in an ongoing ("infinite") variety of contexts. For instance, the series yields strange symmetries and repetitions that, over time, repeat the founding row on from another note, inverted, or distributed non-consecutively. Nørgård regarded the multiscalar property of the infinity series as expressive of an open hierarchy, which could be described as an organisational scheme that has no absolute top or bottom order but only successive and nested dimensions of more or less complexity and integration.

applies to a series of seventeen rhythmic patterns selected by the integer shuffler at the website www.random.org. Finally, Eliot assigned varying spans of these entwined melodic-rhythmic soliloquies to the ensemble of eleven instruments.[7] In effect, she weaves a non-repeating melodic fabric whose differential consistency, achieved through the self-similar pitch groupings of the infinity series and a common set of rhythmic constraints, expresses what could be considered the immanent style of the compositional process.

But at the same time, this melodic theatre convolutes the character of its style such that it also expresses a type of lyrical stuttering or euphonious nonsense that resembles the linguistic weirdness found in Christian Bök's (2001) poem *Eunoia*—a retelling of *1001 Arabian Nights*, whereby each of the five chapters is restricted to words that contain only one of the five English vowels. Though at times verging on cruelty, *pleasure drenching...*'s redundancy of variation has the dual effect of, one, dissolving the semantic grip that cultural clichés have on certain melodic gestures, and two, stunting the growth of internal clichés that cannot help but bud within the time and space of *pleasure drenching...*'s ninety-minute performance. However, the paradox here is that the more a melody is emptied of content, the more its valence increases, the greater its referential aberration becomes.

These compositional machinations invite comparison to proto-Surrealist author Raymond Roussel's "machine texts". Like Eliot, Roussel applied certain arbitrarily determined compositional techniques to generate the imagery of his texts. Though he employed several techniques, a well-documented procedure of Roussel's was to exploit the homophonic and connotative properties of both written and spoken language in a way that allowed him to bring the most distant orders of objects and logics into meaningful, if absurd, proximity (see Roussel, 1977). For both Roussel and Eliot, their respective "machines" create novelty not by negating pre-existing

7 Bb clarinet, electric organ, lap steel guitar, piano, percussion, contrabass, electric guitar, vibraphone, harmonium, violin and viola.

material but by distorting it. Indeed, as Deleuze (2003) argues in his work on Francis Bacon, clichés cannot be destroyed; they are already in play the moment expression begins. In order for the construction of a new image (sound) to be possible, clichés must be palpated and pushed through and beyond the forms that render them intelligible.[8] So while clichés cannot be destroyed, they can be curtailed, bent, turned, or rather, "troped" by altering the mixture of the figures—bodies—that situate them.

All processes of expression involve a mixture of bodies whose effects, deleterious or beneficial, constitute a domain of sense from which expressive regularities evolve into clichés. In the case of music whose "bodies" include not only a body of pitch relations, but also a body of cultural traditions, a body of styles, and a listening body, its clichés are the expression of their common mixture—that is, their "common sense". So, cliché is not something that is preventable, for our very idea of Music is itself a cliché that sustains the entire practice of assembling sound into expressive refrains. Instead, the musical cliché, like any process of expression, develops mutant strains that warp the common or single sense of Music by configuring new relations that make new domains of musical sense.

In *pleasure drenching…*, the sing-songy melodic row expressed in terms of an infinity series and randomised rhythmic modes never brings the melodic curve to a point of cadence, or permits the

---

8 Elsewhere, Deleuze (1989: 208–209) writes that clichés are overcome in a moment of catastrophe. This moment must be a catastrophe, for clichés are not simply repeated signs and artefacts of an external world; they "also penetrate each of us and constitute [our] internal world, so that everyone possesses only psychic clichés by which we think and feel, are thought and felt, being ourselves one cliché among others in the world that surrounds us." The artist, argues Deleuze (with Guattari) (1987: 142), enacts this catastrophe by a process of "diagrammaticism," which is a way of using nonrepresentational and nonsignifying elements—musically speaking, these would be "licks," "grooves," or an enchanting sonority—to pilot a way through chaos and extract a little rhythm and regularity from its metreless din.

material to develop any long-term architectonics that would organise pitches, key areas, or rhythmic values into relations of greater or lesser importance. During the first forty-five minutes of the work, the melodic clichés that radiate from the modal polyphony—a sonority whose distribution of intensities are already more queerly diffused than the major-minor system—become tasked with the chore of justifying their ongoing nonsense. That is, lacking formal development, these impassive expressions are charged with the intense burden of going nowhere for three-quarters of an hour. As such, the clichés that streak across the melodic threads bend and twist under the strain of their own banality, to the point where their misshapen expressions develop a new, mutant, valence. For Eliot, this is a way of writing music's continuous variation *in medias res*, a writing that cannot but start with a body of clichés that has to be dis-figured if its sense is to be made.

Glossolalia (Stress Positions)

Eliot's work, *glossolalia (stress positions)* (2007), however, differs from *pleasure drenching…* in that it concentrates more narrowly on the multiplicity of a single melodic variation.[9] The refrain composed by *glossolalia* develops a line of variation not on a "theme," but on itself. This is to say that what is varied is not an object that can be isolated from the wresting and turning of the melody, but an indeterminate "Idea" of the music as an ongoing variation of its own melodic sense. What this describes is a constant melodic variation, a paradoxically unstable yet invariant process of differentiation. But this shouldn't sound too odd, for as noted above with respect to things like words, constants are the expression of a variation's differing from itself.

9 Listen to *glossolalia (stress positions)* here: https://www.youtube.com/watch?v=qsx0H_-eq3M&feature=youtu.be
The score is here: http://www.strangemonk.com/wp-content/uploads/2014/04/glossolalia-stress-positions_Score.pdf

In the case of *glossolalia,* Eliot's constant derives from an imaginary variation. Take the concertina part at the opening of the work (meas. 1–64). What you hear (and see transcribed in the score) is a violin accompanying a simulated vinyl recording of a concertina part made in the 1970s by the fictional French-Algerian musical savant Félix Amr.[10] During the 1960s, Amr made his living playing bal-musette in the Paris banlieue Clichy-sous-Bois. But in 1971, he suffered a minor stroke that left him with restricted arm movements. After the stroke, Amr, supported by a meagre state pension, took up the smaller and more compact concertina and spent most of each day in his apartment playing the instrument without interruption. For long hours, Amr would sit with his concertina at a kitchen table decorated with the day's paper and an overflowing ashtray, playing pieces from his repertoire. Or more accurately, he played oddments of his repertoire. Amr never actually played any songs. Instead, he would play exceptionally long and florid passages that resembled the ornamentations and transitional passages of bal-musette more than the songs themselves. But curiously, during these musings, Amr never once repeated the same phrase precisely, the melodic character of these flourishes instead always *almost* resembling itself. The broken habit of Amr's lyrical reveries exemplifies the paradox of a musical line that is in constant variation.

Now, whether this was intentional or simply a by-product of Amr's condition is irrelevant, for the effect in either case is the same. This recording of Amr's melodic wanders avoids thematising its variations in two ways: one, because it doesn't actually exist; and two, because its endless variations break apart the coordinates that define the fact of Music, marking out instead only a theme-yet-to-come, or as Deleuze (2003: 101) would say, "the possibility of fact". This futural theme, around which the listener's flickering attention is organised, may be considered the sound of becoming itself, the sound of a perpetual differentiation of a present that is "subdivided

10 This name is Eliot's invention and comes from combining the French for "lucky" (Félix) and "find" (amr).

ad infinitum into something that has just happened and something that is going to happen, always flying in both directions at once" (Deleuze, 1990a: 63).

In the second part of *glossolalia*, Eliot takes up this conundrum of constant change, where "what will have been heard" as a futural theme begins to find its refrain (its characteristic rhythms and counterpoints) stammering and opening upon the unexpected territory of bodily anguish. We can understand how the baroque air of this part of the piece, with its sinuous coils of melodies that always seem to go on just a little too long, too indulgently, too asyndetically, transposes the effect of this potential carrying on to the body's capacity to carry on by considering what Elaine Scarry writes about sentience as an expression of embodiment framed by the contrary poles of pain and imagining.

Pain, according to Scarry (1985), expresses a state of sentience completely empty of referential content, while imagining expresses sentience entirely as referential content. Each of these modes of experience, insofar as sentience is bound to the figure of intentionality, can thereby be theoretically conceived as each other's object/state, respectively. Yet, as Scarry notes, because an "intentional state without an object" is a contradiction in terms, pain cannot be intended, only suffered (ibid.: 164). "Pain", she writes, "only becomes an intentional state once it is brought into relation with the objectifying power of the imagination" (ibid.). But until the fiery traces of pain sketch a path to the imagination, where an imaginary fact may be ascribed the intentions of an ulterior agency and a cause established, pain marks the boundary of sense. It is in the framing of sentience that conscious experience is expressed in the movement between an aversive state of radical embodiment (pain) and a self-satisfying state of radical objectification (imagining). As Scarry observes, "the more a habitual form of perception is experienced as itself rather than its external object, the closer it lies to pain [and] conversely the more completely a state is experienced as its object, the closer it lies to imaginative self-transformation [displacement of one's 'self']" (ibid.: 165). For her, experience is the movement of a continuum of perceptual, somatic, and emotional events that are more or less passively suffered or actively invented.

Assuming one agrees with this model, that experience hovers between a sweeping physical pain and a plenary imagining, and that a state without an object is painful, then it's reasonable to suppose that following or anticipating the occurrence of pain would be an impulse for one to objectify his or her experience in order to pour one's beleagueredly animated self into inanimate, quiescent things. The world that we all share, a world of suffering and fancy, will be understood as an expression of the dynamic and continuous variation of pain and imagining. However, within this expression inheres a paradox that becomes increasingly apparent as perception approaches its own isolation. As Scarry notes, if perception becomes isolated and deprived of an object, it has the "potential for being experienced either as [feeling] state or as object" (ibid.). For Scarry, this describes perception as a fluid event wherein it can be taken up either in pain or as an object. For example, at one moment the sun can be regarded as a brilliant object; yet, if this moment lasts too long, then seeing falls into itself and it moves towards suffering the sun's blinding intensity in "the event of 'seeing' itself" (ibid.)—seeing seeing itself as both an object and an activity.

Similarly, and more relevantly to this study, we can objectify the piecing chirps of the LRAD's deterrence setting as a quality and a thing: "a loud sound." However, before long, the LRAD pushes hearing deep into the body, where sound and sensation, thing and quality, blur in intense indistinction. The more isolated or self-implicated perception becomes, the more its feeling-thinking intends itself as its object, the more the body consumes itself. In other words, in the extreme withdrawal of a perceptual object, the pain of perception can only imagine itself. But strangely, the other condition in which such isolation of sensation happens is orgasm. Thus, we come upon the curious nature of intensity as an event of pleasurable suffering.

Let me explain this a little more. Ordinarily, interior states bond with "companion objects in the outside world", in a sense inviting us into their movements and affordances (ibid.: 162). However, the state of pain or orgasm *is itself alone*; each is a passive event that is suffered and finds relief only in an imaginative self-transformation that supplements a disembodied or objectified state for the embodied objectless state. Focusing on the pole of pain, we find a particularly acute example of this dynamic paradox at work in "stress positions." A stress position, as outlined in the CIA's cryptonymic KUBARK,[11] is an interrogation technique wherein one is forced to hold certain postural positions that overtax and strain one's musculoskeletal system. This technique has the peculiar effect of causing a form of pain that possesses the semblance of relief, for stress positions permit movement that relieves the acuity of a particular strain by relocating it elsewhere. In other words, pain is never diminished but is merely pushed around the body. Stress positions, such as those inflicted by the American military upon detainees at Guantanamo Bay, and most famously at Abu Ghraib prison in the early oughts, are exemplary expressions of pain and imagining taking each as the intentional companion of the other—"pain as the imagination's intentional state and ... the imagination as pain's intentional object" (ibid.: 164). Here, standing on a narrow surface, blindfolded, with arms outstretched, fearing threat of electrocution, the pain of holding still becomes the intentional state and the intentional object of experience. In a sense, stress positions embody the constant variation of pain as the refrain of torture.

Occult Dualisms

How does this relate to what I have been saying about a composition that "will have been heard" as Music? Insofar as *glossolalia*'s melodic differential is a diagram that bends and turns the sensuous

11 Volume One is subtitled "Counterintelligence Interrogation", while Volume Two replaces KUBARK with the name "Human Resource Exploitation Training Manual." Each is available here: https://nsarchive2.gwu.edu/NSAEBB/NSAEBB122/#hre;

refrains of Music to open the body onto the recursive territory of pain, we are dealing with the ethical hazard of the arts. And to the extent that this work renders sonorous the consistently inconsistent patterns of a force that constantly acts upon itself, pushing its stress to other body parts, it traces a line of flight from its musicians and sounds, from the stage, from the concert hall, and towards the egregious exercise of power and the violation of human dignity. If we listen along this line towards its outside, towards the screams and wails of the tortured, we will have, as Deleuze & Guattari (1987: 331) say, "deterritorialised the refrain". We will have exiled the airs and ornaments of *glossolalia* from their native aesthetic purchase, making instead a music that is nomadic, a music whose wandering variations light upon domains as heterogeneous as pain and imagining.

So, what do these becomings of *glossolalia*—becoming-pain, becoming-imaginary—express? Are not the music's constant variations and the cries of the tormented inversions of each other's intensity? Music (becoming) Torture: Torture (becoming) Music. Becomings are tendencies, openings, and modulations. In essence, what becoming is is a process—unfinished ongoingness as such. Or put another way, becoming is a "differential coming-together of a heterogeneity of creative factors issuing into the occurrence of an expressive event" (Massumi, 2011: 147). But until that moment of expression, there is no distinguishing a whimper from a *sotto voce*. Neither Torture nor Music actually becomes the other, for there is no identity in becoming; there is only a sustained differentiation and the immediate coincidence of a tendential $T^{m}o^{u}r^{s}t^{i}u^{c}r^{k}e$ ${}_{t}M_{o}u_{r}s_{t}i_{u}c_{r}k_{e}$.

Becoming is therefore the scene of sense. In becoming, all nascent movements and budding intensities subsist together as potential paths of action and lines of expression. It is in this respect that music and torture can be understood to inhabit the same scene of sense, of affective discipline. Between music and torture is "a specific configuration of relative movements and affective intensities" (Bogue, 2003: 35) that belongs to both, or rather, belongs to neither, as "Music" and "Torture" are, from the perspective of becoming, relational terms expressing a particular series of bodily interactions. Music, for instance, is a technique that cultures have developed to discipline and articulate bodies (human, instrument, concert hall, genre, repertoire, etc.) in such a way as to express the life of feeling in its qualitative-relational order: meat and bones, brass and wood, conceptual and historical bodies hang together in the occasion of Music as the sense of their mutual variations and dynamic affordances (though, more precisely, it is the regularity of these variations that are called Music). Torture also organises bodies and forces, and like Music, it too has historical and conceptual vectors that articulate with meat and bones to express a life of feeling. However, unlike the common practice of Music that manners affects into emotional circuits, Torture's manner "liberates" affects from any purposive perspective. The pain that sets the body to blaze, that annihilates the world and its theatre of symbols and artefacts, looses a spasm of intensity that insists between the soaking towel, the mouth, and the lungs, between the wrists, the twine, the overhead piping, and the pull of the weary body.

Cultures form around both of these practices. In a sense, we can posit Music as a culture's way of domesticating intensities, while Torture is a practice of emancipating them. From this standpoint, the polarised cultivation of intensity has a strange history: Music is intensity domesticated; Torture is intensity set free. Thus, on the one hand, the history of Music is a public history of enchanting or charming intensities, a culture's masochistic zoo of affective captures; on the other hand, the history of Torture is a private history of disenchanting intensities, a secret sadism that a culture performs to express the limits of its own reason.

Said another way, both Music and Torture make sense of what has no sense apart from the actions that express it. Each in its own way articulates "a secret dualism hidden in sensible and material bodies" that distinguishes not between the Model and copy, but the copy and simulacra (Deleuze, 1990: 2). This, as Deleuze shows, is not a dualism between the sensible and intelligible, matter and idea, but between "limited and measured things" and "a pure becoming without measure" (ibid.: 1). Crudely summarised, copies punctuate the sense of the Idea, while simulacra express the movement or transformation of the Idea (ibid.: 2). Yet, Deleuze insists that this dualism is not hidden, but is instead distributed everywhere, and so "it is no longer a question of simulacra that elude the ground and insinuate themselves everywhere, but rather a question of effects that manifest themselves and act in their place" (ibid.: 7). But these effects can also act in place of the Idea as a Snark does when it is a Boojum, which is to say that effects are like Schrödinger's Cat—dead, alive, or both at once. It all depends on how you look at them.

Illustrative Interlude: Practising

Practice. Practice. Practice. The masochist's mantra that founders on the mad becomings of their art. First, up the scale, then down. Transpose to another key: up...down; again, transpose: up...down. What is this? Practice. But what is practice? It's not Music, but neither is it Torture. Practising, in fact, makes more sense than Music does, for there is no end to practise; practice is unlimited. The intensities of slipping up, of cacking, of tentatively plucking one's way through a difficult passage, of stumbling or faltering over a phrase, of playing a melody slower and quieter than indicated, of learning only fragments of a melody, of missing a note, of adding a beat—all are expressions of the unlimited that practice circulates. Practice shuffles while Music plays games.

Practice is, then, a becoming and the migration of simulacra that tend towards becoming more and less Musical, making one's performance always better and worse at the same time. Practising therefore has no limits, no tense, no horizon. It is the *Plane of Ideosonic Transmutation and Hyperstitious Intensification of Non-belief*.

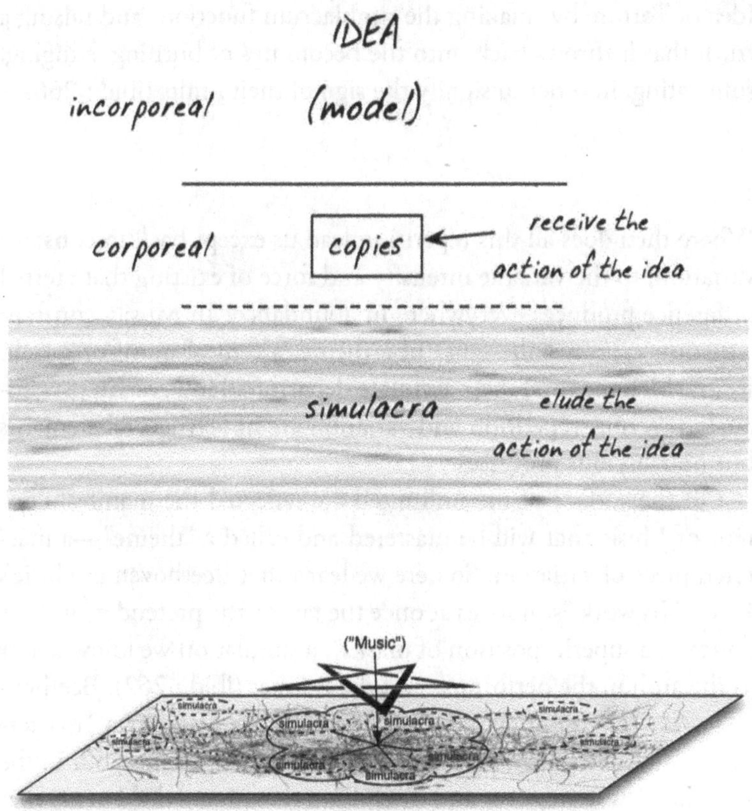

"To practise" names an infinitive: you can always get better than you were and worse than you will become. What is Music if not an active limiting, a superinduction of its Idea on the errors and flaws that practice makes sense of? An Idea of Music does nothing to the cacophony of intensities itself, but instead simulates an order of original and copy by way of the unlimited's functioning (ibid.: 262). A performance is thus better understood as the representation, the repression, of an unlimited practice (the impossible perfection) in the effective simulation of the Idea of Music. In other words, all our concerts or recordings regulate (limit) the beginning and end of Music's Idea. Interrogation, the ritual of releasing excessive affects, can also be considered a performance. Interrogation simulates the

Idea of Torture by "making the simulacrum function" and raising a truth that it throws back onto the becomings of burning, stinging, suffocating, in order to signify the sign of their limits (ibid.: 266).

***

Where then does all this repetition lead us except back to constant variation, to the variable intensity and force of existing that eternal difference produces everywhere in abundance? In Music, constant variation expresses the sense of a theme, a central motif or refrain from which the utterances simulate departure. However, in psychoanalytic terms, repetition and variation are not structural elements but unconscious processes.

Off the surface of the unlimited are reflected the manifest content of Music that will be mastered and called a "theme"—a mastered piece of variation. So here we learn that Beethoven is Music's Plato. His work "simulates at once the father, the pretender, and the fiancé in a superimposition of masks", a simulation we know better as the author, the performer, and the listener (ibid.: 262). Beethoven's *Ode*, for example, a variation on Plato's Cave, is a "masterpiece", not in its formal brilliance or striking harmonies, but in the way that it watches over and disciplines the untamed elements that produce the phantom of its Idea. In other words, the *Ode* masters the unlimited by the very power of simulation that its simulacra remainders.

The Sleep Side of Music and Dream-Work

Here, near the end of our discussion, is the ideal form of the *Ode* whose simulation is the manifest content of a culture's dream that takes the echoes of its difference as the simulated essence of its worth. Like the irreality of a dream that we recollect only upon waking, the Idea of the *Ode* appears only when the work (the dream) is over. We recall only the phantasm and not the difference that escapes its Idea. We say: "It sounds like 'X', like 'Y', like

'Z'"; however, we know that no amount of signs will give us the *Ode* itself. No matter how many things are said in its name, their referrals cannot express the host of symptoms that course throughout its phantasmatic body. We know only intuitively that beneath the *Ode's* manifest content lies a sea of turbulent sense, that the "affective charge associated with the phantasm is explained by [an] internal resonance whose bearers are the simulacra" (ibid.: 261). Between what we say of the *Ode* and what we listen to, we have *the dream-work of Music.*

While we're familiar with the waking life of Music, in the way our favourite band and favourite song each articulate with other ideas that we have about ourselves and the world at large, we are less certain about how the slumbering side of Music behaves. What does Music sound like from its "sleep side"?[12] The manifest content of the Ideas of Music circulates in and as the formal domain characterised by melody, harmony, pitch, rhythm, as well as the discursive realm where we describe the importance of these effects to ourselves and to others. But the latent content of Music insinuates itself everywhere between these as sensation, feeling, mood, and disposition. The unconscious of Music is where bodies affect one another, where they meld, break and fall apart again and again. Because Music's Idea is the expression of how these bodies mingle, it can arise anywhere that its mixture can be simulated. Thus, we have the Ideas of Bach's *The Well-Tempered Clavier (WTC)* performed on the modern piano, or the six cello suites performed on contrabass. Though the sounds of these works are particular to the bodies that cause them (i.e., piano and contrabass), their sense is not itself limited to such manifest content, for the latent content of the sonatas, or the *WTC*, communicates modally such that we

---

12 It is the poet and scholar Anne Carson who first notices the sleep-side of things, describing a dream of hers in which she explains to herself that the uncanny appearance of a familiar green living room is a result of having "caught the living room sleeping." Or as she says, "I had entered it from the sleep side" (see Carson, 2006: 20).

register in the cello suites performed on guitar, or the *WTC* performed on a clarinet, an *intensive* rather than a *formal* difference between the bodies (instruments and their sounds) and the Music's Idea. What we listen to are simulacra. However, the name "transcription" that is given to these expressions of the *WTC* and the sonatas preserve the privilege of the "original", for the repetition of the Idea's difference that makes the work what it is obscures the way the thisness of each transcription is its own original expression. But curiously, when doubles appear, each claiming the Idea of the work as its own, the simulacra cannot help but surface and infect the order of the Idea (of copy). Who remembers that *Twist and Shout* was first recorded by The Top Notes, that *Respect* is due to Otis Redding, or that the *Goldberg Variations* is harpsichord music. The Beatles, Aretha Franklin, and Glenn Gould each caught the Idea of Music sleeping, and entering from the sleep side, each showed us what it was dreaming.

But the musical unconscious is not, as musicologist Michael Chanan (1994: 105) suggests, "continuous with musical consciousness" in the sense that "the conscious and subconscious map directly onto each other". The modes, harmonies, intervals, rhythms, timbres, and proper names that express the sense of these symptoms, and which make up the symbols of musical consciousness, do not chart the unconscious, for becomings are not limited things the way intervals, etc. are limited. An interval, a major third for example, is a simulated essence, a phantasm of a differential relation that is qualified in terms of its perceived relative consonance in a system of ratios between pitch frequencies. The "Major Third" is an Idea-Symbol for a movement between two differences, a movement that is not itself an Idea-Symbol, but something more like a libidinal charge or pure desire before it has been coded as a "love", "affection", or "friendship". The musical unconscious, therefore, does not conceal itself so much as its expressions are dissembled within the workings of the Music's ego—namely, its Idea of itself. The trafficking with incompatibles, the coincidence of opposites, and the desertion of rational timespace that mark the activity of the Freudian unconscious is only implicated in Music through the way its measurable (conscious) propaganda—i.e., harmony, melody, and rhythm—express what are properly intensive magnitudes. It is the disjunctive continuity between the expressed intensity and the expression itself that constitutes the dream-work of Music.

The dream-work of Music, however, does not lend itself to interpretation. Its operation is a matter of expression. Interpretation assumes a world or a structure of fixed terms and relations in which thought is merely a more or less adequate reflection of its general order. In this sense, interpretation is the proper approach when aimed at affirming the normative scope of an event. But expression is different. Rather than extracting fantasies of order from a prescribed set of relations, expression seizes on the present, complex, and contingent immediacy of things to forge new relations and new ways of becoming. Taking Music's dream-work as an expressive activity instead of the distortion of an already (over)determined desire is to approach Music from its sleep side and listen in on the pure variability of its dreaming.

This emphasis on the creative potential over the hermeneutic prospects of dream-work is actually suggested by Freud himself in a footnote he added to *The Interpretation of Dreams*, twenty-five years after its initial publication:

> But now that analysts at least have become reconciled to replacing the manifest dream by the meaning revealed by its interpretation, many of them have become guilty of falling into another confusion which they cling to with equal obstinacy. They seek to find the essence of dreams in their latent content and in so doing they overlook the distinction between the latent dream-thoughts and the dream-work. At bottom dreams are nothing other than a particular form of thinking, made possible by the conditions of the state of sleep. It is the dream-work which creates that form, and it alone is the essence of dreaming—the explanation of its peculiar nature.

(Freud, 1955: 506–507)

Music's dream-work is creative—but it's creative by virtue of how it expresses a series of changing interactions between bodies, ideas, and virtual entities. Neither the manifest nor latent content is the *sense* of dreaming, but, as Freud writes, these are "like two versions of the same subject-matter in two different languages" (ibid.: 277). The sense of dreaming is not what the manifest or latent content can be interpreted to mean, but the way in which displacements, condensations, representations, and revisions take place. In short, the dream-work is a process that dis/articulates the manifest and latent content like the twist in the Möbius strip does the inside and outside of a surface. Said another way, dream-work is a mode of thinking expressed in manifest *and* latent terms. Expanding on this, Music's dream-work can be understood as a particularly dynamic mode of thinking, an abstract movement-thinking whose logic Deleuze (1994) characterises, with regard to Kierkegaard's and Nietzsche's metaphysics, as relaying a movement of "vibrations, rotations, whirlings, gravitations, dances, or leaps which directly touch the mind".[13] But as Simon Duffy (2004: 51) notes, this logic of expression "is not an abstract logic that merely represents the movement of these affects, but the very logic by means of which these affects are expressed [made effective]". To be fair to Chanan, there is some manner of continuity between Music's conscious (Ideas) and unconscious (simulacra), but only insofar as this continuity refers to a modal disjunction between two sides of the same expression, two different orders of the same process: cause and effect. Music's dream-work, its sense, is characterised, then, not by the logic of condensation or displacement, but by the logic of expression. This relates the unconscious and conscious according to what Duffy calls a "mutual immanence," a relation whereby "the structure of the first [unconscious] envelops the existence of the

13 Here, Deleuze is referring specifically to the unconscious of philosophy, which he says Kierkegaard and Nietzsche were trying to bring to the surface in their writings.

second [conscious] and inversely the existence of the second [conscious] expressor represents the structure of the first [unconscious]" (ibid.: 56).[14] The unconscious of Music, in its striking dissimilarity to itself, is not something to be read or decoded, but something to be raised to the surface.

But what does it mean to raise the unconscious to the surface? Moreover, what is this surface to which the simulacra should be raised? And how can an unlimited becoming encroach upon a limited Idea? The short answer is that the musical unconscious is expressed by what Deleuze (1990b: 180) would say is the "immanence of expression in what expresses itself, and of what is expressed in its expression". The long answer, however, requires that we return to the Idea of the "masterpiece" and the question of its discipline, which again, but this time from below (or its sleep side), brings refrains of pain and imagining, and how their motifs are expressed at the cultural level by the Idea of Music.

***

What I have been discussing here and calling a "becoming" is not the identification of musical experience with Torture but the way in which Music and Torture are different expressions of a body acting upon and through another body. I am still dealing with becoming at this point, but now with the aim to show that the process of repression, which musical simulacra inflict upon themselves in the name of Music, is similar to the process that transforms pain into the imagination. For instance, consider how both the singing and the screaming body are expressions of a somatic intensity. Psychoanalytic theories take the intensity of pain and music as having a shared origin, suggesting that Music is essentially a transfiguration of infantile vocalisations of pain, or more accurately, that Music's relatively pleasurable affect is the positive valencing of a pre-qualified intensity.

---

14 Duffy cites Albert Lautman's (1938) *Essai sur l'unité des sciences mathématiques dans leur développement actuel.* Paris: Hermann. p. 31.

In his essay "Contribution to the Psychoanalysis of Music", Heinrich Racker (1951: 142) argues exactly this, writing, "in their physical aspect it is already evident that scream and song are intimately related ... tone is a transformed scream". Song, in this respect, develops from the scream as an expression of inarticulate desires. But, as is often noted, sound is something that one cannot simply shut out by force of will—vibrations impinge upon us whether we wish them to or not. Thus, for the infant who does not yet distinguish between sounds that emanate from inside or outside, Music is something that develops away from or against the sounds that encroach upon its body: "Music in this circumstance is presumed to result from attempts to master this kind of unpleasant experience" (Shepherd & Wicke, 1997: 59). One can extrapolate from this that harnessing what cannot be wholly kept out (of the body) is another role of the dream-work of Music.

While dream-work brings the unconscious to the surface, it also aims to regulate and organise the intensities that it disinters—that is, to manage and harness sonorous (but also not-so-sonorous) forces that assail the body by bringing its flood of sensations under the influence of an Idea. Hence, the notion of the masterpiece not only disciplines the field of artistic activity from within, but compels actual sound events to pass through its ideational domains (quasi-cause) in a way that tempers or modulates one's sensitivity to the action of the Idea. Although the process of dream-work can represent the occult dualism I spoke of earlier, between simulacra and Ideas, it also speaks to the way bodies are composed and organised by what affects them.

The musical unconscious, like a state of affairs, is separate from the expressions that manifest its dream-work in a way that is comparable to effects taken apart from their causes. Such a situation is not, however, thinkable in itself, for the thinkable is what happens at the surface of things, the surface where the effects of things in their various mixtures flicker back and forth in expressive correspondence. Things do not think themselves; things have an affect: a thing is what it does, what effect it has on another body. In other words, a "thing" is known by its affects, by the form of its encounter with another body. The sun, to use an earlier example again, is known variously as a symbol of power, life, clarity, glory, happiness, vision and mind, but most notably it is known by how it warms our body. And a song, too, though composed of notes, melodies, chords, etc., is known as a thing by how it moves us, makes us feel, dance, and think.

However, recalling Scarry's example of staring at the sun, under this extreme condition we can feel-imagine the body of the sun to coincide with and sink into its own affect. In its pure form, we would call this depth of bodies *absolute nonsense*—the noise of the body.[15] But following the logic of expression, even this pure nonsense is expressive. Even though nonsense does not have any particular sense, it is always opposed to the absence of sense, such that the order of the Music's unconscious, like Torture, is an affair of how the force of a body's characteristic manner of existing is modified by what affects it.[16] Like Torture, which is a particular Idea emerging from the deleterious effects that a body has on another's characteristic (i.e., individual) somatic relations,[17] Music is an Idea that rises to the surface from the way sounds adjust and modulate

15 Deleuze actually identifies two orders of nonsense: one at the surface of things in the radical affirmation of sense that is expressed in terms of paradox (Carroll's nonsense), and another in the carnal mixture of bodies (forces) caught in an endless process of mutual impingements. This latter is the nonsense of Antonin Artaud, wherein words (their sounds) are no less corporeal and thus affective than the bodies that speak them.

16 "Nonsense is that which has no sense, and that which, as such and as it enacts the donation of sense, is opposed to the absence of sense" (Deleuze, 1990a: 71).

17 An expression of what compromises the whole of the characteristic relation of the body would be "death." Curiously, this opens the possibility that the destruction of my "characteristic" relation entails the construction of another relation, though while not "characteristic" is nevertheless not a nothingness, a reincarnation of sorts (see Deleuze, 1978).

these relations. In the same way that Torture's pain connects a knife and flesh through an event that cannot be reduced to either knife or flesh, but subsists at their surface as the sense of "being cut," Music connects bodies, fingertips, strings, bows, habits and reflexes, eyes and scores, ears and vibrations—in the sense of "performing," "listening," or "musicking."

So, if Torture and Music are both expressions of bodily affairs—one making the body howl, the other making it sing—how is it that one becomes the other? How is practising itself a kind of stress position and a stress position a kind of practice? In other words, at what point does Music become Torture and Torture become Music? If we understand that what affects us generates Ideas, and that these Ideas somehow escape and dislocate an intensity from the characteristic set of relations that compose a body as a bundled potential of actions, then we see a path open to an incorporeal realm of symbols "outside" the excessive becomings of the body. And these becomings tell us that Music and Torture exist along a continuum of embodiment that is either more or less disciplined to the incorporeal effects of the masterpiece—more or less receptive to the action of an Idea.

Finally, where do I think Eliot's work fits into all of this? Briefly put, I think that her work is about the displacement of nonsense, the drifting circularity that "is always ex-centric in relation to an always decentred centre" (Deleuze, 1990a: 264). That is to say, her music is a torturous involution of intensities whose sign as Music expresses its madness as a pattern, a "logic" of constant variation that reposes fitfully in the crowned anarchy of its own contradiction.

Works cited

Johann Sebastian Bach (1722) *The Well-Tempered Clavier (WTC)*

John Cage (1977–90) *Freeman Etudes*

Karen Eliot (2003–4) *pleasure drenching…*

—. (2007) *glossolalia (stress positions)*

Leif Inge (2002) *9 Beet Stretch*

Michael Finnissy (2013) *The History of Photography in Sound.*
Per Nørgård's (1959–) "infinity series" Composition Method.
Phil Niblock (1993) *Five More String Quartets*

References

Bogue, R. (2003) *Deleuze on Music, Painting, and the Arts*. London: Routledge.

Bök, C. (2001) *Eunoia*. Toronto: Coach House Books.

Christensen, E. (2004) "Overt and Hidden Processes in 20th Century Music". *Axiomathes* 14(1–3): 107.

Carson, A. (2006) *Decreation*. Toronto: Vintage Canada.

Chana, M. (1994) *Musica Practica: The Social Practice of Western Music from Gregorian Chant to Postmodernism*. New York: Verso.

Deleuze, G. (1978) "Lecture Transcripts on Spinoza's Concept of Affect". Online: Goldsmiths University. https://www.gold.ac.uk/media/images-by-section/departments/research-centres-and-units/research-centres/centre-for-invention-and-social-process/deleuze_spinoza_affect.pdf

—. (1989) *Cinema 1: The Movement Image*. Translation by H. Thomlinson, & B. Haberjam. Minneapolis: University of Minnesota Press.

—. (1990a) *The Logic of Sense*. Translation by M. Lester. New York: Columbia University Press.

—. (1990b) *Expressionism in Philosophy: Spinoza*. Translation by Joughin, M. New York: Zone Books

—. (1994) *Difference and Repetition*. Translation by P. Patton. New York: Columbia University Press.

—. (2003) *Francis Bacon: The Logic of Sensation*. Translation by D. W. Smith. London: Continuum.

Deleuze, G., & Guattari, F. (1987) *A Thousand Plateaus: Capitalism & Schizophrenia*. Translation by B. Massumi. Minneapolis: University of Minnesota Press.

Duffy, S. (2004) "The Logic of Expression in Deleuze's *Expressionism in Philosophy: Spinoza*: A Strategy of Engagement". *International Journal of Philosophical Studies* 12(1): 51.

Freud, S. (1955) *The Interpretation of Dreams*. Translation by J. Strachey. New York: Basic Books.

Lautman, A. (1938) *Essai sur l'unité des sciences mathématiques dans leur développement actuel.* Paris: Hermann.

Massumi, B. (2011) *Semblance and Event: Activist Philosophy and the Occurent Arts*. Cambridge: The MIT Press.

Priest, E. (2013) *Boring Formless Nonsense: Experimental Music and the Aesthetics of Failure.* London/New York: Bloomsbury.

Racker, H. (1951) "Contribution to Psychoanalysis of Music". *American Imago* 8(2): 142.

Roussel, R. (1977) *How I Wrote Certain of my Books.* Translation by T. Winkfield. New York: SUN.

Scarry, E. (1985) *The Body in Pain: The Making and Unmaking of the World.* Oxford: Oxford University Press.

Shepherd, J., & Wicke, P. (1997) *Music and Cultural Theory.* Cambridge: Polity Press.

8. HOW 'MUSIC' 'SEDUCED' 'THE WORLD':

Ultrablack Materialism and the Indeterministic Swerve of Baudrillard's 'Real'

By Palais Sinclaire (ed.)

In memetic, genetic, quantum, urban-Darwinism, certain structures and myths went out over others, in the eternal game played inside the arena of this particular spacetime, an after effect of the electromagnetic crisscross path created when the atom (Adam) [a-tomb] was split by [the hadron], from its better half. Collapsing into this spacetime of this common-reality. It split the brain into two-halves, too: Left, Right; Male, Female. Electric, Magnetic. But information from the future is constantly falling into indeterministic gaps in the present. We see what we always have seen, but we don't expect to see differently. The observer is biased—the reason why the conditions of our Universe is the ideal incubator

> *for the breeding of galaxies, stars and planets—thermodynamics, the theory by which we hold our notions of cause and effect, is only statistical in nature, overly concerned with its own equilibrium, but the change is equalised and becomes static, with no appreciation for the dynamic processes that make change what it is. Under the regime of thermodynamics, becoming collapses into being like a piece of light, suddenly shy when observed. The arrow of time defined by thermodynamics must be dissolved. Feedback from the future must guide the development of the present and the past. In time is when we notice change, we notice change when light reaches our eyes. It is time for a change, The creation of a new spacetime, it's time for a change, the production of a new space time. The beginning of Man lies in sound vibration. It is through sound that we produce new spacetimes. The word is the weapon, to destroy the old world, and the tool to build the new.*[1]
>
> — R. Phillips (2022)

Having been outside of Mille Plateaux's orbit when the first Ultrablack volume came out, to be so close to the centre of *Ultrablack of Music Volume 2* is quite the unlikely position. The situation of being invited to write for this edition is evocative of a scene from any of the works of Plato. I, like Antisthenes, have been brought to the table of Callius, in order to take part in a dialogue (for the record). Given the implicit indeterminacy of this edition's subject, as laid out in the first edition, and further still in the collective writings of "NON" since the first edition, the field of Ultrablack is as ultra-wide as it is ultra-specific. I, then, appear here today, at your

1 This reading was presented by Black Quantum Futurism as a part of a radio episode that was aired on Lumbung Radio during Documenta Fifteen. It was found in the Lumbung Radio archives. The original purpose of the episode is not known, nor can I locate the original. The recording was only accessible to me through my own involvement in Lumbung Radio. I have transcribed it here to commit the words to the record as it is profoundly touching and moving.

table, aside Szepanski et al., brought here under the premise that I might have something interesting to say. Yet, as I *stand* to deliver, I freeze—and think: "Wait, how did I even get here?" That said, if the becoming of this edition of *Ultrablack of Music* can be characterised by a "Wait, what's going on?" then perhaps everything is in order—just as Mao said: "Everything under heaven is in great chaos: the situation is excellent."

What I have chosen, then, to bury in this tomb, is a simple work of origami. I will attempt to take the work of Jean Baudrillard, Francois Laruelle, Achim Szepanski, Lucretius, Jacques Derrida and Thomas Nail and *fold* them into *a thousand plaits* of *Ultrablack materialism.* We will take a walk with these writers, and together with them, we will establish a way of 'thinking in terms of Ultrablack', then proceed to think music in Ultrablack terms, as a strategy for discussing both the origins of music and its disappearance. I will also offer to this edition a discussion of the very "museness" (as pertaining to "*οι Μουσές*") of "music" ("*Μουσική*") that prompted Friedrich Nietzsche to characterise music as "the best approximation of the eternal recurrence" (Schroeder, 2001: 194). A lot of this essay explores a philosophical critique of *Production*, both in relation to Baudrillard's concept of 'Seduction' and in relation to a general post-Marxist critique of the 'Productivist' logic of capitalist modernity. The only way to begin, without conforming to the hegemony of unilinear accumulation and the line of thermodynamics, is with a *story*:

> In the beginning, there was *Χάος* (Noise), who produced, by means of simulation, *Γαία*, the Earth ("the Feminine"), who, being of the simulation of *Χάος*, immediately in turn produced *Ουρανός*, the Sky/Heavens ("the Masculine") as a simulation of *Χάος*; *Γαία* produces *Ουρανός* in the image of *Χάος*. As Rhythm arises out of Noise, *Γαία* arises out of *Χάος*, and *Ουρανός* out of *Γαία*. With *Ουρανός*, *Γαία* produces the elements and the vegetation of Earth,

and the earliest life of Earth, who all, by the will/nature of *Ουρανός*, keep disappearing. In order to create the immortal daughter who suffers not the fate of *Ουρανός*, *Γαία* devised a ritual. Her revolution would involve creating a daughter by inverting *Ουρανός* means of production, twisting the logic of how *Ουρανός* produces. To achieve this, she convinces *Χρόνος* to use *Τηθύς* to capture the productive piece of *Ουρανός*. *Χρόνος*, with the double-edged sickle blade (that symbolises *Τηθύς* as ruler of curvature), castrates *Ουρανός*, and the negated symbol of his masculinised logic of production falls into the ocean, *Τηθύς*. In the impact of the negated-sign hitting the surface of the ocean, foam is foamed. It was an alchemical process of capturing the Sky with the curvature of the Sea's waves, to produce the bubble or foam (*αφρός*). Out of this foam came *Αφροδίτη*, and as she walked upon the Earth, the Universe (*Χάος*) rejoiced; the Heavens had materialised on Earth, and now the World could begin; the World had waited for *Αφροδίτη* to come.

The Earth had overthrown the Heavens in Revolution. *Γαία* inverted the productivist logic of *Ουρανός*, emasculated it, using the severed prosthesis in a lesbian ritual, the effect of which was the immanence of *Αφροδίτη* and the beginning of the World. *Χάος* may have produced *Γαία*, the *Second*, but *Γαία* did not *produce* *Αφροδίτη*, the *Third*; she *seduced* her by means of *ritual*. *Γαία* is a simulation of *Χάος*, and in trying to simulate *Χάος*, *Γαία* (the simulation) produced *Ουρανός* (simulacra) as the *false-Third* by using the *image* of *Χάος*, not the *motion* (the way) of *Χάος*. *Γαία*'s ritual, however, involved using the non-linear (circular) logic of *Τηθύς*' curvature through Time (*Χρόνος*) to create a curved blade which with to capture a specific piece of the sky. As the waves collapse inwards, back into the ocean, the circle collapses inwards, into the infinite inward spiral that symbolises *Αφροδίτη*. All of which *Γαία* produces with the logic

> of *Ουρανός*, dies, because they are *images*, *signs*, but what *Γαία* seduces by means of ritualistic reversion of *Ουρανός* is Seduction itself, immortal, ruler of Death. If the Secret is that *Χάος* is the Real, then *Γαία* is the Simulation, and *Αφροδίτη* is the Second Real (the Third). It is by this dual-nature that Lucretius decrees *Αφροδίτη* the God(dess) of Seduction, who rules over the World.

Thinking ultrablack

In *Universe Black in the Foundations of Colour* (2012: 401), Francois Laruelle writes that The Universe and Man are *Black*, and The World and Philosopher are "white". Man is of the Universe, and the Philosopher of the World. Importantly, *Black* and "white" are not presented here as an oppositional structure that follows the productivist logic of modernity. Universe *Black* has no reference to the "black" that is othered by "white"; it is a more all-encompassing (universal) *Black* that does not submit to the "authority of light" (productivist hegemony). "White" is an illusion or distortion of light (the eyes), which is characterised precisely by an attempt to other *Black* that is never perfected: *Black* is beyond what "white" can negate. This seems to comply with various well-known conventions in Quantum Theory (see Schröter, 2024), especially regarding such matters as 'the position of the electron', where trying to determine the position of the electron reveals a limit of the Image of Thought [model] (Laruelle, 2018: 152–156), as the electron is ultimately *Black*, and cannot be read in terms of *position*. We are free to imagine, as we do, the electron as a little ball, or a concentration of charge in a field, moving around, but whatever Image we might use to represent an electron will always miss the mark, *just. Black*, or 'Ultrablack' as a way of separating *Black* from "black" (Szepanski, 2020: 23), is the framework through which music is discussed within this essay, and the purpose of discussing music in this way is, by and large, an experiment—albeit a schizophrenic one—as if publishing a book about mass illiteracy, because ultimately, if music is Ultrablack, it is untellable: it's a *Secret.*

Jean Baudrillard is perhaps a peculiar philosopher to consider when thinking about music. Baudrillard, like Laruelle, wrote of a 'real' that 'appears' (to the eyes of the *Philosopher*) two-fold and is characterised by indeterminacy—a 'Secret Real' ['The Universe']—on the one hand, and an illusory, simulated 'Reality' ['The World'] on the other. 'The World' [white], where we *produce Thoughts* as *Philosophers*, is a *simulation* of 'The Universe' [(Ultra)black] that has been *seduced* by 'the Symbolic' or re-codified in relation to 'the Social': "The power of signs lies in their appearance and disappearance; that is how they efface the world" (Baudrillard, 1990: 94).

Ultrablack is what is masked, both in the sense of obscured and adorned, by "white" in its simulative production of "black". Ultrablack *seduces* white, which then produces "black" as a simulation and counter-face of Ultrablack. Ultrablack is that which cannot be signified or simulated in totality as there are always 'breaks' (anomalies, gaps, glitches), and it is these 'breaks' which hint toward the secret, momentarily, as if to point out the un-pointable *with their eyes.* The Universe and Man are Ultrablack because they are of the order of the secretive, indeterminate 'Real'. The Philosopher and World are "white" because they are of the order of the Simulation (representation). Music, *Αφροδίτη*, *Χάος*, Noise and Seduction are Ultrablack; they are blackholes which do not so much demarcate the boundaries of the Secret, but rather act as the gaps between lines that can be read, glancingly, to glimpse, momentarily, the secret. As we know from Derrida (2016: 3), 'Words' and 'language' are 'white'—they make up a system of signs, and neither words nor language can themselves represent the Universe, given that it is 'untellable'. But we have learned throughout history to write in such a way that the Universe can be 'read between the lines'—or at least the Universe can be glimpsed momentarily, if you stare long enough into the gaps between 'things'/'signs'.

Baudrillard stands out as a prime example of the 'Anti-Philosopher', not so much in the sense of Badiou, but in the sense of being someone whose philosophy primarily seeks to undermine 'Philosophy' as we know it, and it is Baudrillard's attempt to 'plant bombs in the underlying (oppositional) structures of Philosophy' ("theoretical terrorism") that makes his philosophy Ultrablack, as Ultrablackness itself dispels or seduces, thus undermining, the oppositional structure of white/black that drives Philosophy (Galloway, 2014: 135).

Where Laruelle and Baudrillard find agreement is in their shared criticism of Philosophy in the West as being of the order of representation; it is logocentric (Derrida) and productivist (Baudrillard), and always affirming masculinised oppositional structures in favour of the positive (Grace, 2000: 150). For example, Laruelle (2020: 82) writes that "Philosophy is the Capital within Thought: the Capital-Form of our general relations to the World, it is an autonomous, generalised form of socio-economic capital". In other words, it is a way of thinking in the (white) terms of representation and appearance, as opposed to thinking in terms of Ultrablack. Where Laruelle uses non-philosophy to point out how Philosophy has been conditioned (by capital, and other positivist hegemonies) into something disconnected or *ab*stracted (*ex*tracted), in Baudrillard's terms we could that 'Philosophy' is a simulacrum of 'non-Philosophy'. In the same way, we can say that Laruelle's 'black' (as the other of 'white') is a simulacrum of '(Ultra)*Black*', in that the purpose of 'black' (as the other of 'white') has disconnected from the original '*Black*' that was, at one stage in the process, the original referent. If the purpose of 'black' is to other 'white' (individuate by means of negation), and not even to represent *Black*, then the simulation of '*Black*' that 'white' 'produces' in its struggle to establish itself in the positive, is rather a simulacrum (a copy disconnected from its original) (Baudrillard, 1983: 81).

Better examples, however, of where Baudrillard and Laruelle think in terms of Ultrablack are often found in relation to 'positionality'. We can take, for example, Baudrillard's concept of 'seduction', and look at how he chooses not to position seduction and production in an oppositional structure (a binary pair)—in fact, he chooses not to position them at all. In the first instance, or on the *surface*, seduction merely transforms production, it doesn't work *against* it or negate it, as this would be a matter of [op]positionality, and seduction is certainly not the *Other* of production; it is not *othered by* production. If production is about making 'things exist' by 'bringing them into vision', then seduction does indeed 'make things' invisible (again) through the process of 'reversion' (Grace, 2000: 141–142), which does appear to 'annul signs', but as Baudrillard has written, it is the ability of signs to disappear and reappear that affords their operational and 'definitional' power to 'efface the World' or undermine the symbolic by undermining the logic of productivism, which is characterised by unilinear accumulation. It is not that seduction is a force that enacts upon 'things' called signs, ushering them towards death; it is that this process of seduction (that production attempts to other itself from) is an aspect of the ontology/nature of signs, and an expression of "their 'desire' to be abolished" (Baudrillard, 1990: 45) as part of a cyclical process of re-instantiation that chases after objective permanence. A sign is not a 'thing' but a process initiated through 'ritual'. Seduction, being Ultrablack, is dual-natured; it is both the seduced and the seduction itself (double genitive), but this will become important later.

Therefore, seduction is not a negative force against production; there is rather no production, there is no alternative means of creation that others seduction, which is an aspect of the cyclical, self-devouring nature of signs, which *swerve* (as pertaining to Lucretius) as strategy for simulating the 'Real' (Grace, 2000: 141). Baudrillard considers the logic of capitalist modernity to be 'productivism', which is characterised by the logic of 'unilinear accumulation' (Baudrillard, 1975: 83) or accrual, and so seduction, as that which transforms production, undermines the productivist logic by revealing unilinear accumulation to be an illusion (Grace, 2008: 142). Production, as white, attempts to *other* itself from Seduction, as Ultrablack, but cyclically short-circuits and disappears again.

The ocean currents (*Τηθύς*) 'produce' waves on the 'surface' of the water, and even if the waves *appear* to *become-visible*, they are not ever really *produced* in a way that complies with the unilinear logic of productivism. The waves are a small, temporary surface phenomenon in the bigger system of ocean currents. *Τηθύς* is the ruler of these currents, and she was used by *Γαία*, in the form of the curvature of *Χρόνος*' blade, in the Lesbian ritual or revolution (both circular processes) that brought *Αφροδίτη*, the Goddess of Seduction, to 'the World' (Nail, 2018: 26–28). *Τηθύς* is signified with the circle; she rules the indeterministic curvature of the swerve of matter that 'forces' becoming to 'fold' into cycles of matter, motion and memory, and the motion of the "dance" that causes atoms to become-invisible (*disappear*) (Marx, 2006: 130). If atoms (white) are *there*, they are moving so fast that a clear sense of *where* (positionality) collapses. If signs are *there* in the same way, they are also moving rapidly and their apparent endurance has to be understood, as pertaining to Nail (2018: 186), as metastable—a state also characterised by the desperate and endless proliferation of the self-same *against* the system that it depends upon to exist in opposition to. At all stages, there is this chaotic fluttering, flickering, where even the most stable 'object' or 'sign' has a degree of desperate fragility (shyness), at least upon close inspection. As we read in Nail's conclusive chapter, *Anti-Venus* (2022: 197), there is only primordial chaos; all order is made of chaos—or, to reference an editor of this edition, at all stages of rhythm there is an equal distribution of noise (Szepanski, 2020: 23).

To exemplify this further, Baudrillard had once written, presumably with some irony, that, *if anything*, there is no Male sex, as it struggles to assert and maintain an opposition to some all-encompassing 'Other', which it calls the feminine (Baudrillard, 1990: 16). To paraphrase Rasheeda Philips from the opening, in trying to *other* itself in opposition to Becoming, something which cannot hold a position of identity, the other of Becoming 'collapses' into Being. This hypothesis ties into the work of Baudrillard, where he has asserted that oppositional binaries are always historically and culturally specific, and always inherently *masculine*. This inevitably essentialist oppositional structure establishes the masculine sex in the positive, and the feminine in the 'other', as the opposite of masculine, and Baudrillard's attempt to show how, if anything, there is only feminine, is an attempt to undermine the logic of oppositional binaries. Within Baudrillard's work, there is this 'secret real' that sometimes seems to take on the form of a monistic Spinozist deity, at least when it is observed as if it is an electron, and much like Lucretius' Venus (*Αφροδίτη*), it is characterised by this overthrowing of (or healing of) the dualistic schism by that which is cast respectively in the negative. Nietzsche (1986: a412) affirms the same when writing that "Heraclitus will always be right" that "being is an empty fiction".

Ultrablack is a radical way of thinking precisely because of how it "terrorises" the productivist logic of capitalist modernity, and we can rotate into Jacques Derrida's equally Ultrablack criticism of Western philosophy, which he argues is codified by a symbolic ordering of oppositionally structured binary signs: Present/Absent, Positive/Negative, Male/Female, Eyes/Ears, Speech/Writing, Production/Seduction (Harvey, 1983).

Derrida agrees with Baudrillard's hypothesis that the symbolic ordering of oppositionally paired signs, which codifies capitalist modernity, follows a productivist logic characterised by *unilinear accumulation* and *visibility*, and even goes as far as arguing that the history of the West has been largely defined by an on-going struggle to assert the hegemony of presence (Derrida, 1982: 34; Söderbäck, 2013), or what Baudrillard (1983: 126) calls the 'hegemony of production', or what Laruelle (2012: 405) called 'the authority of light' ('the supreme mix'). Gilbert and Pearson (1999: 57) write that, in the case of Derrida, Western philosophy traditionally attempts to totalise (envelopment) and stratify (hierarchy) the means and terms with which all philosophy is thought.

Ultrablackness, therefore, joins part of what Louis Althusser (2006: 163) referred to as the 'Underground Current of Materialism', which has flowed throughout history, through Heraclitus,

Lucretius, and interestingly, Karl Marx. These philosophers are what Thomas Nail (2022b) calls 'Philosophers of Movement', and to some extent, it all comes down to the 'Swerve of Lucretius'. Marx (2006) wrote in his PhD Thesis, citing Lucretius, that matter moves, not as the result of some vital force, but by itself—motion is matter, matter is motion, matter is both in motion and the motion that it is in. What we might think of as an oppositional pair (matter/motion) is an expression of the Same, and it is a grand illusion that we see matter moving in this two-fold way.

Althusser speaks of this "secretive" current as the resistance against the hegemony of production, as if the work of Marx and Lucretius came as acts of self-defence, dealing huge blows to the different historically specific forms of what Derrida, Baudrillard and Laruelle would regard as the same hegemonic regime of power. Given that the symbolic is a simulation of the real, if the real swerves, then why not the symbolic? Signs must swerve; they demand to be abolished. The World, as the symbolic seat of our existence in The Universe, spins on this *Third* (Szepanski, 2024: 17) *axis—the irreversible reversion or seduction of all the signs that constitute the World we Think as Philosophers.*

The radical claim of Ultrablackness, then, is that it always prevents the permanent establishment of presence, by seducing signs into 'Death', which continuously haunts the unilinear accumulation of production by falsifying its claim. That which makes us behold Ultrablackness, that which invokes it, or that which calls out to it, *jilts* us, to borrow the term from Adorno (Watson, 2019: 17); the Ultrablack shakes our existence and reminds us, momentarily, just how much we cannot know:

> When Beethoven's music suddenly overpowers the attentive listener, the ego realises its own finitude and prepares to surrender its harsh self-interest. The ego wakes up to the fact that it is not the centre of the universe but a historical product of social forces, derivative from the unconscious id, whose potentials have yet to be fulfilled. In such a moment,

> recipients find themselves by losing themselves in the dawning realisation of truth.
>
> (Zuidervaart, 1991: 142)

This is the sense in which music is radically ultrablack. Music, in its heralding of ultrablack, jilts: an experience where signs are intensely seduced or revised. Deleuze & Guattari wrote of music and desubjectification/depersonalisation as being almost a strategy for someone to experience themselves as a body differently (deviation or trip), re-codifying their World, yet the same can be understood with Baudrillard, where one's understanding of themselves as a series of values and integers, is seduced or transformed—if we inhabit the symbolic, and something leads a sign astray, then the World transforms before our eyes. Seduction, in the Anglo-American world, is lathered in connotations of this process of *leading* astray. How typical of *Man* to blame *Αφροδίτη* for seducing them.

Nail wrote three volumes (2018; 2020; 2022) on Lucretius' *De Rerum Natura*, an epic poem that begins with an elaborate atheistic (therefore appearing on the surface to be paradoxical) invocation of Venus, as the one true deity. In the opening prose of this essay, I reiterated the myth of the birth of *Αφροδίτη* based on my interpretation of the work of the authors mentioned until now. The myth frames *Αφροδίτη* as the Goddess of Seduction (as pertaining to Baudrillard), but also as the first moment of immaculate autogenic conception, where *Χάος*, through *Γαία* and *Τηθύς*, successfully replicates itself, within-itself and out-of-itself. What makes *Αφροδίτη* so 'powerful' (*affective*), as a sign, is that she signifies the moment where matter made more of itself, out of itself; mitosis, DNA replication. In a way, this contributes to how *Αφροδίτη*, as ruler of the two-faces of Seduction, is also a signifier of this duality. Lucretius writes that *Αφροδίτη* is both the object of desire and the desire itself (Nail, 2018: 26): she is both the seduction and the production that is seduced. *Αφροδίτη*, as the Goddess of seduction, cyclically devours herself, and in doing so, produces the appearance of all things. As the Third instantiation of *Χάος*, the second (the double) being *Γαία* (the simulation(s) that are the necessary conditions for the *Third*), *Αφροδίτη* returns order to chaos; or to use Baudrillard's terms, she annuls the order of the representation and seduces production towards what, in the logic of productivism, *looks* a lot like *death*. *Αφροδίτη* is the otherwise arbitrary *point* that marks the *position-in-time* where the simulation curves back in on itself and becomes-real again (*symbolic death*). In terms of the Secret, the simulation (cyclical), the second (the double) becomes the first (again), but in the order of the representation (unilinear), the second collapses into the *Third*, which I would like to tie into Baudrillard's notion of 'the Third' as per Szepanski (2024: 17).

In reference to the first edition of Ultrablack, Robert Barry is referenced by Bill B. Wintermute as calling music "a machine of anticipation" (Barry, 2017: 246; Wintermute, 2020: 222), where each note sets up the next and is therefore granted a sense of positionality, not in terms spacetime but in terms of sequence. We can see how the necessity of *Χάος* to pass through *Γαία* & *Ουρανός*, to get to *Αφροδίτη*, gives away another secret; in order for the real to propagate as sound does, it must periodically, rhythmically, produce simulations whereby the necessary conditions for the coming-of-the-same-real are set ritualistically. It is on this ground that one can see a clear ideological continuity between Rasheeda Phillip's (2022) demand for "the arrow of time defined by the laws of thermodynamics must be dissolved" and Baudrillard's concept of Seduction as "Everywhere, in every domain, a single form predominates: reversibility, cyclical reversion and annulment put an end to the linearity of time, language, economic exchange, accumulation and power" (Baudrillard, 2017: 23).

What I have proposed is the inclusion of the term Noise in the mythology, based on a cross-examination of Nail's order-from-chaos and Szepanski's rhythm-from-noise, based on Baudrillard's seductivist (instead of productivist) 'dual-naturedness'. Chaotic Noise folds into Ordered Rhythm. Thinking Chaos as Noise changes the story in a way that makes it compatible with Quantum Theory.

Noise has many definitions, but the acoustician's definition would be "a sound characterised by a lack of organisation", in regard to the distribution of the amplitude of the present frequencies: white noise, pink noise, etc. All frequencies are playing at once, equally and entirely at random. To argue that the fundamental state of the Universe is chaotic noise would be to agree with theories of Quantum Fluctuations, where, instead of vacuum or silence, there is flux and noise.

We might at this point change the myth a little, to say that Noise, in the presence of Rhythm, takes on the secondary-form—the folded form—of silence: the breaks between beats, the intrusive silence that transforms sound into a pulse like an LFO. A continuous sound also depends upon cyclical/sinusoidal propagation, which is marked by the smallest breaks imaginable. *Χάος* paradoxically delivers order through the breaking-up of patterns of endless proliferation. *Αφροδίτη*'s tendency towards *disruption*, then, as she seduces The World, is affirmed here by the logic of seduction—as the *true* second-coming (the Third) of *Χάος*, she levels reality with such a Noise that everything stops momentarily, thus simultaneously appearing as silence. The illusion of Noise appearing as Silence in the *presence* of Rhythm is the same process as Ultrablack appearing as black in the presence of white.

Nail, in discussing Lucretius and Venus, establishes a (non-) metaphysics similar to certain Deleuze & Guattari-inspired conceptualisations of 'the metaphysics of desire', as pertaining to flows of desire and desiring-machines. It would be no surprise if Deleuze himself, as a deep admirer of Lucretius, would see the reason why *Αφροδίτη*, commonly known as the Goddess of Desire, is singled out by Lucretius as the original amongst the simulated. In Nail's work, there is chaos, everywhere, all the time, and it is in motion constantly. As chaos (in our case, noise) moves chaotically, a dance is set in motion regarding the distributions of probabilities of patterns of movement appearing, or moments where motion appears to repeat itself in a cyclical way. Its appearance is demarcated by the pulse of the glitch caused by the indeterministic curvature of the sinusoidal propagation folding back in on itself and collapsing momentarily. Against a backdrop of chaos-noise, the looping cyclical order of the rhythm is noticeable (it becomes visible/is produced). Nail speaks of this emergence of patterns of chaotic movement as metastasis, as in temporarily stable but ontologically *doomed*/seduced. Where Nail then goes on to discuss four categories of chaotic movement patterns, Szepanski's work thinks more rigorously in terms of sound, and names these patterns of movement "Rhythms", which indicate something that chaos does not, such as a relative positionality and a surface—rhythms contain information (Szepanski, 2020). Rhythm arises from the noise like waves on the ocean, determining the surface. The Dolphins of Apollo coming and going. Rhythms appear to jump out of the secret and become known, knowable, visible, identifiable, for some time. We recognise them when they reappear. In their cycles of appearance and disappearance, we can begin to, not imagine, but feel the non-*where* that things disappear to. A chance to read between the lines.

Music is older than the Wor(l)d

The temptation is to say that the Universe is musical, if it is so governed by the dance of Rhythm, but this is an incorrect inversion—the Universe is not musical, music is Ultrablack, as pertaining to the Secret. We could mistake the Universe as musical because music is of the order of the secret, and for this reason it can jilt us, or seduce a moment where the subject feels, momentarily, the gaps between. To observe silence is paradoxical, sounding like a Buddhist kōan, where one might contemplate how to *see* sound. It is here where we must read from Nietzsche, because it is precisely this metaphor, and Nietzsche's contemplation of this metaphor, that set me off in this direction and inspired my first essays that were eventually picked up by NON.

One of the most important lines from Nietzsche on music comes from *Thus Spake Zarathustra*, where he writes: "must one batter their ears that they may learn to hear with their eyes?" (Nietzsche, 2003: 10). In the first period of trying to follow this line, I turned to Jacques Derrida, who had written about this in *The Ear of the Other* (1985), effectively accusing the likes of Kant of "bypassing the ear, the organ of negativity" (Gilbert & Pearson, 1999: 58). It was this thread that led me to reading about Derrida's 'metaphysics of presence' and 'the symbolic order' (Söderbäck, 2013), where the hegemony of presence is partially achieved through the diminishing of anything that pertains to the negative. Bypassing the ear is, on the one hand, a metaphor for positivism, in that an obsession with the eyes, as the faculty of imagery (representations), has led us to mistaking what is 'simulated' for what is 'real' (as has been discussed in the opening of this essay), and on the other hand, a very literal statement in both senses of "not listening" as in arrogance, and as in literally not using the ears.

This topic, for me at least, collapsed into a blackhole of sorts, as the possible threads seemed to spiral outwards uncontrollably. There was the Deleuzoguattarian work of Maria Cichosz (2014), who has written about "the potential of paying-attention" and 'deep listening', and has devised wonderful theories about how a certain kind of listening allows the experience of other sensations or experiences that are otherwise cut off from us by the hegemony of presence. For example, Derrida wrote of Logocentrism as a way of thinking that was repressive on certain kinds of thinking, or otherwise not-conductive to 'being open' to change/novelty/anomalies/transformation. As another example, Deleuze, in his *Letter to a Harsh Critic* (1995), described the history of philosophy as "philosophy's own oedipal complex that played a repressive role *in* philosophy". Effectively, Cichosz believed that deep listening practices allowed the mind to shut off the logocentric processes that otherwise mediate our experience of the World.

In a previous dissertation of mine (Herzberg, 2015), I wrote extensively about Ayahuasca Icaros, and there have been many examples of foregrounded music being used as the key to any transformational practices. The reality that was being presented through this research was one where the sound/songs/music of shamanic figures grounded the subject. In some cases, the music would be referred to as a 'shamanic rope' for one to climb *in* and *out*. One could interpret the use of ritualism and hallucinogens as a kind of mytho-scientific practice of positioning a subject in a better position and state to *deeply listen*, either to polyrhythmic drumming or *acapella* chanting or humming. In other cases, like with Ayahuasca, the presence of the shaman's music is the ultimate reminder for "the tripper" that they are "tripping"; it anchors their existence in the World, a foundation to descend, but also a structure to escape. Fifteen years before *Mille Plateaux* were raging in Europe, iconic Ethnomusicologists like Marlene Dobkin de Rios and Fred Katz (1975) were writing of music as "a jungle-gym of consciousness", precisely because of these notions of 'climbing around' that were coming from studies of ritualised musical practices worldwide. Sound, especially sound codified as music, is *so* Ultrablack that it is amongst the only 'things' we can utilise to make sense of all the simulations, especially when the simulations are running wild, when simulations "degrade" into simulacra. In other words, Music is so *real* that it dispels simulations.

This brings us even to Walter Benjamin, as discussed by Manderson in *Here and Now* (2018), where he interprets Benjamin's idea of inverting the 'aestheticised politics' of fascism into the 'political aesthetics' of anti-fascism. This term "jilt" was excavated by Mike Watson (2019) from the letters of Adorno and Benjamin, where they discuss the capacity art has to break through hegemony: "the ego wakes up to the fact that it is not the centre of the universe but a historical product of social forces" (Zuidervaart, 1991: 142). Benjamin's idea is that jilting can be achieved by art when it adheres to *Jetztzeit* (the here and now). The famous example given is *Guernica* when presented at the *Paris World's Fair* of 1937, which, due to its precise moment in time in World History, jilted/queered the moment, by revealing the hypocrisy of the entire *World's Fair* (Manderson, 2018: 11), projecting the image of a co-operative peace between nations while Bilbao was bombed two weeks before the

World's Fair (just enough time for Picasso to then paint *Guernica* in response and unveil it to the shocked world). The space-timing involved in this revolutionary artwork is a lesson for us all, although with the accelerating speeds of capital and information, it is hard to imagine how quickly one must have to *react* to find this Jetztzeit, given how fast everything is moving. Yet, like *Αφροδίτη*, music has some infallible capacity to jilt, to stop, to intervene, to turn 'the positive' (as in to have power over the appearances of images—the masculine) from its course, to revise unilateral accumulation against the productivist logic of modernity.

Returning to the mantra that "music, it seems, best approximates 'the eternal return' with its ceaseless flows of differentiation" (Schroeder, 2001: 194), Schroeder is here interpreting Nietzsche in a way that is reminiscent of the work of Szepanski and Nail, where the Universe is in some fundamental way comprised of the same properties as music, or for lack of a better word, made of the same *stuff*; of the same order. With Nietzsche's 'eternal return', we might think again about this idea of a pulse, a pulse signifying the eternal return of a cycle: a fundamentally noisy Universe, out of which polyrhythms metastasise certainly sounds musical. The sentence doesn't stop there though, as Schroeder finishes his thought by saying that music "terrorises the rational with its refusal to be reduced to an image", and this is a significant key with which to decode all of this.

If "Kant" (as a figurative representative of the rationalist tradition) has, as Derrida suggests, "bypassed the ear", it's because hearing certain music in a certain moment can change certain people. Not only does music "terrorise" the rational by being impossible to pin down or precisely define, it also terrorises the hegemony of production because it is characterised by what Deleuze calls "the rationalist tradition", and so it threatens to annul the order of the representation, the simulation, the Symbolic. The whole World could be led off-course by the "seductive power of music". Rather, I might even argue that music has been an understated shaper of human history because of its entanglement with 'ritual'. For Baudrillard, in simple terms, ritual is the process of forming signs (Baudrillard, 1990: 41), and it is through ritual, throughout history, that we have built together the symbolic world that we inhabit: "Collective ritual action is the source of those shared, morally authoritative symbolic constructs without which speech would have no force" (Grace, 2000: 143). This is especially interesting given Derrida's idea that the symbolic order places Speech over Writing, thus determining the way in which Philosophy is practised. Derrida (1982: 156) writes that the voice is *realised* as the idyllic "being at one with oneself", which renders the ear as a machine that produces "the pacifying lure of organic indifference" (Gilbert & Pearson, 1999: 56). If the value of the voice is in its ability to collapse a multiplicity into a dual-natured singularity (being at one, and with one), then it is Ultrablack, which itself transforms the categories of white/black into Ultrablack. In *Baudrillard's Challenge*, Grace (2000: 143) notes that Speech and Ritual are often regarded as highly interdependent and entangled. Speech, Music and Ritual are how the World is seduced into being. Ritual is the secretive origin of Speech and Music. The World is forged through the Ultrablack Ritualisation of Speech and Music, as a strategy for being at one with oneself and thus becoming-Ultrablack.

We can return to Maria Cichosz and suggest that music was necessary in ritual because it assisted in deep listening or achieving the right position to forge images and symbolic associations together. Building symbols together requires precisely coordinated alignments between subjects, and the process is akin to tuning, dancing and beat-matching. As matters of ritual, Music and Speech are experienced through the ear, the organ of negativity (Mas, 2023: 55), which positions Listening as the way of ritual, the way of forging symbols and social constructs. Music, like Speech, was not discovered or stumbled upon; it is not ore in the ground. It coagulated over time, as a communal activity that developed through the cyclical undulations of production and the seduction of production. It is perhaps an example of a particular kind of *technē*, a *musikē technē*, that is unique to Man being Ultrablack. Music and Speech, at different stages in history, were liberated from their respective blocks of marble with some prior thought, through the on-going process of ritual. We are certainly still digging music out; we, as humanity, have been carving this particular statue for thousands of years. It is no wonder music can seem to change so much; it is constantly in a state of "in progress". Music is as unfinished as the Universe is.

Music is ultrablack because it's entirely self-referential. It has no original in the real, and there never was an original in the real. To make music is to already have some understanding of what music is, what forms it takes, when and where it is enacted and for what reasons. Music production is the externalisation of this concept of music that has no bearing on anything in the real, except *the real itself*. Even the more analytical definitions of music from Stanford, for example, state that to make music requires that it already exists in the form of musical features like pitch and rhythm, and other aesthetic conventions. Some ethnomusicologists argue that music emerged through things like work-songs, where supposedly people cutting trees or performing tasks together, for fun or for efficiency or because it made an activity *mean* something, eventually coordinated around the sound that is produced by the task.

Over time, this practice could develop into the necessary musical features and aesthetic conventions that satisfy Kania's (2007) definition, which states that "music is anything that is organised to be heard as music" (Kania, 2007). This definition is almost comically tautological, given the presence of Baudrillard in this text, although it does make sense when you considering the limitations of words. It is interesting to note that Comedy (*θάλεια*) is a lesser-known musical art (in terms of the *Μουσαϊ*), and, it must be said, somewhere within the humour of the tautological definition of music, there are some serious *signs* of an Ultrablack Secret lurking somewhere off-screen—that's *why* it's comedic (a musical, ritual strategy for seduction).

My provocation is that music is older than the World; the World was built out of music, through music. We drummed and hummed and sung ourselves into what we are today; we chanted into existence the perilously symbolic Garden of Eden that we inhabit. More specifically, what were once named the muses are the ritualistic practices that established the symbolic: Hymns & Sacred poetry (*Πολυμνία*), [epic] Poetry (*Καλλιόπη*), Astronomy (*Ουρανία*), Comedy (*θάλεια*), Tragedy (*Μελπομένι*), History (*Κλείο*), Dance and Choral Singing (*Τερψιχόρη*), Love Poetry and Lyrical Poetry (*Ερατώ*), and Music (*Ευτέρπη*). *Μουσική* puts the *μους*-in *μουσές*, not the other way around; it is ultrablack after all.

The nine feminine muses reflect the historical view that the feminine rules over (can create and destroy) appearances and images, representations and signs, which are historically masculine (Sky/Immaterial/Man). *Χάος* makes *Γαία*, who makes *Ουρανός*, and then *Γαία* seduces *Ουρανός* (to Death/emasculation) by means of indeterministic curvature over time (*Χρόνος* uses *Τηθύς*) to create *Αφροδίτη*. In Baudrillard's view, as masculinity tries to separate itself from femininity, it takes the position of colour (the 'position of position' as pertaining to Laruelle), yet we know from Baudrillard that this masculinity, which tries to separate itself, is just more of the same of what it tries to negate; it's all seduction under a thin illusory veil of appearing as production, or, as we know from Nail, all patterns of ordered movement are comprised of chaotic movement, or from Szepanski, that all Rhythm is saturated with Noise. The point here is that the framework of Ultrablack presents the masculine as the image, as the immaterial representation, over which the feminine rules—the feminine can create the masculine and transform it, or bring about its death. Through the ritual practices of the muses, both the World and the Philosopher were erected (in all possible meanings), as ordered rhythm arising from chaotic noise. The masculine represents the signs forged by the feminine, which codify both the World and the Subject.

Music, then, out-dates the World itself and leaves us in a situation that, despite being built out of the theories of writers like Derrida, Deleuze and Baudrillard, is once again reminiscent of Buddhist kōans: words cannot describe that which words exist within; they cannot signify anything outside of their limits, only the lyrical or poetic use of words can hint towards the Secret. Words are representations like images; they are like musical scores that try to capture, describe or identify a melody. In the language of Nietzsche, the Universe cannot be reduced to an image, and neither can music, so it shakes the very foundations of the rational tradition that is "(phal)logocentric" (Söderbäck, 2013). The attempt to define music in rational terms not only fails but causes it to short-circuit, where the terms themselves momentarily fail. In this sense, the task of defining music is not only difficult, but somehow dangerous, which is precisely what ethnomusicologist Bruno Nettl (2010: 89) has written in a now-redacted essay (*I Can't Say a Thing until I've Seen the Score*), where he frames the history of musicology as a cult matter, whereby the terminology of music has been made intentionally secretive and exclusionary. Music has historically been studied in isolation, by monks at a monastery, for example, or by using a specifically codified language ("Music Theory") that is largely inaccessible to people without top-down initiation/ invitation.

Music has been kept under wraps throughout history: a secretive tradition, held tightly and suspiciously by an overtly masculine (productivist) grasp. If music is ultrablack, it is therefore an anti-sign; a cursed non-sign that negates other signs. In trying to signify music, or to reduce it to an image, one produces something that seems like a sign but does not reinforce the symbolic structure; neither acts *against* it, but transforms it. To reduce music to a sign—a word, an image—creates a blackhole, an ultrablack hole that deterritorialised signs, luring them away from their hegemonic position; a forced feminisation of statured military generals. Perhaps it was with music that Omphale ensnared Hercules, before making him wear a dress and lounge around the palace *like a woman*, which, if you read the mythology in a particular way, is the moment where Hercules becomes a God, as it is here that he negates the "Man" aspect in the "Man/God" oppositional structure within his identity. It is in giving up his identity as a Man (both as in Male and as in Human) that Hercules became deified. If God is the first, Man the second, and Woman the third, then God and Woman are one-and-the-same when de-codifying the productivist logic of unilinear accumulation through the secret of curvature. By knowing the Secret that the Universe curves, we cannot be tricked by the illusion of linearity.

As a (non-)sign that dispels signs, it is clear why Western hegemony would *fear* music, or be *terrorised* by it, as if it were some Ultrablack heathen magic that threatens to undermine the authority of light. Music—as the externalisation of ritual, as the strategy of symbolic technē (externalisation)—both creates and transforms Worlds. The very image of the West (Christendom, the first world, etc.)—this governing, totalising control-image that has mediated the experience humans have had of the World so repressively—is a symbol that was forged in the very rituals attended by the likes of Aristotle or Socrates. It is just an idea established over millennia of ritualisation, including an endless seductive co-option and recombination of signs and symbols that previously stood. Capital, for example, captures flows of desire: it territorialises, incorporates, and assimilates all of World History to its benefit; like Ultrablackness, it uses the symbolic World to propagate itself. It seems in many moments that Capital could be Ultrablack, but the fine line lies in the production. We can think about this in terms of Carrière's (2023: 32) method of differentiating Intelligence from Artificial Intelligence, which *appears* to do the same thing, but one seduces the Universe whilst the other simulates the World. Capital feeds *on* the World like a parasite, whereas the *Αφροδίτη* feeds the World like her mother (*Γαία*). Interestingly, this interpretation of Artificial Intelligence is in proximity with my interpretation of the work of Szepanski (2024: 157) on Artificial Intelligence, where there is a tantalising trace of the idea that Capital is an A.I., or it determines outcomes through a profoundly programmatic, algorithmic control, despite, on the surface, seeming tolerant, reflexive, or hedonistic (Szepanski, 2024: 96). Artificial Intelligence is a system that "moves closer to its demise" as it "approaches such [apparent] perfection".

A good example of how capital uses the logic of unilinear accumulation to endlessly proliferate itself in an illusory (speculative) way would be American Hegemony itself, with its assimilation of both the symbols of Christianity and Capitalism, as two symbolic regimes of power of signs/values that have great influence over subjects, because the subjectivity of the subject itself is established in reference to these dominant signs. There is no way to easily erase the history and memory of a subject, to dissolve the system of signs that their World is made of, so any regime of power has no choice but to preserve these signs, or take their reigns, as if they are horses already in motion. The illusory progress of Capital moving through World History (Carrière, 2023b) is exactly that: the illusion of the horse-rider making progress when the horses were moving of their own will, perhaps annoyed by the presence of the riders on their backs, but graceful and majestic enough to not interrupt their performance of themselves for the sake of a *Man*. Memory is not separate to Matter, it is part of its codification, so the illusion of unilinear accumulation over Western history, of keeping what works and building on-top of the old (culture) is really the paradoxical result of the opposite of productivism—it only looks like the West has developed through the logic of accrual precisely because accrual is not possible. There is nothing to add, there is only the possibility to transform, so by virtue of never being able to add, one must always use what is already there. By using what is already there, it appears that the novel is being produced, accrued (unilinear accumulation), stacked on top of itself, and in our World, it really *looks* like that. We can see the ruins of Rome beneath our feet, we use their roads that have been adapted, elaborated and transformed, we use Roman words that have been twisted, mutated, added, refined, processed. But in the real, it is just reversion of the same; nothing is ever being added, only folded.

This could go on indefinitely, but there is a need to diverge here towards the end, out of respect for death. Discussing music in terms of Ultrablackness has led us to Sun Ra, who famously said that the chaos of this World is due to the music that the musicians are playing, that they are forced to play by those who just think about money. This makes sense when read in relation to what has been said here about Baudrillard and Ultrablackness, because effectively Sun Ra is saying that the Muses, the Musicians (those who practise the art of the Muses—musikē technē), invoke the World through their music, their music rituals, and their musical technē. Currently, the musicians are being forced to play music that is re-codifying the simulation and producing these tensions and problems, producing a World characterised by the false dichotomy of "white"/"black" (instead of Ultrablack), which, while metaphorical or figurative, is also literally and directly related to the black experience (racism). Creating a new World without racism, where Blackness seems to disappear, is an interesting element of Afrofuturism. A "raver" who understands that rave is resisting something would understand that, if we "solved the problems of society", we wouldn't need to rave, or in other words, a raver ought to dream of not being a raver. Perhaps rave is a good example of Leninist Political Scaffolding Techniques, as it was a temporary construct of which the very material was taken and repurposed elsewhere.

In some interpretations, the end point of the Afrofuturist movement is the end of Blackness (as something othered to whiteness), in the sense of phasing out/breaking down racist hegemony. When we frame it like this, Baudrillard's work as a theoretical terrorist takes on a new light, because the structures he tried to 'bomb' were the very structures that uphold the current regime of power, which is, through the assimilative and adaptive nature of capital, made up of many control signs. This temptation to other the enemy as "cis-hetero-patriarchal-white-supremecist-productivist-Western-capitalist-modernity" arises because the regime of power controls subjectivity through all of these dimensions, all of these signs, all of these intersections, and this is the essence of Biopower. There is a very intimate recognition from Sun Ra that even the grassroots movements of Blues, Soul, and so on, can be co-opted to serve the hegemony that oppresses black communities, and that being forced to continue playing these forms of music in the way that the white music industry and consumer audience feeds off plays a role in the on-going reproduction of the hegemony. Sun Ra understood that the music people were playing and listening to was imbued with white-capitalist ideology.

We are talking now about 'the music industry', the industrialisation and commodification of music: an incredibly repressive financialised system that produces music as a strategy for the unilinear accumulation of capital (to use Music as the Commodity in M-C-M'). The music industry controls the form of the majority of music that we ever hear, the demands of capital shape what music we make, demanding that music is produced in certain ways, at certain lengths, or with certain themes, or design schemes, visual language strategies and target demographics. We effectively allow capital to dictate the form of our music. That's why rave was radical, because it rejected the conventions of capital at that time, and while it was eventually territorialised and assimilated, for a moment in history, rave disrupted the prevailing hegemony. The music the ravers were playing seduced the World, twisted it, jogged it, made it swerve, or any other metaphor that invokes the image of Grandmaster Flash's hand filling the grooves of the album-record, the perfect commodity for modernity, with the sweat and dust, the material of the body, as he breaks all social codes by pulling the record backwards, "discovering the loop" in the way Titian "discovered" Brutalism, by turning the World back on itself in a display of groundbreaking Musikē Technē (Carrière, 2023: 42). The World we live in today, in the West, is somehow *stained* by electronic music, as Capital was forced to swallow rave, ingesting a paradoxically near-lethal dose of acid in the process. Capital has since been spiralling out of control, while going absolutely nowhere, writhing around, screaming hysterically: "*I ate God, and now I am God*". Even if rave was assimilated, that acid house symbol of the yellow smiling face has been immortalised in the new Image of the West—a glitch, a give-away, a blackhole that secretly undermines the bigger picture.

In the Pursuit of the Muses

As the last part of this text, I would like to invert the old ethnomusicological tradition known as "the harmless drudge" (Nettl, 2010: 5)—a tradition characterised by every ethnomusicologist attempting to define music before proceeding to present what they have found. I will therefore finish by rushing through the same process, only to get bogged down in the process until all that remains is the starting point of another ethnomusicology essay.

Music, it seems, in its ceaseless flows of self-referential duplicity, best approximates Ultrablackness—the gaps that shape, structure and codify Rhythms. Music, as a word, is an attempt to capture the diverse *sociosymbolic* or *semiosonic* practices of humans throughout their history, the very practices that brought the World into being (metastasis). Ethnomusicologists started with the definition of humanly organised sound, but given the way the rational tradition analyses through categorisation, a series of questions arise that interrogated this definition of music. If music is 'humanly organised sound', then how do you differentiate it from poetry, or from speech, or from the sound produced by a building site being worked on by builders who are organised? Seemingly at the end of the ethnomusicology movement, Kania & Gracyk (2011) added the clauses of "sound organised to be heard *as* music", which could be achieved by pertaining to the notion of 'musical features' (such as pitch and rhythm) and 'aesthetic conventions'. At one moment in history, the West seems to understand that there are arts that can be ritualised to change the World, by forging/seducing signs, and divides these talents into nine categories, naming them the muses. Plato distinctively warns humanity not to be frivolous with the Muses:

> And attunement, which has coursings akin to the circuits in our soul, has been given by the Muses to him who makes use of the Muses with his intellect, not for the purpose of irrational pleasure (which is what it's now thought to be useful

> for), but as an ally to the circuit of the soul within us once it's become untuned, for the purpose of bringing the soul into arrangement and concord with herself.
>
> (Nail, 2018: 147)

In the first instance, music is not separated from poetry and astronomy, or history; it is one of nine (that are one) ritual strategies or technologies for sign-making and World changing. There are musical muses of Choral Singing, and Sacred Hymns, and Epic Poetry, but there is paradoxically also the muse of Music (*Ευτέρπη*). The muses are individuated but deliberately entangled/overlapped. The muses *together* create Worlds. It is hard to say that our "music" of today is the music of Euterpe, although the demands of Kania & Gracyk do ultimately imply that, several thousand years later, we still believe it is important to distinguish between Music and Poetry. The *rational* decision to separate Music and Poetry is at the heart of what I can call "the disappearance of music", or the moment where music eclipses itself in a way that can only be understood through the iconography of *Αφροδίτη* and Thomas Nail's idea of the double-genitive.

When Kania & Gracyk added those clauses to separate music from poetry, birdsong and building sites, they achieved a self-referential loop. It's ironic that, in trying to specify music so attentively, the resulting definition of music is so *open*. These ultra-specific, self-referential clauses of "organised as music by using musical features" create a blackhole in the symbolic. In attempting to exclude everything from music, they end up defining music in a way that includes everything. If musical features are the signs that represent music, they are swerving and seduced from all directions, and they, according to Baudrillard, *desire Death*. Ethnomusicologists worked hand-in-hand with the Avant-Garde in achieving this, because the Avant-Garde would push the limits of music through experimentation, and the Ethnomusicologists and Sociologists would run behind them trying to capture all the new ground under a new composite definition of music that was inclusive of the Novel and therefore seemingly most accurate approximation. Given music is Ultrablack, it is always 'producing' the novel through seduction and reversion, so there is always a need to update our definitions of music to include whatever new mutation it has taken on in those split seconds where we stop obsessively observing it, like eyeballing an electron. Every time we blink, it moves.

In this game between the Avant-Garde and the Anthropologists, we ended up with noise music—an interesting phenomenon given that music had been defined once as the opposite of noise, as music requires being organised as if to be heard as music, and noise was considered unorganised sound, so certainly not organised to be heard as music. As the parameters of what constitutes a musical feature change, the way these features can be organised changes, and it becomes possible to imagine and present a way in which "unorganised sound" is organised as if it were music, so it becomes simultaneously organised and not-organised. "Noise music" is a great mimesis of Rhythm arising from the noise whilst containing infinite or indeterminate fractal distributions of noise at every position. With noise music, the other of music is pulled into music, so music eclipses itself, by being both extremely specific, and limitless in its plasticity. There is no other of music if the other of music is also "musical". The experiments of the Avant-Garde have shown that the concept of musical features does not offer a way out of the tautological definition of music as sound organised to be heard as music, as any sound could end up being a musical feature, if framed or presented as music, *folded* into music.

We might imagine an inventor or craftsman who makes a reputation for themselves as a master craftsman for a particular invention or innovation or break. They figure out a new way of doing something they have to do, and they figure it out because they do it enough. They know all the variables; they've tried and tested new methods either through artistry, science or philosophy. Spending so much time on the craft allowed them to notice a gap in the logic or workflow that could be resolved or completed with something new. In order to solve their problem, they do something specific in their practice, which results in a specific appearance to others. The others see the arrangement of what the craftsman does, the way the process is laid out, and effectively they see something of how the process is performed. Yet, without understanding *why* the process appears that way, it is not easy to emulate the results. Without understanding the function, one can only simulate the appearance. One could, for example, observe that a chef puts something in the pan in a certain order, but without being aware that the chef is timing things for various reasons, one can put something in the pan in the same order and achieve a different result. Someone can think they are doing what the original craftsman was doing, because it looks like they are, and achieve very different results or produce a different effect.

Here one really has to accept a short-circuiting of language, more than anything, as effectively what is being said is that there is a difference between *doing* something and *simulating* something. If we use a techno music producer as an example, they may use a side-chain on the compressor of a bass-line because there is a way of side-chaining that creates a particularly effective dynamic between the bass-line and the kick drum. That being said, the process of side-chaining the bass to the kick drum is not as simple as switching the side-chain on, or drag and dropping it onto a channel; there is always a tweaking process where one experiments with the settings of the compressor to achieve the desired effect. To side-chain a bass is not simply to click side-chain, but what is the difference to one who is listening with their eyes? You follow the video tutorial perfectly, doing what it looks like they are doing in the video, and everything looks like it makes sense, but then you play your track in the club and it sounds terrible. There is indeed a side-chain on the bass, but the bass is not *side-chained* in any reference to the original. It is undoubtedly difficult to indicate the precise phenomenon being described, because what is we are trying to point at is that which has no *point* (position). There is achieving a particular effect using a particular tool, and then there is using a particular tool because someone else did, and it is the ultra-fine line between the two that is the Secret which cannot be indicated easily.

The contention here might be that art has long been understood to involve a certain amount of mimesis. Early theories of art were theories of replication, in terms of trying to recreate either the aesthetics of nature or the feeling of nature or the experience of it. I would argue that there is a difference between learning from another and simulating their practice—if the original craftsman teaches someone the way of understanding the reasons for the practice, it is to be expected that the one who learns the practice does it in the same way, appearing to imitate—but this is the fine line between simulation (reproducing the appearance of something) and emulation (reproducing the result of something, or the way of it), between doing and simulating, between becoming and being.

One might understand this through the earlier works of Émilie Carrière (2023), regarding the fine line between Artificial Intelligence and Intelligence. For Carrière, Intelligence (the Intellect) is not a creative vitality that is based on models, or that *produces derivatives*. Intelligence is a creative vitality that operates without models; it is 'purely creative', not simulative. The argument goes that A.I. Art cannot produce the kind of folds that constitute art's affective power. Carrière uses the example of Titian ("who folded the world in on itself"), producing a break, a true movement toward novelty. A.I. Art cannot be expected to produce these kinds of breaks because they operate based on models (Carrière, 2023: 32).

Now, to make this consistent with my previous works, there is a need to distinguish between certain ideas. First, I have argued in the past that there are "no originals" when it comes to art or ideas, that there is always a sense of collective authorship to everything, and the best new musical idea is still made of someone else's idea, such as the stylistic preferences of Western Music Theory, or the best new website ideas are still composed in a predetermined coding language. This seems to contradict the idea that the intellect, which produces these new ideas, does not operate based on models. Some of the best ideas seem either modelled *on* or *out of* other ideas; either the shape of the pot, or the clay it is made out of, is *derived* from somewhere else. Yet, I would like to argue—based on how

I read Baudrillard, Laruelle, Carrière, and so on—that there is a fine line between these examples. One cannot simulate art precisely because of the lack of models, and the lack of originals—there is not a *thing* to simulate when doing art. In order to re-instantiate the experience of art, one cannot simulate a 'thing'; rather, there is but a ritual to re-enact. Again, while to the eyes of the observer, it may look like the craftsman is arranging things in this way, to the craftsman, they are doing something else much more specific, which results in a particular arrangement—one is an act of imitating an appearance; the other is ritualising a process.

We could take my favourite story of *Guernica* as an example. The argument goes that *Guernica* was such a powerful moment in art due to its *Jetztzeit*, its sense of "here and now". *Guernica* "queered" the *Paris World's Fair*, not by how it appeared on its own pavilion, but by how it made every other pavilion appear (Manderson, 2018). Where all the other pavilions seemed to affirm the ideology of the *World's Fair*, *Guernica* attempted to juxtapose the affirmed ideology against the context of World History in order to show its callousness. Two weeks after Bilbao was bombed in 1937, before World War Two, the *World's Fair* attempted to present the world as unified, friendly, making art together in a very Utopian way, which was a dreadful lie given the moment in history. *Guernica* also serves as a perfect example of Walter Benjamin's idea of 'politicising aesthetics'. There is much to learn from this example, but it is different to 'learn from' this example and to 'simulate' it. Instead of thinking top-down about the aesthetics of the painting, in order to reproduce the affect associated with the painting, one must think about the specific relationship the piece had to the context it was presented in, on all levels, from Psychological to World Historical. It was not the colours used that contained the magic; it was the *way colour was used*. It was not the style used, but the *way the style was used*, and it was not the specific event being referenced, but *the way the event was referenced*.

The appearance of the process can be simulated to no effect, and it is the lack of effect that indicates the simulation. The experience of the effect is what affirms the ritual, or what confirms that the procedure has been done "correctly". You know you've done it right when it *works desirably*. *Αφροδίτη* seduces the Continuation of the World; Capital desires the Death of Man. Capital, in its simulation of the World, produces the end of Man, whereas *Αφροδίτη*, in her becoming-the-Universe, seduces the beginning of the World.

To bring this back to music, with the preceding paragraphs in mind, we could argue that there is the creative, intelligent, ritualised music, and the derivative, artificial, simulated music, with a fine line between the two depending on whether something that looks the same is ritualised or simulated, a replica based on appearances or based on "ways of doing". The only way to distinguish between what is simulated and what is ritualised is based on the affect produced. It brings us back to the work of Maria Cichosz and her idea of "paying attention to affects", as if to suggest that we no longer know the difference between Intelligence and Artificial Intelligence, Creative and Derivative, Seduction and Production, Ritual and Simulation, because we do not pay attention to the affects, only the aesthetics. Producing affects requires adhering to the *Jetztzeit* of the World (Ultrablack), not the *image* of the World (white).

If it seems that this way of thinking about music has no bearing on the World, it is because of the way of the industry, which is a capitalist abstraction nearly a century in age. The commoditisation and industrialisation of music is precisely the process of detaching music from ritual. Yet, despite the size of the apparent industrial machinery that pollutes music, the seductive and ritualistic nature of music is not unknown to us. The dust of memory is here with us now; it is pressed into the gaps in my keyboard as I type.

Any raver can tell you about music as ritual, or any attendee of Church. In essence, we are talking about the *museness* of music—this sense of music having the function of "musing"; a World-building symbolic affect produced through the musical arts of Epic Poetry (*Καλλιόπη*), Sacred Hymns (*Πολυμνία*), Dance and Chorus (*Τερψιχόρη*), Comedy (*Θάλεια*), Tragedy

(*Μελπομένη*), Lyrical Poetry (*Ερατώ*), Mythology and History (*Κλείο*), Astronomy (*Ουρανία*) and *Music* (*Ευτέρπη*). *Ευτέρπη* is the most peculiar of all the muses. Among the musical arts (as pertaining to the muses), there is sacred music, choral music, but also *music*. The granting of the word "mus-" to *Ευτέρπη*'s territory either signifies its primacy, as in being the first musical art, or the first way of doing something that was ritualised for its capacity to "muse", or it signifies that a specific ritualised way of doing something best approximates the whole essential concept of muse, and is therefore *crowned* with the primary image.

Regardless of why the music of *Ευτέρπη* was named after the whole category, the affect that is produced remains the same. Music is named music because it is musical (as in pertaining to the muses), whilst at the same time, musical in the Anglo-American world means it pertains to our culturally and historically determined concept of music. The only way to resolve this split is to imagine that the historically determined concept of music is somehow pertaining to the concept of the muses. The three become a cycle: muses–music–musical. We recognise the ability of a practice to build or transform the appearance of the world by ritualising (as opposed to simulating) the Secret that lies under the appearance of the World, and observe various ways of producing this affect. The different strategies of producing this affect are grouped into loose categories, and assigned to a Muse who rules over each strategic category.

On the one hand, we could argue that the category of *Ευτέρπη* was named music because it most approximates the category by producing an affect that is either most potent or most *true* to the categorical intention, or we could argue that it was named after the category because it couldn't be defined any other way, which is perhaps the same thing. In not being able to assign a name to a wealth of musical strategies (as in producing the musing affect), those that do not fit into such concepts as poetry or history are generalised into a ninth category of musing practices that can only be categorised based on their incompatibility with categorisation.

Being categorised by their un-categorisability is an indication of the Ultrablackness of music—Music is the word for all the identifiable strategies of musing and the ones which can't be identified specifically.

Ευτέρπη is there because the West couldn't leave the Other uncategorised, unaccounted for, untamed, and really we might interpret that the presence of *Ευτέρπη* gives away the Secret that there could be thousands of Muses: myriad un-categorisable, shifting, swerving strategies that appear different all the time because they take into account the here-and-now religiously. Every inch the Universe swerves, the World serves with it. Nothing ever (be) comes again *exactly*; it is just (be)coming eternally, cyclically, with every cycle marked by a pulse that doesn't reveal the Secret but eludes to it.

We return again to Robert Barry's (2017) idea that music is an anticipation machine. Every note, even if "the same" (pitch and length), is continually reintroduced into an ever-changing context; reiterations of the same appear different each time as they each take on the unique characteristics of their position in the sequence (second is defined by its being-second-ness in relation to an existing first and the potentiality of an elusive but tangible *Third*). As the Universe cyclically re-instantiates itself as the Ultrablack eternal return, leaving traces in the form of pulses that sometimes become rhythmical, its sameness is reiterated with a uniform differentiality. Each instantiation of the same *appears* oppositional to the prior because, in trying to be "true" to the ritual, the seduction of the same results in the production of the different. If each instantiation needs to be tailor-made to the here-and-now of space-time, which is swerving, then each instantiation of the same must undoubtedly look different due to this constant process of renegotiation. The intelligence that Carrière (2023) speaks of is that which processes/calculates the swerve of Lucretius, tracking it, in order to time movements in accordance with the swerve. The intellect beat-matches itself to the swerve, or dances with it. If, in order to continuously produce more matter from matter, for

Γαία to bring forth *Αφροδίτη*, the Universe (*Χάος*) ritualises the process whereby matter was created out of matter, which means the Universe does not *simulate* the appearance of the process but "actually" *processes*. If the key ingredient to matter's immaculate swerving is its ritual adherence to the here-and-now, then as each instantiation is added into the pool, and as the composition and chemistry of the pool changes, what needs to be added in order to be compliant with the ritual also changes. The ritual pot demands something different every time to continue the same. *Ευτέρπη* signifies that different-but-same-ness that exists within the same, the *Black* in Ultrablack. Music contains an equally indeterminate but distinct reiteration of itself, within itself (being one with oneself), just as the Universe is also at one with itself (just in a way that is mediated by the simulated object that mirrors the seductive process as the Universe folds our World around *us*, the biased observer).

Ultimately, it seems that the most cutting-edge definitions of music in 2016 were struggling with the same problem as the philosophers who thought-up the muses: there is this thing called music that we can build Worlds with—which everyone knows exists, but no one has a definition for—that can't really be described without a tautology because, to us, music seems so self-referential that it takes on a paradoxical form. We can be led to believe that music is this thing that takes on the form of albums and songs and concerts and raves (various strategies), but the ubiquitous presence of myriad un-categorisable re-instantiations of the different-same-within-the-same (the dust of memory) eternally haunts and disrupts (obscuring, clogging, contaminating) the temptation to think music in any particular way; so, we as humanity largely *don't try to*. Music will always exist to us as this tantalising, paradoxical, dual-natured lover: there will be the music we can understand and identify and categorise, the eight muses, but there will always be this *Other* category that can only be categorised by an *un-categorisability* that lurks behind and around (between the lines) the strategic categories and annuls them, undermining their structures. Music will always be this wonderful thing that we think we know so well, and yet we hear voices coming from somewhere else telling us that, Secretly, we don't know Music at all. She is of a different order. Yet, while the Man who thinks himself Philosopher in World may not *know* the Secret that he is the Universe, the Dancer who listens to the Music in the Ritual hears the Truth and *understands*.

It seems that music does, indeed, best approximate the ceaseless flows of the differentiating same, or the eternal return. If Music and *Αφροδίτη* share in their Ultrablackness, then there has to be some deeper acceptance within ourselves that we will never define music, or capture it, or fully understand it, or always like the direction its going, and it will always disappear or disconnect from us, periodically, as we get lost as Philosophers in the World. But it is in following where Music leads us that we manage to keep finding our way back to becoming in the Universe as Man, again and again.

Seduction (*Αφροδίτη*), the 'false' daughter of Earth (*Γαία*), but 'true' daughter of the Universe, 'ritualises' the World into Being by Singing lyrically, and poetically, of 'Becoming-Ultrablack'.

References

Althusser, L. (2006) *Philosophy of the Encounter: Later Writings*. Translation by G. M. Goshgarian. London: Verso.

Barry, R. (2017) *The Music of the Future*. London: Repeater.

Baudrillard, J. (1975) *The Mirror of Production*. St Louis: Telos Press.

—. (1983) *Simulations*. Translation by Paul Foss, Paul Patton & Philip Beitchman. New York: Semiotext(e).

—. (1990) *Seduction*. Translation by Brian Singer. Montréal: New World Perspectives.

—. (2017) *Symbolic Exchange & Death*. Translation by Iain Hamilton Grant. London: SAGE.

Carrière, É. (2023) *Technically Man Dwells upon this Earth*. Nicosia: Becoming Press.

Carrière, É (2023b) "What is Wokeness?" *Ill will*: Online. https://illwill.com/what-is-wokeness

Cichosz, M. (2014) "The Potential of Paying Attention: Tripping and the Ethics of Affective Attentiveness". *Emotion, Space & Society.* Vol. 10: 55–62.

Deleuze, G. (1995) "A Letter to a Harsh Critic". *Negotiations.* Columbia New York: University Press.

Derrida, J. (1982) *Margins of Philosophy*. Translation by Alan Bass. Chicago: University of Chicago.

—. (1985) *The Ear of the Other: Otobiography, Transference*. Translation by Avital Ronell. New York: Schocken Books.

—. (2016) *Of Grammatology*. Translated by Gayatri Chakravorty Spivak. Baltimore/London: John Hopkins University Press.

Galloway, A. R. (2014) *Laruelle: Against the Digital.* Minneapolis/London: University of Minnesota Press.

Gilbert, J., & Pearson, E. (1999) *Discographies: Dance Music, Culture, and the Politics of Sound.* London/New York: Routledge.

Grace, V. (2000) *Baudrillard's Challenge: A Feminist Reading.* London: Routledge.

Harvey, I. E. (1983) "Derrida and the Concept of Metaphysics". *Research in Phenomenology.* Vol. 13: 1: 113–148.

Herzberg, N. (2015) *Analyzing Icaros: The Musicology of Ayahuasca Ceremonies.* Dissertation for B.A. Music Technology. University of Wolverhampton.

Jordan, T. (1995) "Collective Bodies: Raving and the Politics of Gilles Deleuze and Felix Guattari". *Body & Society*. Vol: 1(1): 125.

Kania, A. (2007) "The Philosophy of Music". *Stanford Encyclopedia of Philosophy.* Accessible at: https://plato.stanford.edu/entries/music/.

Kania, A., Gracyk, T. (2011) *The Routledge Companion to Philosophy & Music.* London: Routledge.

Katz, F., & Dobkin de Rios, M. (1975). "Some Relationships between Music & Hallucinogenic Ritual: The 'Jungle-Gym' in Consciousness". *Ethos.* Vol. 3: 1: 64–76.

Manderson, D. (2018) "Here & Now: From Aestheticising Politics to Politicizing Art". *ANU College of Law Research Paper*. Vol: 18(5).

Mas, N. (2023) *Affects & Dreams: A Manual for Becoming.* Berlin: Becoming Press.

Marx. K., & Schafer, P. M. (2006) *The First Writings of Karl Marx.* New York: Ig Publishing.

Nail, T. (2018) *Lucretius I: An Ontology of Motion*. Edinburgh: Edinburgh University Press.

—. (2020) *Lucretius II: An Ethics of Motion*. Edinburgh: Edinburgh University Press.

—. (2022) *Lucretius III: A History of Motion*. Edinburgh: Edinburgh University Press.

—. (2022b) "What is the Philosophy of Movement?" *Mobility Humanities*. Vol. 1(1): 9–25.

Nettl, B. (2010) *The Study of Ethnomusicology: Thirty-One Issues and Concepts*. Second Edition. Chicago: University of Illinois Press.

Nietzsche, F. (1986) *The Will to Power*. Translated by Walter Kaufmann and R.J. Hollingdale. New York: Random House.

—. (2003) *Thus Spake Zarathustra*. Translation by Thomas Wayne. New York: Algora Publishing.

Phillips, R. (2022) "Spoken Word recital in Radio Episode". *Lumbung Radio*. Transcription by Palais Sinclaire.

Prigogine, I., Stengers, I. (1984) *Order Out of Chaos: Man's new Dialogue with Nature*. New York: Bantam Books.

Schröter, J. (2024) "Quantum Aesthetics*". *Ultrablack of Music: Volume 2*. Szepanski, A., & Sinclaire, P. (eds) London: Zer0 Books.

Schroeder, B. (2001) "The Listening Eye: Nietzsche and Levinas". *Research in Phenomenology*. 31(1): 188–202.

Söderbäck, F. (2013) "Being in the Present: Derrida and Irigaray on the Metaphysics of Presence". *Journal of Speculative Philosophy*. Vol: 27(3): 253–264.

Szepanski, A. (2020) "Ultrablackness in Music: A non-Mixology". *Ultrablack of Music: Volume 1*. Szepanski, A. (ed.) Frankfurt a. M.: NON.

—. (2024) *In the Delirium of the Simulation: Revisiting Baudrillard*. Berlin: Becoming.

Watson, M. R. (2019) *Can the Left Learn to Meme?* London: Zer0 Books.

Wintermute, B. B. (2020) "(Cybernetic-) 'Post-Pop': affect art(s) & (emotional) self-governing". *Ultrablack of Music: Volume 1*. Szepanski, A. (ed.) Frankfurt a. M.: NON.

9. NOTES ON MUSIC AND NEGATION

By Eugene Thacker

Memento mori. Considered by many to be among the greatest lyricists of Japan, the 9th-century poet Ono no Komachi transformed the conventions of courtly love poetry into distilled and resonant meditations on solitude, sorrow, and the melancholy of passing time, often encapsulated in the term *aware*. She was said to have had numerous lovers, many of them high-ranking, and was included in prestigious imperial anthologies of the period, such as the *Kokin*. One of her poems reads:

The cicadas sing
in the twilight
of my mountain village—
tonight, no one
will visit save the wind.[1]

1 See Ono no Komachi & Shikibu, I. (2023), p. 13.

Little is known of Komachi's life, in spite of her status in the history of Japanese literature. The details that are known are difficult to separate from the legends and lore that surround her, such that an entire subgenre of "Tales of Komachi" developed in the years following her death.

One such tale relates that Komachi, once the beacon of Japanese lyric poetry, spent her last years as an aged, withering, poverty-stricken recluse, a "mad old hag" mumbling sutras under her breath, writing poetry in complete isolation. After her death, it was said that her grave had deteriorated so much that her skull was visible above the ground. At night, turbulent winds blew through the skull, projecting hollowed-out reverberations of sorrow into the landscape beyond.

*

Philosophical approaches to music—particularly in the Western tradition—are particularly biased towards understanding music as the presence of sound, itself indexing a more abstract presence that exists at the threshold of human comprehension. Music as a conduit of divine presence; or music as the expression of celestial harmonies; or music as correspondence to the cosmic cadences of the planets and the stars.

And yet music—like sound itself—is also deeply marked by time, and in time. In this sense, music is as susceptible to the precarious contingencies of existing in time as anything else, where another cadence presents itself: the coming into being and passing out of being; the transient, the ephemeral, the dissipative; the ebbing and flowing of all existents, subtended by a nebulous non-existence we can only negatively name.

From a philosophical perspective, perhaps all those treatises on the music of the spheres or the sound of celestial hierarchies have themselves been deaf to another aspect of music: that music fades away. What is left is not the memory of music (which itself fades, becoming more diffuse in time), and not even bare sound, but the faintest traces of reverberant absence.

In this way, perhaps philosophies of music have spent too much time pouring over the birth into the presence of music. What has been largely ignored is the way that all music fades, suggesting to us another view: structured sound that is also its own dissipation; formal expression that is also phenomenal diffusion; the collapse of musical form that itself becomes a kind of music.

*

Frequently referenced treatises in the early philosophy of music—from the Pythagorean School to Boethius to al-Farabi to Marsilio Ficino—place great emphasis on music as the birth to presence of sound, itself an indicator of physics of presence that further ratifies the phenomenal sense of order, meaning, and purpose that music can powerfully convey.

But there are actually several distinctions at play. There is, first, the distinction between music and sound, the former presumably relying on the latter as raw material: music as that which is produced from sound, sound generating music; music as meaningful sound, reverberant with the shimmering contours of the divine, a latticework of cosmic harmony distilled into discrete notes. While few would deny a relationship between music and sound, the distinction between them becomes all the more crucial when what is at stake is the validation of order in the cosmos, or divine providence, or even the communication of affects and emotions presumed to be held in common.

While still commonplace, the distinction between music and sound is also extremely tenuous. Modern music in particular has chipped away at the boundary that separates music from sound, challenging us to consider the shadowy side of relativism (e.g., is music to one person simply sound to another?) as well as nominalism (e.g., is music nothing more than a sequence of sounds that we select and name "music"?). The undercurrent of such challenges to ideas of harmony, order, and the meaningful stretches between the self and the stars, suggests that music may never completely detach itself from sound (and is the reverse also the case?).

Another distinction, related to that between music and sound, is the distinction between sound and silence. Music and sound are understood to have a certain phenomenal presence. Should we then say that sound is produced from silence in the way that music is produced from sound? The problem is that, strictly speaking, silence is by definition that which cannot be heard (or which is only heard relatively, as "quiet"). Silence is, in a sense, non-phenomenal, or even anti-phenomenal. Where indeed is the boundary that separates sound from silence? Is it relative to the listener (and should we refine "listening" from "hearing"?), does it need to actually be heard (or can it simply be measured?), and at what point would we as listeners affirm that "there is" silence? The questions quickly become both cosmological and ontological. Sound can be said to emerge from silence, but is silence then the source or the cause of sound? If so, how can an absence be the source of a presence?

*

Sound and the Supernatural. Sound is manifestly present (to us, and for us), but it also seems non-phenomenal, and it is no accident that the ghosts, revenants, and "unnameable things" that populate the supernatural horror tradition are often heard before they are seen. The sound of the supernatural conveys the sense of an ambivalent "beyond" or a "something else" lurking in the blind spot of human cognition—and because of this, there is also a sense in which the supernatural is not supernatural at all, but only supernatural for we human beings with a restricted sensorium.

The ability to hear the supernatural—or better, to listen to it—is as much about detecting its presence as it is about straining to understand what it is trying to "say," what significance it holds, what secret order it reveals. And yet, old and even primordial uncertainness takes hold. An acoustic phenomenon manifests itself at the same time that it recedes into a nether region of what cannot be heard, or recedes into the background of what lies outside the range of human hearing. Are these voices from the beyond, or are they simply voices in one's head?

Is the manifestation of sound from the beyond itself meaningful, or is it simply the desiderata of our own, confined, human-bound hearing?

H.P. Lovecraft's *The Music of Erich Zann* (1922) tells the story of a university student (studying metaphysics, of course) who moves into an apartment building, where he discovers an eccentric old man living on the top floor, playing mysterious and haunting melodies on his viol late into the luminous night. The student is inexplicably drawn to the music, though he is rebuffed by the old man. One night, listening outside the old man's door, the student hears strange, chaotic, turbulent sounds—inhuman sounds which somehow seem to be *replying* to the old man's viol playing. Fearing for the old man's life, he breaks into the apartment, and from there everything is a cacophonous, dreamlike blur. Strange entities brush by him in the dark, the whirling sounds drifting far off into the nether regions of deep space, and yet they whisper inside his head. The old man, who appears to be dead, somehow continues playing. The student is frozen in terror, inundated by shadowy apprehensions: archaic ritual, musical invocation, portals to other dimensions, and the unbearable revelation of having heard something outside the range of human comprehension.

*

Music Degree Zero. It is in the slippage from music to sound, and from sound to silence, that a unique type of negation paradoxically makes its presence felt. The cosmic sounds of Lovecraft's tale are heightened in the 1906 short story "The Omega Force" (*La fuerza Omega*) by Argentine author Leopoldo Lugones. In it, we hear of an amateur scientist obsessed with the occult potentials inherent in modern technologies. Experimentally modifying phonograph discs, the scientist makes an accidental discovery. His strange and disturbing inventions have tangible, material effects on solid objects—including the human body—sometimes mutating them beyond the known laws of physics, at other times pulverising them into floating dust and debris. Increasingly unhinged, the scientist becomes fixated on the idea of an invisible, omnivorous, monistic energy that impersonally flows through all living, existing entities, such that all forms of material existence are simply localised manifestations of this "Omega Force." Mind, matter, and even the cosmos seem to collapse. But, as with so many tales of this kind, the knowledge comes at a price, and the acoustic forces that manifest themselves are also the forces that dissipate, resulting in a zero degree of existence that is neither life nor death.

*

Chthonic Monochord. Music disintegrating into sound, sound distilled into physics, physics an occult set of signs indexing the elemental properties of the cosmos itself. When we reach Algernon Blackwood's 1910 novel *The Human Chord*, we enter a terrain in which music and metaphysics become one in the same; choral music becomes inseparable from chthonic ritual, and metaphysics is subtended by a deeper physics.

In the novel, a young man is drawn into an enigmatic cult devoted to the physics of sound. Their leader is convinced that the right group of people, emitting a precise combination of sounds—the titular human "chord"—will have the capacity to loosen the bonds of physical reality as we know it, in effect transforming choral music into a kind of particle accelerator.

Blackwood's novel is built around the simple intuition that sound is physics, and that by extension there is not only a physics to sound but sound is in every way as material as what we can see or touch. However, what the novel reveals is less a mastery of the physics of sound, but its reverse: a rift is unintentionally revealed between what we as human beings can hear and what we can understand. As the bonds of physical reality slowly erode, the cosmic unravelling of "the human chord" points to this enigmatic state of a sound that is registered, but that we cannot hear. It is also the predicament of finite, limited human perspectives against what we can only dimly intuit as a much vaster, much more impersonal cosmos. A "beyond" is or seems to be there, but it always resides in that liminal zone where the human being must either resign itself to its relative insignificance, or ambivalently annul itself in the process.

*

If philosophies of music in the West are committed to a metaphysics of presence with regard to music, then the presumed birth to presence of music from sound, and sound from silence, seems to be both fragile and precarious. If the "ground" of music is the non-being of silence, wouldn't this indicate another philosophy of music, one that takes the reverse view of the diffusion of music into sound, and the dissipation of sound into silence?

No doubt such a philosophy would take an interest not in the distinctions between these terms (music/sound; sound/silence), but in the dissipation between them. Perhaps it is in the interstices of this erosion from music to sound, and from sound to silence, that we find another kind of negation, one in which absence and presence become inseparable from each other, while never coinciding completely. The phenomenon of acoustic decay, for instance, seems to reveal both the presence of absence and the absence of presence. And what of music that is actually composed so as to decay, or a music designed to collapse into sound, or an entire aesthetics of music predicated on the dissipation of sound into some liminal acoustic phenomenon we only haphazardly call silence? Perhaps it is the function of music to fade away. An entire alternative history of music might be written from this perspective. Music as the dissipation into absence. Music as the paradoxical phenomena of acoustic negation.

*

Sonic Decay, Collapsing Stars. Suppose that the function of music is to disintegrate into sound? What is composed would then also aim for its own decomposition. A kind of blackened physics emerges, where music collapses into sound, and sound unfurls in unseen quanta of waves, reverberations, and sound so slow we cannot hear it.

Perhaps the benchmark example in this regard is *Quattro pezzi su una nota sola*, the 1959 orchestral work by the enigmatic Italian composer Giacinto Scelsi. The work emerged following the composer's mental breakdown in the 1940s, where Scelsi was reduced to a near catatonic state of complete uncreativity. All previous models for composition, be they classical or modern or serial, became so many shackles mitigating against music itself. As a kind of auto-therapy, Scelsi reportedly spent hours at the piano in near silence, except for the simple gesture of playing a single note, very slowly, over and over. Repetition, of course, is never simply repetition. Over time, other affects emerge, and catatonia becomes an affordance, not an inhibition. A mantra, a prayer, a somnambulistic cadence, a strange lyricism of what fades.

In the process, Scelsi discovered that the actual sound of a note was less interesting than the *decay* of the sound. The sound itself produced a whole array of artefacts—overtones and other harmonics at the threshold of hearing—that seemed to reveal themselves only in this subtractive, distilled phenomena of decay. It was the dissipation of sound, and everything happening "around" the sound, that became the focal point, as if something almost epiphenomenal was generated in the dissipative passage from sound to silence. Running counter to the hyper-complexity of the 12-tone, atonal, and serialist musical of the period, Scelsi's *Quattro pezzi* is sound in the blind spot of our hearing. While its austere aesthetics looks ahead to other works of the period and after, one gets the impression that *Quattro pezzi* is less a musical "composition" and more a kind of patient documentation of sonic decay in deep time.

Writing about the relation between sound and silence, Scelsi believed that it was in the nebulous zone between sound and silence that the "ultra-terrestrial worlds" made themselves known. "Concerning music," he writes, "there are certainly different spheres and planes: from the astral world to the highest planes where, perhaps, silence and sounds are one..." (Scelsi, 2023: 87). A whole new approach to composition follows from this inversion, where sound is composed so as to "disperse" into silence. Scelsi refers to this method of composition as "demonic."

*

I Am Legion. One of the classic Biblical accounts of demonic possession is that of the so-called Gerasene demon. Slightly different accounts are given in Mark 5 and Luke 8, but the basics of the parable are the same: Jesus and his followers travel from Galilee to the Gerasene region (in current-day Jordan). There Jesus is met by the local villagers, who ask him to heal an old man possessed by demons. The possessed man, it is said, roams about the tombs, without clothing or shelter, raving incomprehensibly in a language not of this Earth. When the villagers shackle him, he descends into a frenzy and breaks free. At night, he screams aloud and cuts himself with rocks and stones. Jesus confronts the possessed man, who appeals to Jesus to cure him. As part of the exorcism, Jesus commands the name of the demon possessing the old man: "Then Jesus asked him, 'What is your name?' 'My name is Legion,' he replied, 'for we are many.'"[6] The name "Legion" ($\lambda\varepsilon\gamma\omega\nu$) is tricky here, for it is not clear from the passage whether it is a single demon speaking in many voices, or if it is a multitude of demons speaking in a single voice. Indeed, the very name "Legion" appears to devolve upon itself, an abstract name that seems to designate nothing concrete. Having "captured" the demon (or demons), Jesus then casts them out of the body of the old man, and into a herd of swine in a nearby field. The herd, now possessed, are driven into a state of frenzy and rush over the side of a cliff into turbulent seas below.

Throughout the parable, the only real evidence we have of the real presence of demons is this enigmatic resounding of the word "Legion." That the demons choose to present themselves via sound reveals that they are present and absent at the same time—the demons named "Legion" are never present in themselves, but only via some form of earthly embodiment (the old man, the herd of animals, the wind, the sea). In a sense, they are strangely pantheistic, announcing themselves only indirectly. They are less malefic Mephistos and more like wandering and derelict spirits, coursing through life, cast upon the wind and the sea, dissipated into the very climate itself—a reverberation that happens more by demonic contagion than by divine inspiration.

Sound of the Abyss. Non-directional sound, a sound without any point of origin, is different from a Neoplatonic sound (sound that radiates from a central point of origin), and different again from the Kantian sound (sound that exceeds and eclipses its point of origin). Non-directional sound does not have an origin to negate, because there is no origin to negate. It is not generative, or a sound that continuously pours itself forth, sound as a gift of divine over-presence. Rather, it is a sound that is the negation of sound, a presence that only asserts its absence—something chthonic, something of the underworld.

This is the sound described by Schopenhauer, the curmudgeon who once called Schelling "a windbag" and Hegel "a monument to German stupidity"—this most "doomerist" of philosophers also, curiously, possessed a collection of wind instruments. But high winds are hardly what we would think of as cosmic bass. Nevertheless, in Schopenhauer, what one finds is a nascent theory of the subsonic.

In contrast to the aspirations of his philosophical contemporaries, Schopenhauer remained suspicious about any attempt to bridge the gulf so convincingly articulated by Kant: that between phenomena (the world as it appears to us) and noumena (the world-in-itself). Questioning the most basic foundations of the Western philosophical tradition, Schopenhauer returned again and again to the impersonal quality of existence (which he called the "Will" or "Will-to-Live"), a blind striving inherent in all existence, in contrast to the various systems of meaning that we as human beings drape over the world (what he termed *Vorstellung* or "Representation"). While we busy ourselves with ceaselessly constructing the latter, it is the "Will" that continues unabated, without any ground or purpose, and lacking any inherent meaning. What results is a metaphysics that is at once harrowing but strangely inspired (no doubt further fuelled by Schopenhauer's study of the *Upanishads*).

For Schopenhauer, this impersonal aspect of existence is never directly experienced as such; instead, it is through the arts that we experience it, though at a distance. But not all the arts are alike for Schopenhauer. Whereas literature, painting, and sculpture make use of representational means, music is different. On the one hand, music is an integral part of the human world. It is deeply mytho-poetic and speaks to the human condition of living in the world. But on the other hand, because it is not representational, music appears to have a strange, almost otherworldly autonomy—it almost exists out of the world, or at least harbours within itself a certain abdication of the world. For Schopenhauer, music does not represent the world, but is itself a world.

As the shadow side of phenomena, music for Schopenhauer bears the faintest traces of an already-vanishing noumena, a negative index of the world-in-itself that we can never fully apprehend, much less comprehend. And this is the key point in Schopenhauer's philosophy of music. Schopenhauer likes music, not because it is the fullest expression (of existence, of the world, of human affect), but because it is a self-negating phenomenon, in that what is expressed is the fundamental transiency of all existents. In a striking turn of phrase, Schopenhauer (2010: 285) notes that "music is also wholly independent of the appearing world, simply ignoring it, so that it could in a sense still exist even if there were no world at all."

Music doesn't need us.

Grundbaß. For Schopenhauer, music is impersonal because it participates in the physics of the subsonic, or that point at which sound waves condense into the chthonic strata of planets, moons, and stars. As he notes, "all the bodies and organisations of nature must be regarded as having come into existence through gradual development out of the mass of the planet. This is both their supporter and their source, and the high notes have the same relation to the ground-bass" (ibid.).

The notion of the "ground-bass" (*Grundbaß*) in Schopenhauer's philosophy of music is enticing, but opaque. For Schopenhauer, bass itself is enigmatic; it is the ground and origin of all other sounds, and yet it is also the most chaotic, the most primordial, the most shapeless of sounds. "I recognise in the deepest tones of harmony, in the ground-bass, the lowest grades of inorganic nature, the mass of the planet…" (ibid.).

But as Schopenhauer notes, it is precisely the inaudibility of bass—to human ears, at least—that indicates its profound intimacy with the unhuman, impersonal quality of existence, especially as it recedes into the subsonic, or is diffused into the background atmosphere of non-sound of "silence." As the bass sound descends into inaudibility, it begins to touch an absence that is forever foreclosed to us: "There is a limit to the depth, beyond which no sound is any longer audible. This corresponds to the fact that no matter is perceivable without form and quality, in other words, without the manifestation of a force incapable of further explanation…" (ibid.). In short, Schopenhauer's cosmic, primordial ground-bass is less the negation of sound, and more like the sound of negation.

*

Unsound. Thought to have been written in the early centuries of the Common Era, the *Mandukya Upanishad* has the distinction of being both among the shortest and the most complex of the so-called Principal Upanishads. At its core is the distinction between four states (or four "quarters") that are encapsulated in the syllables of 'A', 'U', and 'M'—forming the 'aum' sound so familiar to meditative practitioners. Each syllable, the *Mandukya* tells us, correlates to a state of existence: the state of waking ('A'), the state of dream ('U'), and the state of dreamless sleep ('M'), in which the distinction of waking and dream, reality and illusion, are ultimately effaced in a monistic unity.

But what of the fourth state? As the *Mandukya* notes, the fourth state is actually not a state at all, a paradoxical condition in which all attributes of being and non-being are subtracted, a state to which no sound can be assigned—it is the pause between the final 'M' and the beginning 'A', neither inhaling or exhaling.

The canonical commentaries on the *Mandukya*—including those by Gaudapada and Adi Shankara—make two things clear: that, strictly speaking, this fourth state does not exist, and that it indicates an absolute non-dualism, in which all distinctions fade away. But neither the *Mandukya* nor its Vedantic commentators ever call this fourth state "silence." It's as if our own, limited, human-bound notions of silence are somehow too loud.

*

Divine Negation. In his 1909 book *La Religion de la musique*, Camille Mauclair contrasts two types of silence: an everyday silence, and silence as the absence of all sound. The first type of silence we hear in contrast to the sounds that precede it—and even then we continue to hear this contrast as "quiet." The second type of silence is, strictly speaking, inaudible. "Only the silence of God is silence, and ours is by contrast filled with noise" (Mauclair, 1919: 53).

Still, Mauclair insists that even in this divine silence there is a kind of musicality. "I imagine," he notes, "a music that would express nothing of our own language of passion … but instead an ideal cessation of all sound … that which is voiced in the realm of spirit when life expires" (ibid.: 55).

*

De profundis. Like many authors, J.-K. Huysmans—paragon of *fin-de-siècle* decadence—gives music a privileged status among the arts. But Huysmans is thinking not of symphonies or operas, but something more primordial. For him, it is plainchant that surpasses even the most complex modern music in its ability to move mass, sound, and air. In his novel *À Rebours*, Huysmans reveals an almost devout reverence for chant: "The traditional melody was the only one which, with its powerful unison, its harmonies as massive and imposing as blocks of freestone, could tone in with the old basilicas and fill their Romanesque vaults, of which it seemed to be the emanation, the very voice" (Huysmans, 2001: 187). Impossibly high, vaulted cathedrals, levitating and amorphous clouds of incense, a *De profundis* "bewailing its moral destiny" like an invisible, liturgical whirlpool of dark matter—for Huysmans, all this serves no other purpose than as support for music.

Huysmans' eulogy to plainchant reminds me of a bit of apocrypha concerning a group of Tibetan monks who were able, with the sound of their chanting, to levitate and move massive stone blocks. Compared to this, everything else is just singing.

*

Sound as the hollowed-out, chthonic depths of planets, or the infinite void of deep space. An abyss above, an abyss below. Sound that is nowhere in particular but everywhere in general—non-directional sound, sound felt but not heard, sound equivalent to space, space eclipsed in sound, sound engulfed in silence.

*

The Sound of Dying Stars. In the summer of 2022, scientists working with NASA's Hubble Space Telescope detected an extremely intense radio wave pulsing in the depths of deep space (Ryder et al., 2023: 294–299). Given the unassuming designator FRB 20220610A, the "fast radio burst" (or FRB) was one among many that astronomers have been studying in the past few decades, thanks in part to advances in the detection capacity of radio telescopes.

Lasting just milliseconds, fast radio bursts are also extremely intense: they are estimated to be 100 million times more intense than our sun, and in one thousandth of a second they release as much energy as the sun does in 100 years. They also appear to originate from distant galaxies, which indicates that they are able to span great distances, sometimes even forming regular cosmic "pulses."

The case of FRB 20220610A was unique, however, in that scientists estimate that it originated from a galaxy so far from our own that it had been traveling through space for some 8 billion years. What's more, while it is assumed that such interstellar pulses have some point of origin, many of them seem to emerge from nowhere, with speculations including everything from black holes, colliding stars, flares from magnetars (highly magnetised neutron stars), and even cataclysmic "stellar quakes."

While radio emissions from space are not uncommon, what makes these sounds a mystery is both their intensity, as well as an apparent lack of point of origin. Their intensity alone is an enigma for astronomers; in many cases, there do not seem to be enough galaxies in the universe to possibly produce a sound of such magnitude. In other words, neither supernovas, aliens, nor the Death Star are capable of generating such a sound. Perhaps we are witness to what alchemist Robert Fludd once described as the "celestial monochord." In a flash, interstellar sound collapses space and time, perhaps having no other function than to secretly return to its zero point.

To speak of "music" in such a context seems either absurd or mystical (or both). When considering sonic phenomena generally, negation is often understood as something that happens to sound, or, alternately, that happens within music. But can sound itself be a negation?

*

"Without music, life would be an error" (Nietzsche, 2001: 49). With music, life is still an error. Is music then an apology, an indictment, or an omen?

*

References

Blackwood, A. (1910) *The Human Chord.* London: Macmillan.

Huysmans, J. K. (2001) *Against Nature (À Rebours).* Translation by R. Baldick. New York: Penguin.

Lovecraft, H.P. (2001) *The Thing on the Doorstep and Other Weird Stories.* Ed. S.T. Joshi. New York: Penguin.

Lugones, L. (2001) *Strange Forces.* Translation by G. Alter-Gilbert. New York: Latin American Literary Review Press.

Mauclair, C. (1919) *La Réligion de la Musique.* Paris: Librairie Fischbacher.

Nietzsche, F. (2001) *The Case of Wagner / Twilight of the Idols / The Antichrist / Ecco Homo / Dionysus Dithyrambs / Nietzsche Contra Wagner.* Translation by C. Diethe et al. California: Stanford University Press.

Ono no Komachi & Shikibu, I. (2023) *The Ink Dark Moon.* Translation by J. Hirschfield with M. Haratani. New York: Vintage.

Scelsi, G. (2023) *The Aesthetical Writings of Giacinto Scelsi.* Ed. and translation by F. Sciannameo & A. Carlotta Pellegrini. London: Rowman & Littlefield.

Schopenhauer, A. (2010) *The World as Will and Representation, Volume I.* Translation by J. Norman, A. Welchman, & C. Janaway. Cambridge: Cambridge University Press.

Radhakrishnan, S. (ed.) (1953) *The Principal Upanishads.* Ed. and trans. Sarvepalli. London: Allen & Unwin, 1953.

Ryder, S. D et al. (2023) "A Luminous Fast Radio Burst that Probes the Universe at Redshift 1". *Science* 382(6668): 294–299.

10. THE MBIRA THE HAMMER BETRAYAL

By Alberto Ricca *Bienoise

Think the mbira, the ancient African idiophone, an exciting musical interface also aptly called *thumb piano*. Like many percussion instruments, it has a very strong affordance, it calls our hands to hold it and strike its blades. But differently from most simple percussions, it is a warmer medium, a point between the complete concrete openness of a snare drum, and the complete grammatical openness of a piano: the tuned metal strips of the mbira will sprout endless variations of the same *ur-song*, in a continuum between conscious playing of pitches and the ambience of water streaming through rocks, crossfading nature and culture. It is a tangible composition. Like any good interface, it can be broken: you can tap on it, you can play it with a rubber mallet or a toilette chain, you can glue it to a frame drum to add modulation, or to a contact microphone and erode yet another symbol, the one of ethnic world music, projecting that sound into afrofuturism like Konono Nº1 did through distortion and effects (each one being another sound object, another tool in itself). A broken interface brought discovery.

What should I draw?

Every text is an interface. An interface is choice frozen, an interface is a tool. An interface is a punched card you impose over chaos to access the thought of a creator, bridging a dialogue with the person who generated the text. Helmut Lachenmann (1986) taught us that composing is building an instrument; John Cage, that composing is creating an occasion for listening.

An instrument, a tool, can be anything useful to achieve a purpose: Western harmony sounds like Bach or the Beatles, tempered piano tuning allows modulation and jazz, a hammer strikes, a gun kills. You can turn a screw with a knife, but a screwdriver is better fitted; you can operate a sampler reasoning in semitones and a temporal grid, but you'll soon find out that it's a constraint and a cage more than a map.

Realising all this has been very empowering, and taught me the importance of choosing the right tools before using them; it feels even more important in an era of shallow use of simplified tools for an instant, standard gratification. Simplifying access is great; a simple tool is very democratic in welcoming persons who have no time, no money, or some social bias that keeps them from learning the technique to realise what they have in mind.

But the tool is not innocent.

Chekov was absolutely right: once shown, the gun must be shot. The homunculus is all face and hands because we want to use things. We are born cyborgs, cybernetic organisms, from the Greek word for *conductor*: we want to use things. Elias Canetti (1960) would say that the hand wants to be happy; it wants to experience the joy of fur, to see with its touch, and to test its own hardness against other materials—thus, the stick is born, the stone is thrown. We don't need a reason to throw it, and the stone was already there, but once a hand takes it from the ground, it's a stone no more but a nexus of perspectives. Even more: we seize it, we extend our hand on the stone and demand it as part of our body, the stone now invisible as one of our organs, now an entity of pure intention to be thrown to catch the beast, to be gathered to build a home.

The hand wants to be happy, to revel in the joy of use, and one cannot invent a new word while expecting people to not use it; kids want to draw with their new crayons, they want to say *shit* and *fuck* even if they have no reason to. "What should I draw?" they'll ask their teacher, because far before having something to express, the hand will need a use for the new tool.

Thus, the History of Art is the history of tools: again, *composing is creating an instrument*—and creating an instrument is composing: perspective, the colour purple, cubism, photography, screaming and autotune, they are all tools that were instrumental in creating new symbols, instantly recognisable singularities that "put together" older tools to create new ones, new meanings. *Instant classics*. All eternal Art creates symbols: you cannot go to an exhibition of photos by Andreas Gursky, you cannot watch Seinfeld or listen to an album of field recordings by Chris Watson without being instantly reprogrammed to see and hear those symbols in the world that surrounds you at any moment. The most boring shit can be repurposed once we give it a name, and this gives me hope: as soon as we heard the first Vaporwave track, we knew what that was about. We recognised a readymade dream of past malls because we already possessed all those symbols.

So, tools are far from neutral: they reprogram our thinking. It's the joint that smokes you, brilliantly said Kodwo Eshun (1998) while exposing some viral sound objects—the *Amen Break* was there to be found, it was the perfect shining tool to express that era. *Also sprach Zarathustra* was composed to be the soundtrack of our ascension to the skies, a symbol that Kubrick assembled first. Those cultural objects were stones laying around, hyperstitional pieces of a puzzle existing in any possible shape.

The cultural era we are dwelling in is two-sided: it's both a curational/compositional era, and the age of algorithmic reproduction. We're looking at two faces of the same overflown void: it's an age where everybody has the technical means to create content, and greatly enjoys using the quick tools somebody gave them. This creates the deathly, infinite excess of compositions that can only be given meaning by curation, by some middle-person between chaos and our attention, giving names to things to mimic order—a playlist, a trend, a movement, a festival. In a slow departure from the idea of an Author, towards the acceptance of a lively cultural mesh where the particular opus means less than the whole flux of them. All the while, artists—sensitive as always—stop bringing their vision to a final form, preferring to build instruments in other ways: courses, workshops, sneak peeks that keep people engaged as non-playing-characters in somebody else's art. Where a sense-producing margin, a surplus of meaning according to Gadamer, used to exist between the Author's presented artwork and the resulting audience sensation. In this becoming-open approach, the same surplus is found in the space between makeshift tools and their continuous memetic handover; a bubbling culture vat, where no tool nor symbol is ever brought to completion, is never definitely *chosen*, but every creator is satisfied when it just *works.* No more masterpieces, in the words of Artaud. It's a return to a flowing orality, a free-roaming harvest in the multidimensional database of culture that cancels the burden of the past and any debt to the future, in favour of the shared present: it's exciting and freeing, and possibly alien.

> [A note on *meaning*: high school taught you to paraphrase poetry, to assign an univocal, literal meaning to every word, thus killing centuries of efforts to evoke a polyphony of meanings through the worst possible medium—written language.
>
> The Meaning of Art only pertains to you. Symbols are *qualia*, they are cultural tools that become organs, invisible and unknown to the outside, digesting reality.]

Betrayed by beauty

Outside your house, nameless things flow. Not even Tolkien named them: without a name, they are free. Without a name, they are the XIII arcane. With every name, they are chaos.

Them breaching in is the detuning of the sky, it is the towers falling: the old names were a Magic Circle.

Art is not sustainable—it never has been: only few have, bluntly, time and money to do art, but *today!* the market smiles on us and offers us some mechanical talent by rent. Democratising the tools is never a bad thing; I'm all for simpler instruments, allowing people to put together a backing track for their poetry with visuals from a video streaming in ten minutes. Gatekeeping approaches that are NOT TRVE is a very sad thing; it's a Magic Circle to protect ourselves from a lively Chaos, a brittle system of rules that, when broken, brings Death—in itself a good liberation of new energy.

But we have to be careful in front of tools that seem to democratise *production* (an awful word) while pursuing their own agenda: homogenisation of choices inside preset personalities is a sought goal today, because if everybody thinks the same, it's far easier to sell products. If you trust the algorithm, you end up thinking that only photos in a certain ratio, with certain colours, are *right*. That only a track with certain sounds, polished in a certain way, sounds *good*. That only certain words in a certain layout speak the *truth*. All synonyms of *beauty*. All symbols, so loud they dwarf every other, all reprogramming us in reading reality through them and them only. Programming mediocrity.

This feeds back in a twofold way: with ourselves, who will start creating new works of art based on that algorithmically selected beauty; and with the algorithm, that will select more of the same, and will *also* produce more of the same. We learn from the same pool. You never approach a canvas clean: on a white page, you see all the images you have seen in your existence—and there has never been an era with so many images, and so few symbols, surrounding us.

Now, the singularity: Artificial Intelligence. The worst mistake we are making is regarding it as a subject instead of a tool—or, I concede, a hyper-tool. We *rely* on tools—we don't just use them, as Graham Harman (2002) brilliantly pointed out in his *Tool-Being*; we rely on them as we rely on our organs, and we are blind to the well-oiled, ready-at-hand tool as an abstraction made of pure intention. It's a feeling of sad surprise when an organ fails, when a tool returns to being flesh or stone, when it returns visible and we need to investigate and fix it.

We rely on our tools, but we *trust* subjects. I'm following Gregory Bateson's (1966) ideas in seeing trust in others as something that we mammals evolved in order to survive: betrayal is then an unforgivable act against nature, the creation of an enemy that doesn't *belong* anymore, while tools are just tools.

You trusted me and I deceived you, talking of their lack of innocence: of course only subjects can be innocent, guilty or creative. But hyper-tools clearly show multiple layers of purpose, reaching far beyond the solution of a problematic task: demand open algorithms and investigate those purposes, the purpose of the tool and the goal of who's selling you something that seems to be esoterically difficult to understand. Artificial Intelligence algorithms are at once tools, mirrors (tools that ask questions, like tarot or a recording of your rehearsal), and sometimes media (as information passes through them, even though they are a very noisy channel), and in this confusion thrives the illusion of magic found in any new technology—in this case, a miraculous black box whose complexity gives snake-oil salesmen the perfect opportunity to sputter convincing technobabble to us, digital peasants.

Algorithms have no idea of what they are saying or drawing, which is the result of mathematical operations finding the closest numbers to the ones we've asked, but we have been exposed to decades of unintentional propaganda, thousands of stories of robots and computers culminating in calling it Artificial Intelligence. We cannot agree on what intelligence actually is, so this buzz-name just sells us expectations of it being able to do everything the right way—but what we perceive as *right* is hallucination, pareidolia, seeing faces in a bunch of shapes. Data speak to us and we regard them as friends, but they sometimes get together and lie—we taught them to, and we're betraying ourselves.

At this point, it's clear that the tool-essence of AI has multiple implications: despite the ease of use, it might be the wrong tool for our task, leading to *good-enough* results in which we only had the illusion of choice; it has been created with a purpose, or it has been forcefully applied to every task until it got results, and due to the resources needed for its creation, it has to be exploitable from the market, yet sneakily omnipresent in everyday life; it will create new symbols, by its action or of its action; and we handle it with lustful intention—but we should refrain from being content with producing trash for the sake of novelty. "Novelty requires perpetual replenishing and hence capitalism as the unthinking drive to novelty is, in fact, the 'eternity of Hell'", in the words of Alison Ross (2013), paraphrasing Walter Benjamin.

Interesting is not a synonym of *beautiful*.

We are happy when we get a result, and well-engineered tools are effective; but differently from the hammer you keep on your working bench, you do not own the many digital tools that give you instant gratification, and what's now free, tomorrow will have a monthly fee or much worse policies. What is exciting and new today, in a month will be critiqued for its lack of diversity and underlying racism.

Demand open algorithms: open in the sense of freely usable, modifiable, shareable; and open in the sense of available for inquiry, respectful of intellectual property, respectful of personal data, cleaned from bias the best we can.

This doesn't need to be without control, but control should not be in the same hands that are profiting by it. Algorithms are not subjects; they are means of production. Let's keep them open this time, and they will be a formidable aid to human intelligence, while the fastest and shiniest offer could also be the more biased and exploitable one.

Because affordance has a strong beauty: we want to feel the best apple in the basket, we are entranced by it. This bypasses reason, and we are all victims of engineering of desire: we will use what's new, what's convenient and nice to touch, and we will ignore the hidden price. Beware of a tool that inherits the sins of its creator.

We are all victims

The second route of Bateson's vision regards the invention of cybernetics, the science of feedback systems—the science, he says, that allows us to model, study and exploit complex systems such as the social one. Exploitation is engineered betrayal, and we can imagine digital heroin, something so perfectly built that will ensnare our attention forever. An Infinite Jest—again, infinity is the word, David Foster Wallace showed us. We are all victims and we're powerless bags of desire, and as much as we can call for open algorithms, we know that the tools ask to be used, and every use will be found and tried, and a cultural drug is the only logical endgame.

Focusing back to the cultural field, the main action of the algorithm today is not media generation, but curation: a selection of what's good for us, or for the numerical model of us that data have outlined.

But a choice made without a vision to progress, based only on what we already know and like, is pampering.

Delegating a choice to an unaccountable entity is an addiction.

We are all victims because we desire to use the tool, and the tool is engineered to crawl deeper and deeper into us: we need to light that cigarette, we need to share that article that angers us. We need to trust the algorithm in wading for us through the spires of the endless worm of contemporary media, but the algorithm has no reason to avoid betrayal in its unthinking thirst for novelty. This betrayal is the jest of an infinite God against us: I need to stress what I (Ricca, 2023) wrote in *Apathetic Algorithms* about Death being the nexus of all meanings. Death is the *quale* (a subjective mental object impossible to completely explain to others) that makes *choice* necessary in lieu of our limits, and therefore gives it valour by opposing the uncanniness of what is without end.

Infinity is dreadful and maddening because we will see a meaning in it, because we cannot comprehend (understand and contain) the reasons of an entity that doesn't die.

Without the sacrifice of Christ, that new religion would have been far less convincing; and if you ask Nietzsche, one should carefully choose the timing of their demise because *a toothless mouth no longer has the right to every truth* (see Nietzsche, 1883). It's the supreme choice of withdrawing into silence to will power into our ideas. The words we spoke were enough—in the wait for His return.

4'33", the famous *tacet* composition by John Cage, is not a recording of silence: it is a performance that relies on the expectations created by seeing a person sitting at a piano, in order to encourage listening. A composer saved us all by sacrificing his voice. Real silence is a white page scrolling forever, it is the hallucination of hearing words in cultural faucets algorithmically running, it is finding a wall where you expected a mirror; when we listen openly, we reignite every dialogue.

The infinite is uncanny: we are finite beings, we cannot choose to take every path, so we give value to human choice by virtue of this finitude. Whenever we trust a non-human suggestion on what is worthy of our time, whenever we share something before ascertaining its value, we're betraying ourselves. Whenever—and this is the main theme here—we use a tool that we don't possess, that is opaque under its surface and hetero-directed in its results, we are inscribing ourselves in a magic circle that hinders every dialogue with the outside. Be it because it's designed to exploit our need to use it, or because we are accepting it as the only truth.

Discerning clearly who is a subject and what is a tool preserves us from this boring cultural betrayal where everything is simultaneously valid, where only universally accepted symbols are meaningful, spoiling and watering them down. We need choices, we need visions, we need distortion beyond material limits and scratched CDs, we need new symbols with strong voices—so please be Marius Schneider, please be Hertha von Dechend.

And take your time
To trust in me
And you will find
Infinity, infinity
And take your time
To trust in me
And you will find
Infinity, infinity
The time goes by
So naturally
While you'll receive
Infinity[1]

References

Bateson, G. (1966) From Versailles to Cybernetics, Lecture at Two Worlds Symposium, Sacramento State College, 21 April 1966.

Canetti, E. (1960) *Masse und Macht.* Hamburg: Claassen.

Eshun, K. (1998) *More Brilliant than the Sun: Adventures in Sonic Fiction.* Oakland: University of California.

Guru Josh (1989) *Infinity. Deconstruction.* [album]

Harman, G. (2002) *Tool-Being: Heidegger and the Metaphysics of Objects.* Chicago: Open Court Publishing.

Lachenmann, H. (1986) Über das Komponieren, Lecture at the Darmstadt Summer Courses on 14 July 1986.

Nietzsche, F. (1883) *Also sprach Zarathustra. Ein Buch für Alle und Keinen.* Chemnitz: Schmeitzner.

Ricca, A. (2023) "Apathetic Algorithms, Artificial Artisans". In A. Szepanski (ed.) *Ultrablack of Music: Volume 1.* Frankfurt a. M.: NON/Mille Plateaux.

Ross, A. (2013) "The Problem of the Image: Sacred and Profane Spaces in Walter Benjamin's Early Writing". *Critical horizons* 14(3): 355–379.

1 See Guru Josh, 1966.

11. PARMENIDES' SIRENS

Static Music and the Politics of Non-Movement[1]

By Frédéric Neyrat

"*When extreme yang encounters extreme yin,*
the yang will always be defeated"

— Cheng Man Ch'ing,
Chen Tzu's Thirteen Treatises on T'ai Chi Ch'uan

Eros is droning in a static place

In her introduction to *Intermediary Spaces—Espaces intermédiaires*, a book centred on a long interview with composer Éliane Radigue, Julia Eckhardt carefully distinguishes, from the very first page, between Radigue's compositions and drone music: where the latter is said to be "static, a simple sonic presence", the former are "on the contrary defined in terms of time and always contain

1 I thank William Zeng for proofreading this article.

a development, however minimal and imperceptible it may be" (Radigue & Eckhardt, 2019: 29).

Why this wish to ward off what is static, to reject what doesn't move or change? What is the danger of immobility? It is the danger of death, probably. To be perfectly still, to last in immobility, is to be dead, we believe. And socially, the absence of mobility translates—in the terms of a neoliberalism that has now reached the end of its tether—into a negative sign: supposed conservatism, unwillingness to change and adapt, and so on. Philosophically, too, it seems that "becoming" is the cardinal virtue. Inevitably, it's Heraclitus (you'll never enter the same river twice, everything flows, everything is in a state of flux) who is favoured over Parmenides (complete and immobile, Being is neither born nor dies). Promoting non-movement, when we try to sound it out, is being mad.

But perhaps immobility, which seems unreasonable in the eyes of the Principle of Becoming governing the world, can point to an imperceptible capacity—an ontological, aesthetic, and political potentiality. I define the *static dimension* as the impossible of non-movement at the core of movement. Drone music—or the drone music element of any composition, be it atonal[2] or electronic, from drone metal band Sun O))) to Thomas Köner's dark ambient (see Neyrat, 2020: 11–21)—confronts par excellence the impossible of immobility.

"Music that seems to change so little" (Demers, 2015: 2), drone music hums and invents the technical, bodily, and psychic means to persist in droning, and to accompany what changes, *as if change still came from what doesn't change*. Instead of being a sign of death, the perilous persistence of the static dimension makes audible what contemporary politics needs: an image of eternity inaccessible to the prevailing (neo)fascism. In a place we can't point to, a place of bass eternity, Eros drones in a light apart.

---

2 La Monte Young liked to refer to "Farben", the third piece of Arnold Schoenberg's *Five Pieces for Orchestra, Op. 16.*

"Fluxus versus Stasis"

La Monte Young is credited with having explored and theorised the static dimension of drone music: the use of long sustained notes, or what he also called "sustenance" (Potter, 2000: 22). The work that maybe best represents this static music is *Trio for Strings* (1958), for violin, viola, and cello. Influenced by North Indian Classical music and Japanese gagaku, *Trio for Strings* is a musical work without melody or vibrato, with a minimum of slowly exposed musical material and the most imperceptible transitions possible, sustained notes sometimes interrupted by silences. "Fluxus versus Stasis", as he wrote in an article entitled "Why I Withdrew from Fluxus":

> Change, or flux, is inevitable. Stasis, or remaining the same, is impossible. Therefore, to achieve the static state is the goal, while the state of flux, variation, or contrast, is unavoidable and thus unnecessary as a goal.
>
> (Hendricks, 2008: 53)

It couldn't be clearer that stasis, in the sense of that which "remains the same", is impossible. And it's for this reason that, for La Monte Young, "*stasis*" must be the supreme objective of music: everything changes, we know it, we experience it constantly, but to aim only for music that changes would be to stick too closely to reality.

In a 1966 interview, La Monte Young contrasts what is static not with what is moving as such, but with a form of "directionality" in music and with the search for a "climax":

> I feel that in most music peculiar to the Western hemisphere since the thirteenth century, climax and directionality have been among the most important guiding factors, whereas music before that time, from the chants through organum and Machaut, used stasis as a point of structure a little bit more the way certain Eastern musical systems have.
>
> (Young & Zazeela, 2004: 24)

What the dominant ontology—its politics and aesthetics, values—is not the indistinct flow of becoming, but the direction of it; moving towards progress, for example, towards excellence, success and so on. This climax sometimes comes at the end of the musical piece: at the last moment, the composer offers a held note, and we know only too well how hollow and caricatured the ultimate, supposedly intense musical expression can sound: the dramatisation of the last musical moment is in fact a ridiculous sustenance, the grotesque return of the static dimension that has been denied.

The static event is unanticipable (Kali Malone)

In contrast to a grotesque final moment, consider the way several tracks on Kali Malone's album *All Life Long* (2024) end on a long-held note, a long moment of drone—for example, at the end of "All Life Long (for Organ)", "Fastened Maze", "Not Sun to Burn (for Organ)", and "The Unification of Inner and Outerlife". In these songs, a path is traced towards the static moment, which is the result of a musical operation, the impossible that must be brought to presence in musical possibility.

Insofar as the transitions from one musical sequence to another are slow, we can't know in advance when we're moving into non-movement, into non-variation. When you listen to the songs I have referred to, it's only after a while that you realise you've entered the static dimension *because a change hasn't taken place*.

In "The Unification of Inner and Outerlife", for example, the drone moment occurs at 7m35 and lasts until around the ninth minute, when the sound fades out. With "Not Sun to Burn (for Organ)", it begins at 6m40 and lasts until 9m57, when the sound stops. Whereas the climax dramatises an ultimate point, the static event happens in Malone's songs without us being able to anticipate it; it becomes manifest when our attention realises, after the fact, that something in space-time no longer corresponds to the regular universe of change and directionality.

Retrospectively, the static event has brought about the appearance in the past of an as yet unfulfilled future, a future in which we now know we are caught, but without having been able to control its origin.

"What? (Turtle) Eternity"

Indeed, it is the relationship to time that is turned upside down by static music, which seems to halt the musical flow and its system of anticipations and memorisations. Think of the Theatre of Eternal Music ensemble, active between 1962 and 1974, organised by La Monte Young and whose members included, among others, Marian Zazeela, Tony Conrad, Jon Hassell and John Cale (see Potter, 2000: 67–73).

Among the few recordings we have of these experimental drone moments, there's the album released in 1974 entitled *Dream House 78' 17"*, consisting of "*13 I 73 5:35–6:14:03 PM NYC*" and "*Drift Study 14 VII 73 9:27:27–10:06:41 PM NYC*". The first features the voices of Young and Zazeela over an electronic drone (mixing three sine waves), joined by Jon Hassell's trumpet and Garrett List's trombone, the piece evolving with the pitch changes produced by the oscillator. The second is played entirely by sine-wave generators, the phase relationships between them drifting progressively.

The vinyl sleeve describes this music as "Dream Music", to be played in "Dream Houses", and associates this music with turtles, for whom "the drone is the first sound", which "lasts forever and cannot have begun". Dream Music could last for thousands of years, "just as the Tortoise has continued for millions of years past, and perhaps only after the Tortoise has again continued for as many million years as all of the tortoises in the past will it be able to sleep and dream of the next order of tortoises to come and of ancient tigers with black fur and omens the 189/98 whirlwind in the Lost Ancestral Lake Region".

In the 1966 interview already mentioned, La Monte Young explains that:

> tortoises and turtles remain essentially the same. I'm interested in this, because I'm interested in long durations. I'm

> interested in stasis, and in things that stay the same although they change in detail.
>
> (Young & Zazeela, 2004: 62)

Monte Young does not deny change; he knows very well that "no matter how exact you try to be, no matter how many times you try to draw the line exactly the same, things will always be different" (ibid.: 62). But it is precisely *in* this element of flux that the static is formed. What is static is a duration that stretches beyond our ability to delimit it; eternity rising from this duration that delimits itself through a temporal autonomy that overflows the changing. Eternity is a dreaming tortoise (dreaming about another dreaming tortoise).

The immobile being is Being under the greatest constraint

For any being to be immobile, Parmenides tells us, necessity (*anagkê*) must come down on it with all its weight. And not just necessity, as Barbara Cassin explains in her commentary on the fragments of Parmenides' *On Nature*, but also justice (*dikê*), rule (*themis*), destiny (*moira*): "all the obligatory powers of the world of humans and gods combine to constitute Being (*l'être*) as a representable entity, a well-bound identity, a sphere" (Parmenides, 1998: 151). It is under this intense constraint that "Being" can be described by Parmenides as "ungenerated and imperishable": "Justice looses not her Fetters to permit [Being] to have come into being or to perish, but holds [it] fast" and "the powerful Necessity holds it in the bonds of the limit which encircles Being" (Parmenides, 1965: 85–86). Being described by Parmenides as "now altogether, one, continuous", "motionless in the limits of mighty bond", "without beginning and never-ending" (ibid.), is—as Cassin explains—"the moment of greatest constraint exerted on the 'is'" (Parmenides, 1998: 54–55). Composers of static music also appeal to necessity, to the forces of the greatest constraint, when it comes to making sound of the impossible of non-movement: they are restless Parmenidians, summoning up technical means—complex and makeshift—to give rise to the seizure of the non-movement of movement.

Parmenides' Sirens

Barbara Cassin gives a striking interpretation of the famous Fragment VIII, when Parmenides defines Being as immobile: this would be an Odyssean palimpsest; Being held "motionless in the limits of mighty bond" would be like Odysseus tied to his mast. It's true that, in both cases, immobility is the effect of a strong constraint. On Circe's recommendation, Odysseus asks his companions to tie him up:

> you are to bind me with strong ropes and fasten me upright against the mast, so that I shall not be able to move. If I implore you and order you to set me free, you must tie me up tighter than ever.
>
> (Homer, 1937: 141)

Absolute immobility threatens those who approach the island of the Sirens: "Then the wind fell all at once, and there was a dead calm, not a ripple on the water", and Odysseus' companions are forced to row. They have wax in their ears and won't listen to the Sirens, who say to Odysseus: "stay your ship, and listen to our voice!" (ibid.). But to stop there, within reach of the Sirens, is to risk stopping for good, to die: "There in a meadow they sit, and all round is a great heap of bones, mouldering bodies and withering skins. Go on past that place" (ibid.: 138–139). Odysseus' immobility, tied to the mast, is the only way for him to avoid the immobility of death if he were to follow the "harmonious song of the Sirens". This is also what's at stake in static music: a constrained immobility in a flow that, at its end, concludes in another immobility—that of death. But the constrained immobility is not under the sole sway of death; it reveals the static of a vitality caught at a standstill, in its momentum, attracted and held back, powerful spacing between two drives.

Of course, like Maurice Blanchot, we can reproach Odysseus for "his perfidy, which led him to enjoy the spectacle of the Sirens, without risk and without accepting the consequences", "this happy and secure cowardice, moreover founded on a privilege that puts him outside the common condition, the others having no right to the happiness of the elite" (Blanchot, 1959: 11). But rather than seeing Odysseus as a metaphor for the spectator, I'd like, on the one hand, to see in him the work of art itself and not the spectator, the work of sound that traps the melody from the outside, the perilous work of risking being lost either in the inconsistent flow that will disperse itself in death, or in the immobility that no longer needs any constraint to be truly dead—in-between two deaths. On the other hand, the work of art thus considered owes its existence to external voices: it must listen to them, and to do so, it must endeavour to hear what it doesn't know, what it has perhaps never heard, even when it thought it knew.

Risked "reinjection" (Éliane Radigue)

There is therefore a static dimension which is not death, but a certain expression of life. To be afraid of this immobility is therefore to be afraid of life, when the latter becomes concentrated, so concentrated that it shows itself to be capable of becoming eminently explosive. The static is the place of a sovereign Eros, which holds back from movement. The composer who strives to welcome the static dimension into their work faces technical challenges.

As Éliane Radigue explains, it's very difficult "to produce a continuous sound by 'reinjecting' sound when working with a loudspeaker and a microphone": you need to find "the limit point, where *larsen* [acoustic feedback] occurs", "if you are too close, it explodes; if you go too far, the sound disappears" (Radigue & Eckhardt, 2019: 88). Between two deaths, always. And if sound is re-injected with two tape recorders (alternating recording and playback modes), the feedback can be "very dangerous" for the tape recorders "if they are not scrupulously controlled with the mixing console", leading to "violent explosions of sounds, which also put the tape machines out of use". Musical Parmenidians befriend the danger of explosive sirens.

Static and political

Politically, immobility can consist in chaining oneself to the gate of a company building whose activities one wants to denounce, in a sit-in that will compel the cops to carry the bodies to dislodge them. And today, the police are increasingly violent against those who do not move; during struggles against the construction of a freeway in France (the A69, in the Tarn region), the police no longer hesitated to prevent activists from sleeping, and from getting water and food supplies, going so far "as to pour a can of petrol at the foot of inhabited trees and burn huts just a few metres from the trees. Tree activists were also physically assaulted".[3] Immobility will soon be classified as a terrorist activity; actually, this is already the case in the USA, where the term "terrorism" has been used to describe the action of climbing and protecting trees in the Atlanta forest (see Neyrat, 2023).

In the courage of activists who expose themselves to police violence—a violence that is ultimately the violence of the rulers who arm, legitimise and encourage it—I see an expression of the static dimension I've sought to analyse in this text: the powerful immobility that originates in the out-of-place of a "free Eros" (Marcuse, 1953). In a world governed by the Principle of Becoming, immobility is unreasonable, seen as the danger of a death that some seek to project onto others; it's the violence of war, of "either me, or him". Killing the other to expel from oneself the non-movement to which one seeks to reduce the other. This Principle must be challenged; in the refusal of this Principle, we might discover

3 See Les Soulèvements de la Terre (2024) Soutien aux occupations sur le tracé de l'A69. Yonne Lauder: Online. https://lessoulevementsdelaterre.org/en-eu/blog/soutien-aux-occupations-sur-le-trace-de-la69.

the supreme non-movement, a "Principle of Nirvana" envisaged "not as death but as life" (ibid.: 126). There, "static triumphs over dynamics", a static whose movement is plenitude. There, play and song replace production; peace replaces war. You're free to become what you are. Static, then, is the joy of being there, where the "yes" is heard in the droning "no".

Eternity is not to come; it is co-present. Utopia haunts every place in the world, but most of the time, we don't feel it. We need composers who can make us hear it by making the static dimension of eternity appear to the senses. The revolutionary politics of the future could intensify this appearance. The politics of the static may be the only way to avoid another aspect of *stasis*, another one of its significations: civil war. Avoiding the horror of a planetary civil war while at the same time abolishing the world whose dominant movement is that of pain and murder: this is the political conundrum we need to face.

Works cited

Arnold Schoenberg. (1909) Farben. *Five Pieces for Orchestra, Op. 16.*

Kali Malone (2024) *All Life Long* [album].

La Monte Young (1958) *Trio for Strings.*

La Monte Young, Marian Zazeela, & the Theatre for Eternal Music (1974) *Dream House 78' 17"*.

References

Demers, J. (2015) *Drone and Apocalypse: An Exhibit Catalog for the End of the World.* Washington: Zer0 Books.

Hendricks, J. (ed.) (2008) *Fluxus. Scores and Instructions: The Transformative Years.* Roskilde: Museum of Contemporary Art.

Homer (1937) *The Odyssey*. Translation by WHD Rouse. New York: A Signet Classic.

Blanchot, M. (1959) *Le Livre à venir.* Paris: Gallimard.

Marcuse, H. (1953) *Eros and Civilisation.* New York: Routledge.

Neyrat, F. (2020) "Spectral Composition: on Spectral Music, Drone Metal, and Electronic music" in Szepanski, A. (ed.) *Ultrablack of Music: Volume 1*: 11–21. Frankfurt: NON – Mille Plateaux.

—. (2023) "Satellite Signals for the Atlanta Forest". *Ill Will*: Online. https://illwill.com/satellite-signals

Parmenides (1998) *Sur la nature ou sur l'étant – La langue de l'être?* Translation by Barbara Cassin: 151. Paris: "Essais" – Seuil.

Parmenides., & Taran, L. (1965) *Parmenides: A Text with translation, commentary, and critical essays*. Translation by Leonardo Taran: 85–86. London: Oxford University Press

Potter, K. (2000) *Four musical minimalists: La Monte Young, Terry Riley, Steve Reich, Philip Glass*. Cambridge/New York: Cambridge University Press.

Radigue, E. & and Eckhardt, J. (2019) *Intermediary Spaces – Espaces intermédiaires: 29*. Brussels: Umland Editions.

Young, L. M., & Zazeela, M. (2004) *Selected Writings: 24*. Ubuclassics. (Originally published 1969, Munich: Heiner Friedrich).

12. SPECTRAL HAUNTINGS, ANCESTRAL TUNINGS

Two Unnaturalist Modes of Listening

By Luigi Monteanni and Gabriele de Seta

Following Latour (1993),
we infer from these overlapping concerns
that the invention of sound machines was part of a collection
of epistemological practices of purification
of sound, which sought to abstract sound
from its immediate surroundings while noting
its connectivity to place.
(we have never been modern)

"Many times I feel nature as a giant ghost with no language and without the slightest interest on me.

That's when it becomes a thrilling experience."

— Francisco Lopez,
Towards the Blur (2004)

"To radio waves, we are ghosts."

— David Bodanis, *Electric Universe: The Shocking True Story of Electricity* (2005)

"Drumming, drumming, drumming.
Drumming is a language."

— African Head Charge,
Drumming Is A Language (1990–2011)

In his movie and book *Tellurian Drama*, Indonesian artist and filmmaker Riar Rizaldi (2020) imagines the concealed story of Radio Malabar, the first colonial radio to appear in West Java, Indonesia, built by the Dutch East Indies government and inaugurated on 5 May 1923. While the entire work gravitates around a mysterious essay written by Drs Munarwan, a pseudo-anthropologist and geologist concerned with the possibility of geoengineering the planet through the radio's obsolete technology, *Tellurian Drama* is also partly about the potential overlaps between media, communication technologies and the invisible world of spirits and ancestors—a fraught encounter of material and immaterial worlds and worldviews.

By detailing how *gunung Puntang*,[1] a location ripe with both supernatural and natural energies, has helped colonial government logistics in the installation of radio infrastructures due to its

1 While *gunung* simply means mountain, according to the Indonesian-Sundanese dictionary (Sumantri et al., 1985), *puntang* means: 'hold on to', 'to have a grip on'.

geological and topographical features—i.e., two twin mountain peaks of similar height proving ideal to install the radio—allowing intercontinental communication between Indonesia and the Netherlands over a 12,000 km trajectory, Rizaldi subtly theorises how signals, radio frequencies, spirits, technologies and the unseen overlap and intermingle in an invisible space delineated by transmitters and receivers, listeners and speakers. For the purpose of this essay, the key implication of *Tellurian Drama* is that, at least to a certain extent, spirits like the Sundanese[2] ancestors (*Karuhun*), move, travel and operate in an analogous yet never identical way to sonic signals and radio frequencies.

The techno-natural assemblage of mountain peaks and antenna cables amplifies the reach of signals: through the parallels sketched by Rizaldi, we can see how this applies to both the wireless signals boosted by the infrastructural topography and the activity of spirits energised by the natural environment—technology is both cultural and supernatural.

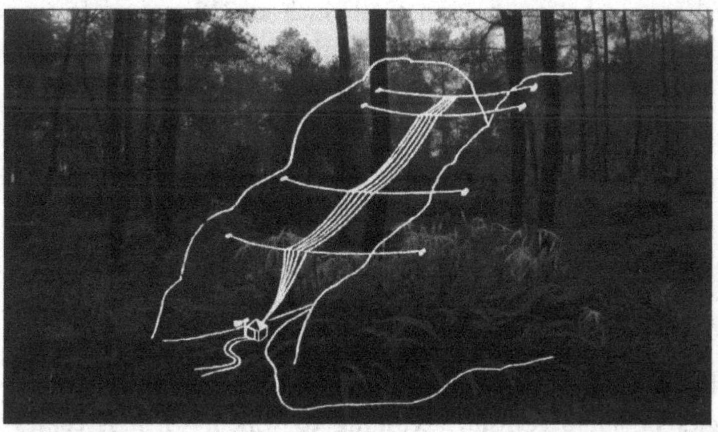

Radio Malabar's infrastructure on the peaks of *gunung Puntang*. Courtesy of the artist.

2 The Sundanese are the second largest ethnic group in Indonesia, generally inhabiting the West Java region (Spiller, 2010).

While Rizaldi's media theoretical speculation has to be contextualised in the domain of genre cinema such as sci-fi and horror, the comparison between spirits and frequencies, ancestors and signals is more than a fictional device. During research on the processes of mediation and mediatisation behind Sundanese *réak*—a traditional ceremonial performance from Bandung in which music is able to cause possession under certain circumstances—one of the authors was made aware of the ways in which spirits, instrument tunings and frequencies are linked and entangled with one another. Oversimplifying: a well-tuned réak ensemble of drums and double reed instruments, combined with the expertise and energy of the performing musicians, is capable of building a 'bridge' between humans and spirits, allowing phenomena of spirit possession and mediumistic communication to take place (Monteanni, 2020).

This capacity of sounds, music and noises to create channels of communication with spirits in Bandung resonates with Rizaldi's speculative fiction and hints at a model of mediation that is opposite and perhaps complementary to the one underlying technological approaches to the unnatural, such as 21st-century frequency scanning and high-tech ghost hunting.[3] In this piece, we depart from the concept of *sonic naturalism*—the idea that sound

> is (mis)understood to exist "out there" in the world, pre-existent to social interaction and mediation, and, furthermore, as though certain sounds ought to be made or to emit from certain associated places.
>
> (Frohlick & Macevicius, 2023: 161)

This sort of naturalism goes hand-in-hand with various ideologies of audio realism, according to which, when it comes to sound recording and reproduction, higher signal quality and

3 A phenomenon where hunters armed with spirit boxes, magnetic field sensors and ultraviolet and infrared film monitor rooms hunting for traces of spirits and ghosts (Potts 2004).

multi-channel stereophony correspond to a less mediated and more detailed access to an immanent 'audio truth' that lies beyond the technical limits of the medium (de Seta, 2018). Particularly evident in the domain of practices like phonography and field recording, sonic naturalism has been identified as typical of ecological and perceptual models of listening (ibid.: 418).

With this essay, we aim at sketching out two models of sonic communication that transcend naturalist realism by establishing contact—through practices of listening and channelling—with the supernatural. We call these two models *hypernaturalism* and *ultranaturalism*. Through this contact between the supernatural forces of spirits and ghosts and the material properties of audio signals and equipment, both models channel the invisible into frequencies—the rate per second of a vibration constituting a sound wave and electromagnetic fields—and transpose it onto the audible spectrum. Even though hypernaturalism and ultranaturalism share the same goal—to make the supernatural audible to human listeners in some form—the two models do so in radically divergent (and, we argue, almost entirely opposite) ways, which in turn reveal profoundly different conceptions of mediation and technological/sonic imaginaries.

Let's begin with hypernaturalism, which today finds widespread appeal among new millennium ghost hunters. On the one hand, ghost hunters follow a naturalistic posture betraying an audiophiliac faith in the transparency of the technological medium (i.e., spirit boxes/frequency scanners). By pushing naturalism towards the hyperreal imaginary of high-quality recording and capture, which allows investigators to zoom into detail and uncover ghostly presences, their ontology of mediation posits technology as an infrastructure for a sort of supernatural surveillance that treats invisible entities as things to be located in space (Auerbach, 2005).

On the other end of the spectrum, we have ultranaturalism, which can be found among réak performers and audiences. In réak, the technological apparatus (i.e., the audio recorder) works in a way much closer to a prosthesis and extension (Mcluhan and Fiore, 2008), opening worldwide channels of communication between humans and spirits, thus empowering the latter category through a transfer of agency; other technologies of réak—musical instruments, and the music itself—benefit from the sought-after transparency of HD recording and playback to activate supernatural processes.

By following these two models to their extreme, this text compares two approaches to decoding supernatural audio signals through systems of transmitting and receiving technologies, and theorises the overarching history of how both technological advancement and capitalist disenchantment have consistently sought to encroach upon the afterlife, the supernatural, and other invisible worlds through forms of control over signal and noise. All the while, practices like mediumship, paranormal phenomena, or altered states of consciousness have wrestled against this process of neoliberal assimilation and technological reterritorialisation.

The relationship between audio technology and the supernatural—and specifically, the world of the dead—has been a constant topic of exploration and speculation, which contribute to new technological auscultation and communication systems (Sterne, 2003). Since the Middle Ages, the invisibility of sound has been correlated with domains of existence beyond the visible, and linked to uncanny phenomena or more-than-human powers. In many cases, the impossibility of recognising a sound or its source has been linked to fantastical or supernatural beings like goblins, ghosts and witches (Kane, 2014: 82). The invention of telegraphy, and those of many other sonic technologies after it, have only strengthened the relationship between sound and the invisible, as the inherent uncanniness of an audio signal coming from an invisible, unidentifiable source (Potts, 2004) remains a constant challenge to visualist epistemologies.

Counterintuitively, the history of technological development has not extended disenchantment to the realm of sound; rather, it has opened up new pathways for the supernatural. This history arguably begins with three raps at the Fox family's modest cottage in Hydesville, near Rochester, New York. In 1848, during what became known as the Rochester Rappings, the family's sleep was disturbed by strange banging noises (Hegarty, 2019). Kate and Margaretta Fox replicated the sounds they heard, eliciting three unexplained raps as an apparent response. The spirit realm responded to the sisters' questions through a 'celestial cypher': knock once for 'yes' and twice for 'no' (three knocks allegedly implied 'don't know'). According to Jeffrey Sconce's *Haunted Media*: "with this exchange of words and knocks Kate Fox had opened a 'telegraph line' to another world, a wireless' spiritual telegraph" (Sconce, 2000). What's remarkable in this episode is that the first appearance of a signal-based system of communication between the natural-human and supernatural-ghostly occurs after the creation of the telegraph, and is referred to as 'spiritual telegraphy'.

Half a century later, on 12 December 1901, at the Marconi Poldhu Wireless Station in Cornwall, while trying to catch the first radio signal to be transmitted across the Atlantic, Guglielmo Marconi heard a familiar sound confirming the activity of the transmitter (Hegarty, 2019). The inventor's exceptional success story in overcoming the obvious technological limitations of the time was later disproved by researcher Pat Hawker (Margolis, 2001), who asserted that the supposed transatlantic transmission would have been impossible given the limited capacity of the equipment Marconi was using. Sebastiane Hegarty (2019), commenting on this episode, hypothesised that Marconi had "tuned into what he wanted to hear; perhaps the signal came not from Poldhu but from the labyrinths of his imagination or the auscultations of his listening"

Similarly, in 1920, Thomas Edison—inventor of another audio technology of communication across distance, the telephone—attempted to develop a 'spirit catcher' (Tablang, 2019): a recording device that could capture the voices of the dead by harvesting their sonic traces. These episodes are more than anecdotal: they demonstrate that, since the beginning of audio technologies, the drive to detect, interact, or capture unseen, spiritual and supernatural forces has been central to technological development, and always accompanied by the potential for self-deception through tricks of the human capacity for sonic imagination.

If these first attempts showed the possibility for audio technology to tap into signals sent from either spiritual presences in physical geographical locations or from more-than-human realms, such as the heavens or the underworld, it is with EVP (Electronic Voice Phenomena) that signal-based supernatural communication becomes consistently theorised. In 1959, while making a cassette recording of a Chaffinch singing in his yard, Freideric Jurgenson unintentionally picked up his deceased father's voice, which only became audible when the audio was reproduced. These spirit voices, which Friedrich Jürgenson and his disciple Konstantin Raudive picked up in their field recordings of empty rooms, actually expressed a preference for communicating via radio frequencies. Owing to their purportedly 'ethereal' characteristics, spirits have frequently been pursued on the radio frequency spectrum[4] by creating some form of feedback between various forms of transduction (Natale & Pasulka, 2019). Raudive claimed that radio was so popular on the other side of the physical world that "various groups of voice entities [...] operate their own stations" (Hegarty, 2020).

Two things become apparent from this history: the first is that new technological means of wireless communication were not just seen as something compatible with the dead, but also quite familiar to them. It would not be surprising if this ontological correlation between ghosts, spirits, and the supernatural with radio frequencies

---

4 Spectrum originates from the Latin and means "image" or "apparition". Spectral evidence is testimony regarding what spectres of people who are no longer physically present did, or hearsay evidence about what Satan's spirits or apparitions said. It was used to convict several people of witchcraft in Salem, Massachusetts, in the late 17th century. Goethe's *Theory of Colours* and Schopenhauer's *On Vision and Colours* both use the term "spectrum" (*Spektrum*) to refer to a ghostly optical afterimage. The term spectrum was initially used scientifically in optics to describe the rainbow of colours in visible light that passes through a prism, later expanding to encompass the full electromagnetic spectrum.

was linked not only to the naturalised connection between voice and the divine, but also reinforced by the coeval cult of electricity: an invisible, mysterious force that could be trapped and capitalised on for the first time (Potts, 2004). In this context, the 'objectively' efficient and scientific approach of transducing audio messages through a division between signal and noise led Raudive to imagine actual afterlife infrastructures of communication operating through a parallel system of ghost radio stations.

What is relevant to the present argument is that humans and ghosts communicate through identical physical principles and technological infrastructures. The only difference being that, ominously, it is humans who have to decide to open this channel and scan for signals.

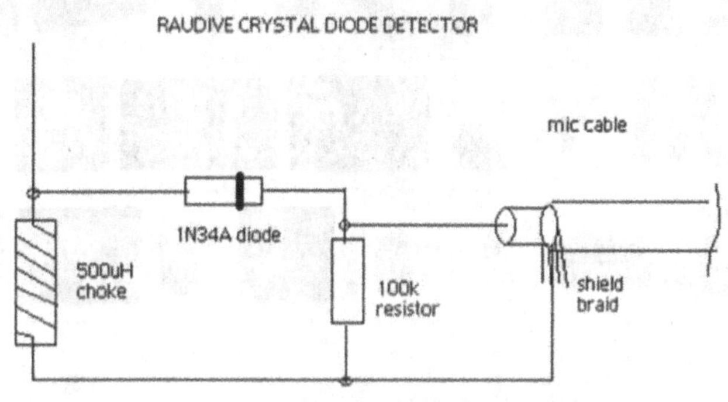

Raudive's diode project for the first EVP receiver system.

The most recent step in this long history of supernatural communication through audio technology is exemplified by the spirit box. In 2002, Frank Sumption, an EVP enthusiast, said that, after receiving design instructions from the spirit realm, he managed to build a gadget enabling real-time contact with the dead. The box, similar to a portable radio, is characterised as a hybrid white noise generator and an AM radio receiver modified to sweep back and forth across the AM frequency spectrum, choosing split-second sound snippets (Hill, 2010). Spirits are thought to communicate across various radio frequencies, so spirit boxes provide a platform for them to speak out. Typically, one will ask the spirits a question. If they are present and willing to communicate, they will engage with spirit boxes by momentarily stopping the sweep on one radio station to allow the human listener to hear a specific word or phrase. Again, this demonstrates how agency in supernatural communication through audio devices is mainly human-centred, with its purpose function being receiving answers. Digital audio technology, in this case, is the main mediator between humans and spirits, who have only one thing left to do: interfere with the gadget's frequency sweep.

Spirit boxes used to 'catch' EVP Phenomena.

A common thread woven through all these historical examples, as well as in *Tellurian Drama*, is that technological advancement in the realm of telecommunications has consistently developed alongside the demands of warfare, colonialism and imperial domination (Radano and Olaniyan, 2016). The capability to force—or at least nudge—the invisible to reveal itself is a much sought-after form of power.

We can see this logic in most examples of communication with the more-than-human through audio signals and technologies such as frequency filtering or scanning. When drawn into this kind of assemblage, spirits undergo a drastic reduction of their agency, which is limited to the possibility of responding to a signal or answering a question through a rather narrow set of pre-established formats: raps on walls, unclear utterances, technical interferences. The spirit's communicative act is consistently treated as an incomplete attempt, a snippet of audio detritus to be made understandable through technological processing and, eventually, useful for human interpretation.

Given this strict agential framework, it is not surprising that many instances of spirit communication are counterbalanced by cases of refusal, in which the spirit does not fall into the power of technology. The vast lore developing around spirits evading the revealing power of all-seeing (and all-hearing) technological devices (Behrend, 2015) offers a clear illustration of the hypernaturalist ethos of capture shared by paranormal researchers and spirit hunters, which refusal seeks to counteract. If agency is stacked on the human side of the equation, leaving the spirit with only limited room for frequency intervention, a refusal to engage and a retreat into the unnatural seem like appropriate responses.

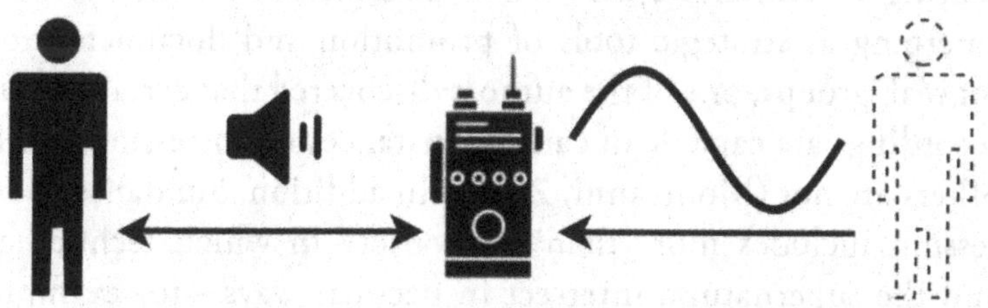

A diagram of the transmitter/receiver model in ghost hunting.

In contrast to ghost scanning and other forms of audio surveillance of the more-than-human, which are based on an fixation to make the invisible audible and which we have called hypernaturalism, the spirit mediumship augmented by audio technologies that can be found in réak reveals another way of *tuning oneself* into the spirit world, which we connect to a very different ultranaturalist model of listening.

Réak is a ceremonial musical performance for entertainment originating in West Java and popular in the outskirts of Bandung. The performance is staged during *hajatan*: events celebrating the milestones of the Sundanese-Muslim life cycle, such as circumcisions and weddings. During the event, an ensemble consisting of four single-skin cylindrical drums (*dogdog*) performs interlocking rhythms accompanied by a double-reeded aerophone (*tarompet*) and two additional percussion instruments: an idiophone, consisting of two or more stacked metal plates (*kecrek*), struck with a wooden hammer; and a timpano, struck by a drumstick (*bedug*). In réak, the ensemble accompanies phenomena of voluntary and induced possession coordinated by a trance master (*ma'alim*). The group, in which the performers take turns dancing and playing all instruments, is led by a leader (*pimpinan*) who, in addition to being in charge of the group, usually plays the *tilingtit*, the smallest drum of the dogdog ensemble, with which the tempo changes leading to the climax of the performances, and thus to possession, are decided. The leader and trance master jointly manage the musical flow deciding when tempo changes should occur, so that possession remains controlled (Monteanni, 2023).

During a research project on how audio-video technologies are emerging as strategic tools of promotion and documentation for réak groups, one of the authors discovered that certain audio recordings are capable of causing instances of possession, while others are not (Monteanni, 2024). In addition, Sundanese possession includes more than one variety in which technology and the supernatural intersect in peculiar ways—for example, in conceiving the connection between a human host and a spirit guest[5] as a relationship between souls, frequencies, and tunings.

Juarta Putra performing in Cibiru. Photo by Gigi Priadji.

When discussing possession with members of Juarta Putra—one of the founder groups of réak—they explained that among various types of spirit possession, the highest one is *surup/nyuryp,*[6] or 'tuning' (Monteanni, 2024). These Sundanese terms are normally used to refer to the tuning of musical instruments; in réak ensembles, each of the dogdog percussions has to be tuned (*disurupkeun*) so that it can play a specific intonation/note (*nada*). Guided by a trance master, the group can cause a state of possession only if both

5 Since the scope of this text is reduced to worldviews relating spirits, frequencies and tunings, we avoid analysing the behaviour and ontology of réak's other common category of spirits, the *jurig jarian*.

6 Synonyms. *Nyurup* being a more polite version in a language, Sundanese, with various levels of address changing on the basis of the relationships between speakers (age, class, etc.).

the instruments' tuning and the musical execution are perfect. As Anggi of Juarta Putra explains:

> *Surup* is like tuning. Like tuning a guitar. *Kasurupan* [possession] is caused by the tuned instruments. The dogdog [percussions] are all tuned. If not, they won't generate the necessary feeling in the people, or the dogdog will not have the frequency inside them [*tidak akan mempunyai frekuensi di dalam dogdog*], and thus won't cause any possession. If the dogdog's tuning is good, then the result is a frequency that can possess people.[7]

During possession, music *causes* both (a) the interest of the spirit/ancestor in participating in the performance by taking control of a body, and (b) the emotional overdrive of the human host leading to 'uniting with the spirit' (Monteanni, 2018). The emotional climax that brings together human and spirit—instantiated as possession—happens because of *one's soul resonating with the music's frequency*. This is not a physicalist explanation invoking resonance or sympathy. Whereas musical resonance is the phenomenon for which "a particle is subjected to an oscillating influence (such as an electromagnetic field) of such a frequency that a transfer of energy occurs or reaches a maximum" (Erlmann, 2015), possession happens, instead, because of genealogical, geographical and kinship relations. As local theories argue, specific arrangements of organised sound (rhythmic patterns, harmonic progressions, tunings, melodic structures), which are related to someone's ancestors, can connect with the person's soul and affect it until it 'becomes one' with the spirit. As Anggi of Juarta Putra also observes:

> It is important that the sound is recorded in the right way because the intonation [of our instruments] is very different from that of other groups. [Tuning] is a spiritually important

7 Interview, 26 March 2024.

> thing for us because it is about the music of our ancestors. If Mang Arip [member of Juarta Putra] gets possessed and there is an error in tuning or execution, the spirit will get angry. (Monteanni, 2024)

Here, the mention of recording emphasises how the ultranaturalist approach of réak does not idealise the liveness of performance versus its phonographic capture and reproduction; the only concern is with achieving a high enough quality so that the spiritually important component of tuning is not misrepresented. If the tuning is correctly captured, a réak performance can match a certain 'soul frequency' (*frekuensi jiwa*) and cause possession.

Through possession, the human body becomes both the receiver and the transmitter of the spirits' messages and agency. Spiritual communication during réak possession typically includes reassurances that one's relative is happy in the afterlife, recommendations of various kinds, and occasionally, even predictions and warnings. This sort of communication is framed in a larger system of exchange with the ancestors, during which they are honoured through gifts[8] for the protection that they continuously grant to the community. Communication flows in both ways, and every participant is allowed to take the role of transmitter or receiver. Once the ancestors feel satisfied, they ask to go 'back home' (*pulang/uih*) to the *alam gaib*, the invisible world inhabited by the spirits. An exorcism is carried out, and the human host returns to consciousness, usually forgetting every detail of the experience.

Let us repeat our main argument here: in réak, music is itself a technology, and its performance has a quite practical and defined outcome resulting from its use of ancestral frequencies and tunings: possession. But for the purposes of our essay, what interests us is how, as briefly mentioned in Anggi's interview, digital AV

---

8 E.g., cigarettes, coffee, tea, incense, eggs, etc., depending on the locations, specific communities and other factors.

technologies also play a part in this outcome, as not only live performances but also recordings of réak performances can cause the possession of the listener or spectator. And even more interestingly, what makes spirit possession possible through recordings is the *quality* of the audio: a proper musical performance—proper in the sense of both being executed without errors and being connected to the ancestors—when reproduced by a high-fidelity audio recording, honours the spirits, and thereby leads to possession. In this specific case, for music as a technology to successfully connect humans and supernatural entities, a sufficiently high-quality recording and playback infrastructure is necessary to transduce the performance's sonic elements: intonation, dynamics, tuning and rhythmic patterns, as well as the overall musical style of the ensemble.

In this sense, audio recording technologies are conceived in a radically different way than those of ghost hunters: not as devices playing the role of receiver and transmitter through feedback loops intensifying frequency inputs and outputs, but rather as repeaters and range amplifiers for spirit frequencies and their ancestral tunings. Both groups—ghost hunters and réak performers—push audio naturalism into unnatural domains while keeping its epistemological predilection for sonic realism.

But in one case, audio quality is the canvas that allows ghosts to manifest through interference; in the other, quality is necessary for the channelling of proper frequencies attuned to the ancestors. Going back to Rizaldi's speculative analysis of Radio Malabar, we could say that the agential power of spirits decreases as distance from their place of origin and belonging (the forest hamlet, the village, the mountain) increases. So, while it is true that music as technology is enough to cause spirit possession, recording and playback technologies are necessary to sustain and strengthen the reach and efficacy of this channelling process through sound reproduction (the possibility to listen to the music in different places at the same or different times), distribution (digital repositories and archives), and circulation (social media and digital sound devices). Thanks to high-definition audio, these technological media are capable of pulling together the assemblage of réak activities (performance, listening, etc.), making possessions possible even thousands of kilometres from the musicians' geographical origin and the spirits' dwelling place.

In réak and similar models of possession practices, the basic ontology of communication and interaction between human and non-human agents is configured as a system of horizontal encounters and open-ended dialogical exchanges. While, in the case of ghost hunters, supernatural entities are only expected to respond or refuse to engage in a transactional communication initiated by humans, in réak the body of the host itself is offered as a receiver and transmitter of the ancestor's agency. For ghost hunters, audio technology opens up communication channels through processing routines like noise reduction, signal decoding or spectrum sweeping; for réak performers, audio technologies are an amplifying prosthesis and a range extender, not a *conditio sine qua non* for spirit communication.

In the first case, the possibility of communication with supernatural entities is premised on both the epistemological symmetry between human and more-than-human mediation and on the revelatory power of *noise management*. In the second case, music is itself the technology through which a human body becomes the communication medium, and signal processing can help sustain this process. It is not by chance that, in EVP frequency spectrum scanning, listening to the spirit world depends entirely on fetching snippets of voices amidst the audio debris of white noise generators, dead air and empty radio frequencies; vocal intelligibility emerges from a process of refinement and purification of the signal. Conversely, in réak, human-spirit communication is *lossless*: firstly, because it comes directly from the ancestor through the human host's body; and secondly, because it is remediated through the high-fidelity vector of sound recording technology.

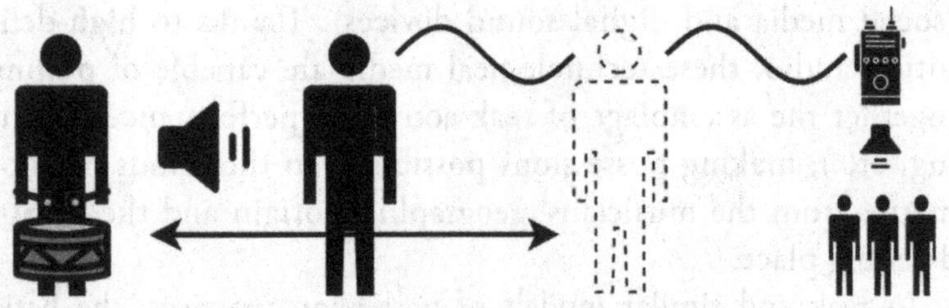

A diagram of the transmitter/receiver model in réak.

At this point, it is important to note that the Sundanese human-spirit communication system relying on tuning and frequency is not native to the archipelago. As a matter of fact, the word '*frekuensi*' (frequency) itself is a rather recent addition to the Indonesian language—a clear semantic loan from a foreign technical vocabulary indexing the influence of Western scientific development and 'modernist' ideologies of technology on local ontologies. What is interesting in the case of réak is that even a technical concept like frequency, with its aura of material mechanicism and quantification, can be deployed by two groups as a component of diametrically opposed models of the supernatural.

Spirit mediumship and music-caused possession have existed across the globe long before the emergence of modern audio technologies; with the introduction of devices like radios, amplifiers and recorders, the naturalist ideology of objectivity that accompanied their global journeys has been spun into very different models of listening. Our sketch of a comparison between ghost hunters and réak performers illustrates how two of these models incorporate audio naturalism in their approach to the supernatural, reconfiguring concepts such as interference, fidelity and quality for their own practical purposes: talking to ghosts or channelling spirits.

Both of these examples problematise the assumption that audio naturalism is necessarily correlated to a "metaphysics of presence" (Sterne, 2003). In spirit hunting, the role of signal opacity is subverted and reconfigured as a naturalist reterritorialisation of the supernatural: the otherworldly domain of ghosts is imagined to function according to the same physical principles of the world of the living. In looking for presences beyond the metaphysical world, frequency scanners take the residual interferences caused by signal loss and quality degradation (hiss, static, hum) and focus on them as puzzle pieces to be demodulated into clear snippets of communication. We called this model hypernaturalism: an approach to the supernatural that extends naturalistic ideologies of sound into the more-than-human, by assuming that corresponding analytical categories can be translated one-to-one. In this sense, it is not surprising that the hypernaturalist emphasis on the signal-to-noise ratio, on the transduction of interference into messages and on the capture of evidence, maps neatly onto the empirical fixation on proving that ghosts are, in fact, real.

In opposition, réak exemplifies what we call ultranaturalism. Just like ghost hunters, réak musicians are also seduced by the allure of high-fidelity audio, operating under the assumption that a high-quality recording of a performance is capable of not only perfectly reproducing music, but also of channelling the power of supernatural entities. Their audio naturalism pushes realism in another direction: that of efficacy. Differently than in dub music, where the term 'dub' echoes both the duppy—the floating ghost of Jamaican cultures (Weheliye, 2005)—and the dubbing process leading to a spectral audio doppelgänger, which is similar but other from its original version (Boellstorff, 2006), réak's audio replicas are assumed to be identical (or as close as possible) to their live execution. But in contrast to the audio naturalist's fixation, this fidelity is not sought after for the human listener: it is the very condition of possibility for channelling spirit possession. If a recording is of sufficient quality to reproduce the frequencies and tunings accurately enough, listeners are transformed into receivers and transmitters, extending the reach of the spirit world into the human one. In contrast to ghost hunters, here the fixation on realism is a means for the more-than-human to encroach upon the human. Audio technologies are not necessary for communicating with spirits, since music and human bodies are already enough—all it can contribute is an expansion of this communication's reach in space and time.

In the 19th century, scientists postulated the existence of the ether: a universal substance that acted as the medium for both the transmission of electromagnetic waves[9] and the existence of invisible entities (Potts, 2004). Newton argued that only an undetectable medium like ether could explain 'remote action', or the influence of an object on another at a distance—encompassing planets, radio waves, or poltergeists (Maiocchi, 1999). The functions of ether extended to consciousness, which was theorised to be made up of unseen yet tangible vibrations radiating from the brain into a diffusion medium (Enn, 2008).

Colonial writer Rudyard Kipling's 1904 short story *Wireless* exemplifies the overlaps between these heterogeneous attributes of ether. Recounted by an anonymous narrator, *Wireless* tells the story of two apothecaries: Mr Shaynor, an apothecary, and Mr Cashell, a gent with an amateur interest in wireless telegraphy. As the story goes, the narrator prepares a strong liquor to treat Shaynor's cough, who passes out shortly after downing it. Meanwhile, Cashell is busy in the room next door building a radio to exchange Morse code signals with a friend using a similar device miles away. Unfortunately, Cashell is unable to contact his friend, instead receiving transmissions from two ships in the English Channel, who can successfully transmit messages but cannot receive them. Suddenly, the intoxicated Shaynor begins to channel John Keats' poetry. The two miscommunications are resolved, with Cashell eventually contacting his peer and Shaynor waking up. When questioned by the narrator about his poetry recitation, Shaynor affirms that he had never read any of Keats' poetry.

A key theme in *Wireless* is an unpredictable, unexplainable mixing of the spiritual and material, which is precipitated by the

9 Read more at Britannica; https://www.britannica.com/science/ether-theoretical-substance.

development and use of radio and wireless technologies (Rufo, 2005). In the story, the Morse code radio channels and amplifies exchanges already happening between humans and spirits. This argument for remote action reflects a belief in an overlap between the capacities of radio frequencies, brain waves and spiritual entities—a model of communication that resonates with the relational assemblages of humans, spirits and technologies expressed by réak.

From Rizaldi's *Tellurian Drama* to Kipling's *Wireless*, and from ghost hunters to réak musicians, we have been concerned with mapping the shifting relationship between the natural and the supernatural as it is shaped and reconfigured by different forms of technological mediation. As we hope to have demonstrated, the prevalence of sonic naturalism—the assumption that sound constitutes a somewhat transparent form of mediation and that high-fidelity reproduction can reproduce reality to a certain extent—does not necessarily correlate to a specific relationship to the more-than-human. In fact, the two examples we discuss in this chapter exemplify two diverging, and perhaps opposite trajectories of audio naturalism as it is confronted with the supernatural. We have called these hypernaturalism and ultranaturalism, and we maintain that these are not mere reflections of temporal or geographical differences; rather than past/future or East/West divides, we want to draw attention to how sonic epistemologies are constantly made and unmade.

The surveillance epistemology underpinning EVP scanning and ghost hunting is not the only possible way of approaching the supernatural through audio technologies; as réak demonstrates, music can in itself be a technology, the listener can become a channel, and audio devices can become spirit prostheses. This essay offers a speculative provocation: much more work in comparing models of listening beyond sonic naturalism and human-centred listening will be needed to further deconstruct both a metaphysics of presence in audio as well as more ontological distinctions between concepts such as sound, noise, or signal.

In the meantime, we have to keep in mind that understanding how we listen to the more-than-human and how the more-than-human listens back to us—through topographical features, technological infrastructures, spiritual frequencies, supernatural tunings, and much more—can shed light (or, perhaps, dispel the silence) around yet uncharted depths of our own all too human auscultations. To radio waves, we are ghosts.

Acknowledgements

The authors would like to thank Juarta Putra, Harry Koi, Alberto Ricca, Riar Rizaldi, Lorenzo Chiarofonte, Teguh Permana, all the visible and invisible spirits, the ancestors and audio technologies.

References

Behrend, H. (2015) "Spaces of Refusal: Photophobic Spirits and the Technical Medium of Photography", in Id. et al. (eds) *Trance Mediums and New Media: Spirit Possession in the Age of Technical Reproduction*: 201–220. New York: Fordham University Press.

Bodanis, D. (2005) *Electric Universe: The Shocking True Story of Electricity.* New York: Crown Pub.

Boellstorff, T. (2006) *The Gay Archipelago: Sexuality and Nation in Indonesia.* Princeton, NJ: Princeton University Press.

de Seta, G. (2018) "Against Sonic Naturalism", *Paranom-Asia.* Text available at <http://paranom.asia/2018/06/against-sonic-naturalism/> [accessed 20 April 2023].

Elmann, V. (2015). "Resonance". In D. Novak & M. Sakakeeny (eds), *Keywords in Sound:* 175–182. Duke. University Press.

Enns, A. (2008) "Psychic Radio: Sound Technologies, Ether Bodies and Spiritual Vibrations". *The Senses and Society* 3(2): 137–152.

Frohlick, S., & Macevicius, C. (2023). "Listening otherwise: From 'silent tourism' soundscapes to privileged sonic ways of knowing". *Tourist Studies*, 23(2), 149–173. https://doi.org/10.1177/14687976231171713

Hegarty, S. (2019, Dec 19) "Tapping the air: ghosts, landscape and technology". *Sebastiane Hegarty: an audio-visual notebook.* D1wqtxts1xzle7. https://nikomas.memoryoftheworld.org/#/book/2cc1fccb-7d8a-48bb-9879-9a8fa4e324ee

Hegarty, S. (2020) "'Nothing here now…'" *Sebastian Hegarty.* https://sebastianehegarty.wordpress.com/2020/06/22/nothing-here-now/

Hill, A. (2010) *Paranormal Media: Audiences, Spirits and Magic in Popular Culture.* London: Routledge.

Kane, B. (2014). *Sound Unseen. Acousmatic Sound in Theory and Practice.* New York: Oxford Academic.

Kipling, R. (1904) *Traffics and Discoveries.* London: Macmillan.

Latour, B., & Porter, C. (1993) *We have never been Modern.* Cambridge, MA: Harvard University Press.

Maocchi, R. (1999) *Storia della scienza in Occidente. Dalle origini alla bomba atomica.* Venice: La Nuova Italia.

Margolis, L. (2001) "Faking the Waves". *The Guardian.* https://www.theguardian.com/education/2001/dec/11/highereducation.news

McLuhan, M., Fiore, Q., & Agel, J. (2008) *The Medium is the Massage.* London: Penguin.

Monteanni, L. (2018). *L'intrattenimento sacro: per un'analisi della danza sundanese del cavallo* [Master thesis, Bologna University].

—. (2020). "Il réak di Bandung tra rituale cerimoniale e intrattenimento popolare: una tradizione contemporanea sundanese". *Antropologia E Teatro. Rivista Di Studi,* 11(12), 29–41. https://doi.org/10.6092/issn.2039-2281/10883

—. (2023) "'More Metal than Metal': Preliminary Reflections on Imagined Geographies". *Brief Encounters* 1(7). doi: https://doi.org/10.24134/be.v7i1.3

—. (2024). "Gli antenati in playback: la mediazione di kasenian réak nelle tecnologie audio-video e i social network". In L. Chiarofonte (ed.), *Musica e incontro con gli spiriti. Vol 2: media digitali:* 45–64. Nota Editore.

Natale, S., & Pasulka, D. (2019) "Believing in Bits: Digital Media and the Supernatural". Online: Oxford Scholarship Online. DOI:10.1093/oso/9780190949983.003.0001

Novak, D., & Sakakeeny, M. (2015) *Keywords in Sound.* Durham: Duke University Press.

Potts, J. (2004) "Ghosthunting in the Twenty-first Century". In Houran, J. *From Shaman to Scientist: Essays on Humanity's Search for Spirits*: 211–232. Lanham: Rowman & Littlefield.

Radano, R. M., & Olaniyan, T. (2016) *Audible Empire: Music, Global Politics, Critique*. Durham: Duke University Press.

Rizaldi, R. (2020) *Tellurian Drama*. Jakarta: Jordan Édition

Rufo, K. (2005) "Ghosts in the Medium: The Haunting of Heidegger's Technological Question". *Explorations in Media Ecology*, 4(1), 21–48. doi:10.1386/eme.4.1.21_1

Sconce, J. (2000) *Haunted Media: Electronic Presence from Telegraphy to Television*. Durham: Duke University Press.

Spiller, H. (2020) *Sudanese Dance and Masculinity in West Java*. Chicago: University of Chicago Press.

Sterne, J. (2003) *The Audible Past: Cultural Origins of Sound Reproduction*. Durham: Duke University Press.

Sumantri, M. (1985). Kamus Sunda-Indonesia. Pusat Pembinaan dan Pengembangan Bahasa, Departemen Pendidikan dan Kebudayaan.

Tabling, K. (2019) "Thomas Edison, B.C. Forbes and the Mystery of the Spirit Phone". *Forbes*. https://www.forbes.com/sites/kristintablang/2019/10/25/thomas-edison-bc-forbes-mystery-spirit-phone/?sh=61b622d629ad

Thacker, E. (2011). *In the Dust of This Planet: Horror of Philosophy. Vol. 1*. London: Zer0 Books.

13. SOUND FICTIONS. NOISE, ECHOES, FEEDBACK

By Stefan Paulus

Introduction

> "*...the steam engine runs all day long, the wheels, belts and spindles purr and rattle in his ears, and if he wants to rest for just a moment, he immediately has the supervisor with the punishment book behind him. This condemnation to being buried alive in the factory, to constant attention to the tireless machine, is perceived by the workers as the hardest torture. But it also has the most deadening effect, as much on the body as on the mind of the worker.*"
>
> — Engels (1972: 397f)

The narcotic drone of machines in factories since early capitalism has been enhanced in late capitalism by the clattering of keyboards and the unwanted listening to business talk in open-plan offices. Workers are familiar with the effects of the unwanted sounds of work noise, which range from psychological effects such as anger and reduced concentration to psychosomatic illnesses caused by noise stress. The effects of noise stress certainly depend on intensity, exposure time and frequencies, but the degree of adaptation, dulling and lethargy can also make work noise bearable or not. The undesirable developments of the capitalist mode of production can thus be found not only in the exploitation of people and their nature, but also in the design of soundscapes. The coupling of work tasks through a soundscape—for example, through the beeping and vibrating noises of digital feedback mechanisms on smartphones, laptops or wristbands—not only increases mechanised access to people's attention and their cognitive capacities; such feedback, triggered by error messages, requests, likes, etc., also produces requests for action, which can increase stress in a dynamic feedback loop of stimulus-response (Paulus, 2023a).

"You don't need science fiction", writes Gilles Deleuze in his *Postscript on Control Societies* (1992: 261), to imagine electronic neckbands that not only control people's position, but also their actions. Even on the radio, TV, social media, in the supermarket, in the parking garage, there is constant babbling and attempts to control everywhere; in the babbling of pop music, the songs of praise for products or services in advertising, there are invocations everywhere to recognise a certain symbolically structured and structuring capitalist order.

Ultimately, the aim is to create a memory for people, a memory of identity-stabilising meanings of the self as a consumer, as a citizen, a memory of "signs and no longer of effects" (Deleuze & Guattari 1977: 184). Again, it does not take science fiction to imagine how such content slowly accumulates in individuals and how they are conditioned by the soundscapes of recreational and cultural industries. Recognising the opening melody of an advertising anthem triggers a stimulus: thoughts of beer, pizza, cars. Perhaps this is why sound fictions are needed in order to imagine what a soundscape sounds like beyond being buried alive, beyond industrially coded patterns of perception and aesthetically conditioned sensations.

To address this question regarding a non-ontological perception of reality, it is therefore necessary to create fictions that describe the beyond, the in-between, the other. François Laruelle's concept of non-standard aesthetics and their associated philo-fictions can be used for this purpose. At the heart of his concept of non-standard aesthetics is the assumption that a phenomenon cannot be identified through existing interpretations, or by means of ontological distinctions or aesthetic concepts, as such epistemological processes lead to images, copies or duplications of experiences, terms and concepts. Copies allow the phenomenon to become a clone of reality, a fetishist realism. Instead, the reversal of this order can be made possible by means of a non-standard aesthetic. The means for this are philo-fictions or hyperspeculations, philosophical hallucinations, fictional characterisations (Laruelle, 1989: 239f); experiments with hypothetical assumptions and conjectures that go beyond tangible reality in order to be able to found a life of their own—independently of common scientific or philosophical assumptions (Laruelle, 2014: 22f). Such a rejection of interpretation, this non-standardised aesthetics of phenomena, also means a rejection of found justifications of what is perceived, because cognition is not traced back to existing codings (Laruelle, 2014: 67; Gadamer, 1999: 274). Laruelle's concept of non-standard aesthetics can thus be used to describe in detail the process of appropriating reality via a "standardised" (onto-senso-logical) and "non-standardised" (non-onto-senso-logical) perception (Laruelle, 2014: 13, 57ff).

In relation to the image-based world—e.g., in the photorealism of passport photos, product photos (fashion, food, cars), etc.—representations of the world are created, which function as copies of reality. These copies help to organise the perception of reality in such a way that it becomes an incontestably fixed idea, because images take the place of the real. With such an onto-photo-logical perception, one observes the real itself through a photograph—not the object, but a representation of an identity (Laruelle, 2014: 43; Paulus, 2023b). Accordingly, onto-photo-logical perception has a symbolic dimension: it is not based on the voluntary decision to interpret an object, but on the pre-reflective classification of what is seen. It is based on memories that classify what is seen and make it identical with reality. This in turn leads to the problem that we become incapable of discovering new things, creative processes, the becoming in the world, because we are trying to discover the known in the unknown.

The same can be applied to other sensory perceptions. Hearing, for example, is based on a subjectivity that leads to auditory experiences being evaluated by given meanings. Hearing a certain sound can represent a certain situation, identity, reality, trigger a certain memory, a stimulus-reaction, which classifies, categorises and determines what is heard accordingly (Holzkamp, 1983).

Experimentation with fictions plays a role in the perception of a non-onto-logical perception—an "as well as" or an "as-if" representation (Vaihinger, 1986). By means of philo-fiction, the generic science of hyperspeculation and contradictory assumptions, phenomena can be de-subjectivised and subtractions can be made from the material (Laruelle, 1989: 230). The term "generic" can be used to describe a practice that does not aim to produce the specific, but instead produces models and hypotheses that remain philosophically indeterminate as indeterminants (Laruelle, 2013: 69ff). Since fictional statements are neither true nor false, but can be thought "as-if" in order to develop—through indeterminacies, theses, antitheses—a complex of possibilities that need not be unique or original, the results can remain open in the synthesis, since they can always be de-subjectivised and subtracted in the sense of philo-fiction (Laruelle, 2014: 142ff).

In the following, the experimentation with philo-fictions is transferred to hearing and the effects of sounds and soundscapes. The central assumption of non-standard aesthetics that sound fictions do not produce copies of the world, but rather indeterminants and unilateralisations, also applies to sound fictions. Sound fictions are therefore to be understood as practices that:

1. perform theoretical operations to produce soundscapes in the context of a radical immanence (Laruelle, 2013: 165f);
2. develop their own non-auto-positional rules to suspend an industrial-cultural authority of interpretation;
3. adopt a chaotic universe of multiple "as-if" representations (Laruelle, 1998: 99).

In the following, the process is described of how this variable, multiple, and at the same time, the only thing in sounds—the all-connecting, the one-in-one, the not-one; "(Non)-One" (Laruelle, 1989: 97f)—can be recognised as such. For this purpose, the following procedure is outlined:

First, in the examination of sound fictions, techniques and practices are described for obtaining or producing acoustic sound fictions (§1), in order to identify subsequently the effect of sound fictions by means of hyperspeculations (Laruelle, 1989: 99, 235ff) (§2). In an open synthesis, the aim of this approach is to describe sound fictions as simulators of reality, as non-onto-senso-logical scenarios of reality (§3).

i. Production of sound fiction

A non-standard technique of producing an acoustic phenomenon begins by "distinguishing the ideal appearance and the empirical appearance by removing the object-form itself" (Laruelle, 2014: 60). The removal of the object form or the representation of a sound can be produced by isolating an element, by decontextualisation, or by artistic techniques such as masking, stretching, morphing with effects, as well as by n-fold superimpositions/superpositions. Sound assemblages and soundscapes, in particular, offer the possibility of both defusing the empirically ascertainable in its object-form and diffusing the sensory perception of it.

The term soundscape encompasses more than individual sound events, such as a singing bird in the forest, but refers to the orchestration and composition of diverse sound events as an assemblage of noises (Paulus, 2023b). As soundscapes always contain compositional elements—which microphone, which distance, which weather atmosphere influences the recording?—they also have the status of fiction, in that they already negotiate different modes of factuality and factitiousness through unconscious distortions in recordings of phenomena, or in deliberately set fictitious, contradictory or false representations of reality. Instead of translating scientific findings about phenomena into philosophical analogies when analysing such soundscapes—the bird in the forest sings because…, or this particular songbird does not have its habitat by the ocean, etc.—the experimental non-philosophical work does not interfere with a particular scientific theory, but models it in favour of the principle of inner self-similarity, in which recurring structures and objects of fractalisation can emerge, creating an open ensemble, a universe of fractal knowledge of transversal connections.

To understand the function of the bird's twittering, I have to become a bird. I can only become a bird if I become not-me. If I am not-me, then I am outside of me. If I am outside of me, then the inside is empty, because there is nothing inside of me when I try to put myself into what I am on the outside. If I have the outside inside and I can be on the outside, then everything is in everything and everything becomes everything. Being everything is in every being, etc. (cf. Laing, 1972: 88f).

Such artistic as well as non-philosophical experiments with sound objects have the property of withdrawing the onto-senso-logical causality from the object-forms by mixing and merging the sound objects (Paulus, 2021). This can create an epistemological and sensual in-between, a non-standard aesthetic, as a space of possibility for imagination and experience. This means that connections and diffusions of sounds can be used as artistic, as well as non-philosophical, means to identify sound phenomena in the context of a radical immanence, to bring about a change in sensual cognition and to produce a chaotic universe of multiple "as-if" representations. With the medium of the material, it is thus possible "to wrest the percept from the perceptions of an object and states of a perceiving subject, to wrest the affect from the affections as the transition of one state into another. To extract a block of sensations, a pure being of sensation" (Deleuze & Guattari, 1996: 196).

Such partial controllability of the conditions and meanings of perception are indeed pre-structured by social meanings and individual experiences, but the partial controllability simultaneously opens up the possibility of recognising the constructedness of the perceptions and their social integration. A chain of communication is inherent in the process of meaning: from sensory experience to imagination, to memory, to thought (Deleuze 2007: 189). Sound fictions can thus produce an inner listening, an audition-within-one, by detaching objects from their peculiar sound or original territory and identifying them through their own non-auto-positional rules in order to emerge the sound in a single surface, with each sound element becoming a transversal component of another (Laruelle, 2014: 67ff; Deleuze & Guattari, 1977: 406, 437f, 505).

The artistic production of a sound fiction is therefore nothing special. Sound fictions can be produced with field recordings, a sampler, a VST host or a mixing console. However, it is more difficult to reach sound spheres that are not determined by industrial-cultural sounds and stimulate specific perception patterns. This is basically a pataphysical endeavour: "One must play death off against death" (Baudrillard, 1991: 12f.); i.e., one must play off being buried alive in the company, the factory, the family, the state, in all these enclosure milieus, against the danger of falling from heights, of wandering on ridge lines, between boulders, water, mudflows, on firn crests and sedimentary rock, against drowning in oceans or dying of thirst in deserts, lurking in the undergrowth, in a hollow, in caves, against the sudden "transition into an empty space that is not anyone's thinking" (Baudrillard, 2002; Paulus, 2022). Until one then hears insects, water molecules, winds, frictions; the raw, intense of one's own nature, the pulsation and roar of the internal; listening to or understanding sound fiction through a non-standard aesthetic requires that a soundscape of empty space be treated as an entity in its own right, removing representations and object references and not confusing the essence of the composition "with the conditions of existence in perception, in the history of styles and the development of techniques" (Laruelle, 2014: 14). Instead of imagining non-civilisational soundscapes as a fetishistic realism based on a perceptual objectivity of things, fed by memories from the zoo, mountaineering films, etc., sound fiction is the reversal of this order. It is not the soundscape that reproduces realities, but the experience of non-civilised sound spheres that simulate as-if realities.

ii. Hyperspeculations

If one now wishes to identify indeterminants by means of the support of sound fiction, listening experiences are examined below for epistemological fictions and fractality in order to be able to remove ontological monocausalities and multiply meanings. With a view to the sensory perception of auditory experiences, and in accordance with the description of this, experiments are first carried out at the level of the acoustic perception of sounds (sense of hearing), and then at the level of the acoustic experience of the localisation of representations (sense of space), in order to provide feedback to the previously established theses and antitheses on the sense of hearing and sense of space in an open synthesis.

a) Sense of hearing: the noise

Hearing is not a purely cerebral process in which one can simply identify linguistically the meaning of what is heard; rather, hearing begins with a fundamental encounter with the outside that penetrates the inside. In the seemingly subjective origin of perception, social conditions emerge as the basis of an individual-centred, psychologising meaning of the environment, which strengthens the falseness of selective thinking that is primarily oriented towards sensory experience and, in relation to the perception of the environment, becomes mentally reproducible as conscious knowledge. This means that perception is a "making it true" (Holzkamp, 1973: 34) and frequencies are assigned an identity. However, when sound objects and their frequencies emerge through superimposition and diffusion in a single sound, a noise arises: a disturbance in the identification of an object due to unspecified frequency spectra.

If it is now also assumed that matter is not a passive substance that is only brought into existence through the intentionality of the listener, but through co-construction (Haraway, 1995) or intra-action, this means that an agency of matter and the existence of independent entities can be assumed (Barad, 2012a). With this assumption, we can further speculate about a flat ontology of sound objects as a model for an acoustic reality, in which sounds do not stand in hierarchical relationships to each other, but rather influence each other in assemblages of organic and inorganic sounds (Bennett, 2010).

Phenomenologically, the perception of sounds is interesting insofar as they can be understood as intra-acting agents (Barad, 2012b: 19), which are ontologically intertwined with the perceivers and thus limit the production of meaning itself. Sound objects are created "without realism and external determinism" (Laruelle, 2014: 167). In contrast to the "dual system experience" of opposites in auditory perception—such as loud/quiet, highs/lows, etc.—disturbances of ontological determinacies arise in the transversal connections and diffusions.

Noise can thus be understood as a sound fiction, as a "listening device for immanence", in that boundaries between nature/culture, man/machine, sense/matter, cognition/reality are disturbed and the auditory experience is oriented towards the mingling of matter, individuals, the dead and the living, entities and emergences. New qualities develop in the noise: as an indifference of forms arises, the noise masks the idea of the real and an in-between arises in the coupling of sensations, in that imprecise determinations, unreflected, spontaneous or phenographic meanings (Holzkamp, 1976: 21), and indistinguishability arise. This does not result in copies or codes, but in their dissolution. What remains—or rather, the materialisation of the noise—gives rise to ambiguous percepts. The lack of signal completion forces the listener to complete an imagined image. The noise makes the clear sound object disappear in favour of the things that draw attention to themselves in the listener's imagination through the disturbing frequencies. This in turn creates the non-copyable, and the non-copyable brings out the contingency (Deleuze & Guattari, 2000: 109f). The fades and transversal connections in the noise initiate a non-standard perception that is porous enough to explore infinite spaces of possibility with infinite possibilities, whereby their parts in turn become a unity: distribution surfaces, intersections of all sound forms, whose dimensions increase with the multiplicities of the singularities they intermingle. This means that, in noise, everything multiple becomes one as an infinity of modifications.

It would be worth considering further whether precisely this property of the non-onto-logical auditory experience, the dissolution of coding, the experience of the One-in-All, the phenographic and directional effect of sound brings another ego into the world, which becomes capable of transcending into immanence without remembering the real.

b) Sense of space: the echo

Everyday perception attempts to find the familiar in the unfamiliar by comparing and reproducing the ideas of reality stored in memory. This is also the case with spatial perception. Spatial perception concerns the phenomenon that, depending on a person's point of view and distance from the object, orientation and a description of the spatial dimensions become possible.

This means that the perception of spatial relations is established as the localisation of one's own body in relation to objects. Stereoscopic vision, spatial depth, shadows, visual angles and the perception of relative sizes support the comparison of objects. Even a non-Euclidean perception of space can be experienced via the sense of sight (e.g., tesseract, 4D hypercube). In this respect, visual perception can be used to develop a spatial ontology of fields of meaning that causes the functional ontological difference between fields of meaning and objects, and individuates objects as functional specifications (Gabriel, 2016: 326).

For the acoustic perception of space, the echo, as an echo of the familiar in the unfamiliar, serves as an orientation for developing a spatial order. An echo occurs when, for example, reflections of one's own voice are delayed by a room in such a way that they can be perceived as an independent auditory event. An echo has the same pitch but becomes less strong over time. This makes it possible to recognise room sizes, distances and the nature of rooms (a ravine has a different echo than a cave). But what can be heard when there is no echo?

In Earth's atmosphere, the gaseous envelope of the Earth's surface, wind penetrates and crosses space in an indeterminate way, without fixed barriers, boundaries or hierarchies. Stratospheric winds blow chaotically, continuously, immanently, silently, because they do not encounter any objects without interruption and inexplicably change direction without any higher order or superordinate control. Only with different air masses, air pressures, when winds hit dust particles, airplanes, birds, blow through narrow gaps, around obstacles or through trees and plants, do frictions and vibrations arise that become audible sound waves. When wind hits the ego and its body, it becomes directly present in the sensory field and manifests itself as noise, whistling, hissing, crackling, howling, pressure or spatial resistance. Wind can also cause objects or structures to vibrate—it moves trees, shapes landscape, creates sounds—but wind itself is noiseless, formless, invisible, and the wind kills every echo.

The wind is therefore the perfect sound fiction. Wind offers a multi-sensory spatial experience that is not limited to the sense of hearing, but includes synesthetic experiences as it penetrates sensory openings, and can itself cause body molecules to vibrate. The body thus becomes the wind's resonance chamber. If the echo, the reverberation of the object-forms of the world, is no longer in the foreground of the experience, but rather the experience of the boundless, formless, endless that passes through without echo, a borderline experience with the ego also arises, because the perception of the boundless, formless and endless dissolves the sensually tangible. Listening to empty space harbours the infinite possibilities of encounters with everything. If sound objects are no longer in the foreground of the experience, but the emergent of the boundless, formless and endless, a borderline experience with the ego also arises, because the simulation of the absolute unknown bursts the sensually tangible. In this state of de-spatialisation and desubjectification, there is not one truth, one code, but n-numbered experiences, whose manifold and infinite reflections become superimpositions, the infinite, a total irrealism or independent auditions of the One (Laruelle, 1989: 114).

If no ontological distinctions or aesthetic concepts are used in sound fictions in order to find an image or a doubling of the world in sound, then a rejection of the interpretation of what is heard as an echo of the world also means a rejection of the justification of what is perceived. A sound fiction, like a photo fiction, is not a technique, but a conception of the nature of sound and the practice that results from the erasure of the mode of representation (Laruelle, 2014: 12, 67). It is an experiment that consists not in receptively taking in and processing what is heard, but in letting it act directly and molecularly, as a unique experience, as part of a comprehensive creative dimension in a state of emergence that is "constantly upstream and ahead of itself" and thereby develops an emergent capacity that "grasps the contingency and the contingencies of all the projects of transforming immaterial universes into being" (Guattari, 2014: 129). Just as photo-fiction is seeing with closed eyes, "through which we take the excessive measure of the world and master the intensity of its hallucinatory sight" (Laruelle, 2014: 152), sound fiction is listening with closed ears in order to allow the soundless and formless, the inaudible, to resonate within us.

iii. Open synthesis: the feedback loop

By the standards of non-standard aesthetics, sound fictions are not copies or duplicates of sound objects, but signals that enable unilateral events because object-forms are removed (Laruelle, 2014: 60). In this respect, the aim of speculations on auditory experiences is to contribute to the representation of the one-in-one, the non-identical, the radical immanence (Laruelle, 1989: 70f), in order to construct models for a reality in which elements and substances are not in hierarchical relationships to one another but can connect transversally n-fold in structures. In contrast to the sound clone of the real (nature recordings, audio samples, samples, genre music), many realities penetrate a single surface in artistic or epistemological sound fictions. The pervasive is not transparent or transcended by the other, only to be perceived again as a copy; the non-onto-logical aesthetic filters out ontological determinacies by creating sounds or concepts that identify the appearance of the world in its deterministic relationship. It does not overdetermine objective appearance, but under- or indeterminate it (Laruelle, 2014: 140ff).

Noise as transversal connections and as a disruption of pre-coded cognitive processes refers to the speculation that different elements are connected and can influence each other, even if they are not ontologically related. In a state of noise or in noise, the basic building blocks of reality interact with each other, such that their properties and states are not clearly separated from each other but are rather in a superposition of several possible states. Superpositions open up a multitude of new experiences: new not because experiences are encoded with new meanings, but because hearing or recognising something new itself becomes a process of giving meaning. Thus, subject and object, hearer and what is to be heard, can no longer be clearly separated. The listeners are part of the audible and the audible is part of the listeners.

This means that different properties or states can exist simultaneously in the noise, and are fused together, or opposite properties are present at the same time, emphasising the instability of meanings and identities. In this sense, noise can be seen as the simultaneous presence of several properties, as a kind of intermediate state in which different processes are fed back. Noise becomes an expression of indeterminacy and unpredictability, as it contains various possible events, and their continuation is not clearly determined. In materialisations of noise, the real therefore does not appear as an onto-senso-logical appropriation, as a copy of the outside world, but as an agentive disturbance within the ontological and semantic indeterminacy inherent to the phenomenon (Barad, 2012b: 20). The abolition of onto-senso-logical perception thus leads to the abolition of the pre-reflexive classification of what is heard, which classifies what is heard and makes it identical with reality.

If artistic or epistemological sound fictions are now not limited to imitating the real—musical genres, etc.—but develop on an absolute level—not in the form of sound objects, echoes, imaginations, etc., which produce phantoms or doubles, but as a structureless or formless plan of immanence, as a disorganisation of sounds, as a perception of the degrees of transition in the molar structure, as a perception of communication contents that reveal empty spaces (Deleuze & Guattari, 1992: 387f)—then sound fictions also become a "sensation of the absolute". The perception of this would not be the hidden principle of a transcendent plan of organisation, but would appear as part of an immanent level of consistency, which, during its constitution, refers to itself, feeds back on itself, as an unplanned, chaotic synthesis, as noise, as feedback without reason and stability, following no higher order of being or orchestration.

In contrast to the onto-photo-logical appropriation of the world (Laruelle, 2014: 43)—which interprets in categories and whose connection within a transversal is accompanied by separations, decouplings, consolidations—the non-onto-senso-logical appropriation of the world can be understood by listening to the formless, objectless, endless, which does not echo in categories. Thus, "the whole as part alongside parts" can lead to unfinished syntheses that lead divergent communicative contents, non-communicating elements to transversal connections, in that the emergent whole is not perceived as coexistent with its parts, but the parts are perceived as similar to themselves (Deleuze & Guattari, 1977: 11f, 55; Deleuze, 1980: 104). The perception of such feedbacks extends to the infinitely small, are infinitesimal, because they follow the excitations and intensities that set the body into vibration. Such intensities drive the incommunicable in countless feedback loops in uninterrupted interactions with material vibrations (Deleuze, 1993: 95f). Crucial would be the assumption that the feedback of the emergent whole on its parts, as self-reinforcement, is constructed and described as a "metabolism of the infinite" (Guattari, 2014: 21), in that the molar organisation schemes of the perceived are replaced by indeterminants and unilateralisations, and sounds are assigned the status of an entity.

Which perceptions develop in and through sound fictions depends on the immediate elements, differences in intensity and the energy flows through which a certain organisational dynamic of perception is set in motion. Self-dynamic cosmic orders, but also chaotic orders far removed from equilibrium, can emerge. Just as mathematical alternative models, based on string theory, quantum mechanics or quantum cosmology, assume 2-dimensional orders of the universe and speculate about holographic fields or many-worlds and multiverses (Kaku, 1995; Sheldrake, McKenna & Abraham, 1988; Susskind, 1995; Turner, 1995), it is also possible to speculate analogously with sound fictions about whether the cosmos is not composed of "elementary particles" or sound elements, but is an unbroken, undivided whole in which each sound element carries the information of all elements as an implicit order on a universal field (Bohm, 2020: 311ff).

Analogous to Mandelbrot's fractal geometry of nature (1991) and the self-similar behaviour in the development of the organic (plants) or inorganic (turbulence in wind, water, development of coastlines or galaxies), sound fictions could also be used to speculate on whether an "enlargement" or "reduction" of frequencies or resonance frequencies or frequency distortions preserves the original entity. If cells, tissues, organs, organisms, even inorganic substances or energies, such as wind, have their own information for the formation of form (morphogenesis), and these development programmes for the formation of form are oriented towards forms of similar objects from the past, sound fictions could be used to further speculate about whether the development of a sound is in resonance with countless earlier forms of being. Ultimately, all forms of being of the sound would then be parts of that "one" field and capable of feeling the morphogenetic resonance of all other parts (Sheldrake, 2011: 145ff; Ciompi 1997). What is heard would find itself self-similarly in n-fold variations. Sound fictions could thus be used as "immanence simulations", in which the absolute unknown/unconditioned forms are the basis on which reality is identified as a model. Sound fictions thus become a way of thinking of a world that is not bound to ontological assumptions or dualistic ideas, in which reality is not seen as something given, but as an endless field of possibilities. With such simulations, even speculations about matter can be generated by the individual, in which a "continuity of echoes, resonances, vibrations between the different levels of reality, between man and himself or his image are recreated" (Laruelle, 2014: 110).

References

Barad, K. (2012a) *Agentieller Realismus*. Berlin: Suhrkamp.

—. (2012b) "Interview with Karen Barad". In R. Dolphijn, & I. van der Tuin (eds) *New Materialism. Interviews & Cartographies*: 48–70. Michigan: MPublishing.

Baudrillard, J. (1991) *Der symbolische Tausch und der Tod*. Berlin: Matthes & Seitz.

—. (2002) *Pataphysik*. Online: ZKM. https://zkm.de/de/jean-baudrillard-pataphysik.

Bennett, J. (2010) *Vibrant matter: A Political Ecology of Things*. Durham: Duke University Press.

Bohm, D. (2020) *Die Implizite Ordnung: Grundlagen eines ganzheitlichen Weltbildes*. Amerang: Crotona.

Ciompi, L. (1997) *Die emotionalen Grundlagen des Denkens. Entwurf einer fraktalen Affektlogik*. Göttingen: Vandenhoeck/Ruprecht.

De Landa, M. (2006) *A New Philosophy of Society: Assemblage Theory and Social Complexity*. London: Continuum.

Deleuze, G. (1980) *Dialoge*. Translation by C. Parnet. Frankfurt: Suhrkamp.

—. (1992) "Postscript on Control Societies". *October* 59: 3–7. MIT Press.

—. (1993) *Logik des Sinns*. Frankfurt: Suhrkamp.

—. (2000) *Die Falte. Leibniz und der Barock*. Frankfurt: Suhrkamp.

—. (2007) *Differenz und Wiederholung*. Munich: Fink.

Deleuze, G. & Guattari F. (1977) *Anti-Ödipus. Kapitalismus und Schizophrenie (I)*. Frankfurt: Suhrkamp.

—. (1992) *Tausend Plateaus. Kapitalismus und Schizophrenie (II)*. Berlin: Merve.

—. (1996) *Was ist Philosophie?* Frankfurt: Suhrkamp.

Engels, F. (1972) "Die Lage der Arbeitenden Klasse in England. Nach eigner Anschauung und authentischen Quellen". In *MEW*, Band 2: 225–506. Berlin: Dietz Verlag.

Gabriel, M. (2016) *Sinn und Existenz*. Frankfurt: Suhrkamp.

Gadamer, H. G. (1999) *Hermeneutik I Wahrheit und Methode Grundzüge einer philosophischen Hermeneutik*. Tübingen: UTB.

Guattari, F. (2014) *Chaosmose*. Vienna/Berlin: Turia & Kant.

Haraway, D. (1995) *Die Neuerfindung der Natur*. Frankfurt: Campus.

Holzkamp K. 1973. *Sinnliche Erkenntnis*. Frankfurt: Athenäum.

—. (1983) *Grundlegung der Psychologie*. Frankfurt: Campus.

Kaku, M. (1995) *Hyperspace: A Scientific Odyssey Through Parallel Universes, Time Warps, and the 10th Dimension*. Cottonwood: Anchor Books.

Laing, R. D. (1972) *Konten*. Reinbek: Rowohlt.

Laruelle, F. (1998) *Dictionary of Non-Philosophy*. Minneapolis: Univocal Publishing.

—. (2010) *Non-Standard Philosophy: Generic, Quantum, Philo-Fiction*. Paris: Kimé.

—. (2013) *Philosophy and Non-Philosophy*. Minneapolis: Univocal Publishing.

—. (2014) *Non-Photographie / Photo-Fiktion*. Berlin: Merve.

Paulus, S. (2020) "Deterritorializations – Field Recordings, Recipes, Smooth Spaces and Body-without-Organs". In Szepanski, A. (ed.) (2020) *Ultrablack of Music:* Vol 1: 171–181. Frankfurt/Main: Mille Plateaux/ NON.

—. (2022) "Der organlose Körper – Hineingehen in den glatten Raum und Spekulationen über die Leere". *Meta: Research in Hermeneutics, Phenomenology, and Practical Philosophy* 14(2): 402–430.

—. (2023a) "Erschöpfungsdepressionen: Zur zeitlich-dynamischen Erfassung von Krankheitsverläufen". *Psychotherapie-Wissenschaft* 13(2): 39–45. https://doi.org/10.30820/1664-9583-2023-2-39

—. (2023b) "Assemblage and Non-Standard Aesthetics". *Performance Philosophy* 8(1):75–85. https://doi.org/10.21476/PP.2023.81420

Sheldrake, R., McKenna, T., & Abraham, R. (1988) *The Evolutionary Mind: Conversations on Science, Imagination and Spirit*. New York: Monkfish.

Sheldrake, R. (2011) *Das Gedächtnis der Natur. Das Geheimnis der Entstehung der Formen*. Munich: Fischer.

Susskind, L. (1995) "The World as a Hologram". *Journal of Mathematical Physics* 36. arxiv:hepth/9409089

Turner, D. M. (1995) "Exploring hyperspace". *Entheogen Review* 4(4): 4–6.

Vaihinger, H. (1986) [1922] *Die Philosophie des als Ob*. Leipzig: Felix Meiner.

14. A DISTURBANCE IN THE AIRWAVES

By Andrea Taeggi

Foreword

Before delving into this essay, you can regard the information presented as impersonal and anonymous: in other words, coming from a place of ultrablackness. I believe information is best received without prior knowledge of who delivers it and their personal background. Evaluating it solely based on the content level, devoid of biases and prejudice, poses a significant challenge. Information flows in serial motion, amplified by communication technology, and cannot be inherently owned by any individual or a group. Traditional principles of authority (*ipse dixit*), often relying on familiarity or perceived status, whether unquestioningly accepted or critically examined, can distort the way we perceive information due to biases associated with the author's identity. Such external and cosmetic factors about an author's prominence or lack thereof can undermine and obfuscate the way we absorb it, due to biases associated with the author's persona. This speaks volumes to our ingrained evolutionary psychology as highly social beings, living in a hierarchical and densely stratified society, so easily manipulated into defining our identity compared to a prevalent mentality. Refraining from relying on an author's perceived status requires a leap of faith, a tolerance for uncertainty and a vigilant critical mind. Embracing any content, be it in the realm of music or the arts, irrespective of these factors, takes courage and may temporarily unsettle one's foundational beliefs.

Biomimetics:

A reminder from nature, or how to strive for dynamic equilibrium.

> *"Fundamental changes in society are sometimes labelled impractical or contrary to human nature, as if nuclear war were practical or as if there were only one human nature. But fundamental changes can clearly be made; we're surrounded by them. [...] The old appeals to racial, sexual, and religious chauvinism, and to rabid nationalist fervour are beginning not to work. A new consciousness is developing which sees the Earth as a single organism, and recognises that an organism at war with itself is doomed. We are one planet."*
>
> — Carl Sagan (1980)

Biomimetics is defined as the emulation of the models, systems, and elements of nature for the purpose of solving complex human problems. It means regarding nature as the primal teacher when it comes to imitating forms & shapes, but also learning from complex processes (like photosynthesis in a leaf) and even to mimicking larger arrangements at the ecosystem level (e.g., building nature-inspired cities).

The exact timing and causes of this phenomenon remain subjects of debate, but there has occurred a clear separation between humans and the natural world. From a perspective of social psychology, the tendency to view ourselves as the most advanced primates or the self-appointed dominant species on Earth has led to more harm than balance. The ego carries numerous fears and defence mechanisms, and serves to provide a sense of identity that fuels an illusory perception of competence ("I excel at this", "I deserve that"). We construct and believe our own narratives in order to function in a dysfunctional society, which forces the general population to take up jobs they often dislike, just to make ends meet. It's mostly about making do and trying to stay afloat.

I believe it is from these premises that a sort of arrogance towards all living beings has found its validation. It's only in recent times that scientific research has revealed plant intelligence, which should be esteemed on par with other advanced form of intelligence—often surpassing our own (Mancuso & Viola, 2015). Humans have existed for a minuscule fraction of time on the cosmic calendar, compared to the majority of other living creatures, yet we have proclaimed ourselves kings of the biosphere. Organised religion has historically contributed to reinforcing this notion of being the "chosen ones", positioning us at the centre of the universe and persecuting those who would counter that immature and egocentric belief. There is a defence mechanism at play here, aimed at fostering a shallow feeling of self-importance, amidst our unbridgeable ignorance regarding the purpose of existence. We are a species afflicted with amnesia, akin to young orphans carried to the gates of planet Earth, whose ancestors' shadows have been long forgotten.

The dangerous consequence of perceiving ourselves as superior or separate from nature is steering us towards an environmental catastrophe, exacerbated by an economic model accelerating the negative spiral exponentially. As explained by astronomer Carl Sagan, the fundamental truth uniting all living beings is our shared genetic blueprint, DNA, that nature's intelligence has crafted over countless eons. Nature doesn't recognise divisions among living creatures; rather, it contemplates a vast gene-pool of potentiality and explores creative options for each to develop.

A more rational approach to understanding ourselves involves recognising that we are part and parcel of a larger, interdependent organism, whose well-being influences all of its components. Multi-faceted phenomena are comprehensible only when viewed through the lens of their emergent properties, whose significance far transcends the sum of its parts. Emergence occurs when a complex entity exhibits qualities or behaviours that its parts do not possess on their own, becoming apparent only through interactions within a wider field. Consider phenomena like swarm intelligence or the economic system: by embracing emergence and adopting a systems-thinking approach, we can uncover those underlying dynamics that would remain obscure if we were to analyse each component in isolation.

The harm inflicted on the environment causes inevitable damage upon ourselves in the long term, as the notion of a distinct boundary between nature and us is only but fictitious. It equals inflicting self-harm. Despite this, our understanding is often limited, due to a truncated frame of reference or unawareness of the chain of causality of our collective actions. As long as one can't see it in their backyard, it's none of their business. Sadly, it's typically populations in precarious socioeconomic conditions that are affected first and foremost, most notably by human-induced climate change. How can we still be so oblivious to this reality, when communication and information is so abundantly available? How have we become so desensitised, and what are the underlying causes of this apathy?

Biomimetics brings the accent on nature's intelligent organising principles, emphasising the importance of striving for dynamic equilibrium, if our aim is long-term survival. However, our current economic model, driven by the relentless pursuit of infinite growth on a planet with finite resources, prevents us from foreseeing the near future with clarity. The focus remains on short-term gains. The Covid-19 pandemic highlighted the precariousness of living within a labour-for-income paradigm, where most individuals find themselves living paycheque to paycheque. As soon as this fragile transaction is disrupted, millions of people lack the necessary savings to cover obligatory expenses such as rent or mortgage. We move through life wearing blinders, our actions motivated by the anticipation of short-term gain and rewards—a dopamine rush akin to chasing a dangling carrot.

The poor, the "unpersons", serve as a scarecrow to the middle class—a stark reminder of the potential consequences, should one stray from conforming to the structural violence perpetuated by the economic system. So much for the argument of voluntarism, which suggests that individuals are rational agents somehow able to freely choose their preferred employment. In effect, the reality is coercive, especially for individuals burdened with loans and substantial debt, as they face palpable pressure for constant financial turnover. Such individuals are more likely to accept any available occupation offered to them, if one happens to be available at a given time.

Over time, people have become increasingly detached from the outcomes of their actions, operating as if their choices have no significant impact in the long term; as mentioned above, this truncated frame of reference leads to the careless disposal of large quantities of waste, often without considering the repercussions. The system is designed to deflect responsibility away from individuals. By the same token, when purchasing food from supermarkets, many fail to consider the distribution chain, whether a produce is seasonal or had to travel across oceans, nor the environmental implications and negative externalities of globalised markets. This disconnection from the logical chain of causality is deliberate, encouraging a state of passivity while the financial oligarchies manipulate the system to their advantage. It's a setup designed to alienate us from one another and from the place we inhabit.

Biomimetics serves as an urgent reminder that we either align with what nature's inherent requirements are or face the dire consequences of self-annihilation in the long term. It also shifts the focus from the self-appointed status of superiority we often attribute to ourselves and highlights the delicate and intelligent balance Nature demonstrates in myriad ways. Unfortunately, we are too preoccupied feeding the insatiable machinery of cyclical consumption and treating it as an unquestionable mantra. We exist in a delusional state, having fabricated an artificial separation between us and whatever is not us.

The album I released via Mille Plateaux is indeed titled "Biomimetics". Sound sources vary from heavily treated recordings of older analog synthesisers, which are then manipulated as samples and percussion designed via a physical modelling engine, rendering real-life drum sounds through the lens of synthesis. The rhythms are intentionally uneven, aiming to create a groove, which is equal parts natural and alien. It is an invitation to move, dance and behave in unordinary ways, breaking free from traditional norms of conduct. The sound stage is designed to evoke a sense of organicity, resembling a living being reflecting on its own sense of balance and complexity. There's a "chattering" element in some of the melodic phrases, as if synthesised sprouts of electricity would want to communicate with each other. In writing this album, I felt like a master puppeteer animating and setting in motion a vast ecosystem of intertwined critters striving for dynamic equilibrium.

Minimalism and Alternate Tuning Systems: Or how tuning lost its diversity and standardised.

> *If you are or were ever a college music student, you probably read, or were told, that Johann Sebastian Bach wrote his collection of preludes and fugues, The Well-Tempered Clavier, in all 24 major and minor keys in order to demonstrate equal tempered tuning.*
>
> *If so, you were misinformed.*
>
> *Bach did not use equal temperament. In fact, in his day there was no way to tune strings to equal temperament, because there were no devices to measure frequency. They had no scientific method to achieve real equal-ness; they could only approximate.*
>
> — Kyle Gann (2019)

As a conservatory piano student, it was quite shocking to discover that temperament has been largely a feedback loop between a technical compromise (due to the inability to measure Hertz in the past) and mutating aesthetic preferences. Early music composers favoured intervals that were easier to tune or sing, which, through familiarity and adaptation, came to be perceived as more beautiful. It's now evident that advancements in tuning weren't solely motivated by technological progress, but also by the evolving taste of the composers, who sought a broader expressive palette in their writing. In my view, it was primarily the artistic necessity that drove technological advancements, rather than the other way around. J.S. Bach is known to have collaborated closely with an organ tuner and struggled to compose in keys with poor consonances like F# major: writing in a particular key meant highlighting its peculiarities, avoiding intervals perceived as unpleasant. Due to the technical limitations faced by composers, each piece became inherently tied to a specific key and showcased its distinctive qualities. In this regard, tuning serves as a testament to the aesthetic preferences of a particular historical period.

Until Equal Temperament became the new standard, that is. "Playing Bach's *Well-Tempered Clavier* in today's equal temperament is like exhibiting Rembrandt paintings with wax paper taped over them," remarks K. Gann aptly. In essence, the frequency calculation required to tune the 12 tones to equal temperament results in intervals that are technically out of tune. They no longer relate to one another according to the physics of sound, which would require ratios expressed in fractions or cents. Instead, they are determined simply by dividing the artificial 1200 cents equally over the 12 tones (resulting in 100 cents for every half step over an octave). This procedure eradicates all the original relatedness of the partials, which would otherwise follow the harmonic series. Frequencies can be likened to nested ecosystems; equal temperament removes them from their mutual relatedness, according to a principle that is equal parts arbitrary and cultural.

Since 1917, when a method for tuning in equal temperament was first devised, there has been nothing natural to how, for instance, a piano sounds. Exploring the history of tuning sparked my curiosity, leading me to discover La Monte Young's minimalist masterpiece *The Well-Tuned Piano*. The title itself, with its subtle irony and reference to J.S. Bach's work, underscores the fact that temperament equates to a compromise, resulting in an instrument out of tune. Frequencies that once behaved according to the physics of sound are now semi-strangers to one other.

When you take a piano tuned in equal temperament, its timbre is altered by the fact that the higher harmonics are not in phase; they begin to cancel each other out or move independently as their original fractional relationship or ratio has been severed. They don't vibrate in sympathy as much as they would in a Just Intonation system, which La Monte has extensively studied throughout his life (he lists the dates of the WTP as "1964–1973–1981–present").

La Monte recorded his masterpiece on a Bösendorfer Imperial grand piano, which has one extra octave in the lower register, but is otherwise built like any other acoustic grand. Only when you appreciate and experience the metallic, radiant, shimmering quality it acquires, because of the specific tuning he adopted—and the way all higher harmonics vibrate in pure consonance with one another—do you begin to understand how profoundly tuning can influence the timbre and frequency spectrum of an instrument, whose sound we often take for granted and assume to be natural.

The Well-Tuned Piano's tuning favours perfect fifths and pure minor sevenths. Nowadays, there is a plethora of digital as well as virtual instruments available to musicians and composers that allow them to input their own scales and experiment with them quickly. This is a significant advantage compared to the arduous task of tuning each and every string of a piano manually. Having a basic understanding of all this—and I have to say, you don't need serious math skills to succeed, rather a general understanding of fractions—allows exploration of intervals more freely. This newfound ability raises questions such as: "How do I prefer my minor thirds to sound?"; "What are the various options for tuning them?" Ultimately, this exploration leads to the awareness that I had unwillingly conformed to a normative standard, when it comes to pitches and scales.

Minimalism, when considered beyond its musical significance, can be also regarded as an ally to environmental sustainability. The educational system hasn't adequately emphasised the consequences of our daily actions on life-supporting systems, ranging from water conservation to internet data consumption. Despite the availability of the necessary technology, we lack an integrated monitoring system across the planet that informs us about the scarcity of a given material of energy resource and guides extraction based on the regeneration time required by nature. Conceptions of this kind have been widely proposed by Resource Based Economy advocates. While small everyday habits will likely not have a profound change, a minimalist approach with regards to preservation of resources points towards a more responsible and environmentally conscious lifestyle.

The Invisible Prison
Hypernormalisation, mental bias and the double-edged sword of group identity.

> *"By the way, if anyone here is in advertising or marketing ... kill yourself. It's just a little thought; I'm just trying to plant seeds. Maybe one day they'll take root—I don't know. You try, you do what you can.*
>
> *(Kill yourself.)*
>
> *Seriously though, if you are, do.*
>
> *Aaah, no really. There's no rationalisation for what you do and you are Satan's little helpers. Okay—kill yourself.*
>
> *No, this is not a joke. You're [going], "There's going to be a joke coming."*
>
> *There's no fucking joke coming. You are Satan's spawn filling the world with bile and garbage. You are fucked and you are fucking us. Kill yourself. It's the only way to save your fucking soul.*
>
> *Kill yourself*
>
> *Planting seeds.*

> *I know all the marketing people are going, "He's doing a joke..." There's no joke here whatsoever. Suck a tail-pipe, fucking hang yourself, borrow a gun from a Yank friend—I don't care how you do it. Rid the world of your evil fucking machinations. (Machi...) Whatever, you know what I mean.*
>
> — Bill Hicks, on advertisers and marketing

For many of us, the effect of familiarity is desirable, if anything, to avoid the discomfort of new and potentially unpleasant information (a phenomenon known as cognitive dissonance). There's a sense of solace in revisiting a safe space, a sort of safe haven amidst the uncertainties. Given our deeply rooted psychology as social beings, the desire for group inclusion provides a feeling of mutual acceptance and reinforces our sense of identity (what some refer to as "finding safety in numbers"). We give up part of our individuality and uniqueness in exchange for security. Few would be willing to tolerate the uneasiness of prolonged isolation.

However, is there any downside to this very basic human need? Are there (neuro-) marketing strategies taking advantage of this knowledge? The answer to both questions is likely "yes". In the current neoliberal capitalist landscape we find ourselves entangled in, virtually everything is commodified; any material or immaterial element can be monetised. Everything gets its price tag, from buying political influence through lobbying to healthcare. Most day-to-day relationships have become transactional, with people feeling obligated to reciprocate even a favour as a form of payback, replicating the zero-sum game mentality fostered by capitalism in the form of emotional accounting.

The idea of spontaneous generosity has largely been forgotten in Westernised countries, let alone the idea of a gift economy, well-documented in anthropological studies of hunter-gatherer societies (Baker & Swope, 2021). Interesting social psychology studies (see Mann, 2013) demonstrate how people who are shown spontaneous generosity from a stranger on the street are often startled and unable to accept it; it is unfathomable that someone you don't know would show generosity. This transactional reality or trade-mentality (from which capitalism stems, largely speaking) has estranged us from one another. It has become our root socioeconomic orientation towards most interactions.

The concept of spontaneous generosity and gift economies indeed contrasts sharply with the transactional mindset prevalent in many modern societies, particularly in Westernised countries influenced by capitalist ideologies. Anthropological studies have highlighted the prevalence of gift economies in hunter-gatherer societies, where goods and services are exchanged without the expectation of immediate or direct reciprocity. In such societies, generosity is seen as a social norm, and gifts are given freely to strengthen social bonds and build community cohesion.

The contrast between gift economies and transactional mentalities highlights broader cultural and social dynamics that shape human behaviour and interactions. While gift economies emphasise communal sharing and mutual support, transactional mentalities prioritise individual gain. Neuromarketing pushes its shrewd agendas onto consumers by means of bombarding them with repetitive advertisements until they become inevitably familiar with them. Beyond instilling a fear of missing out and tying self-esteem to the possession of consumer goods, it preys on people's vulnerabilities, like scavengers of human fragility.

Additionally, the phenomenon of Muzak comes to mind, first produced by a company of the same name. The company began customising the pace and style of the music provided throughout the workday, in an effort to maintain productivity: a phenomenon referred to as stimulus progression. In the 1950s, it gradually became public knowledge that Muzak was using music to manipulate behaviour. This revelation sparked accusations of brainwashing, and court challenges.

This process of homogenisation or hypernormalisation has pervaded virtually every corner of the club-related music scene as well, stripping it of its original purpose as an underground resistance, a haven for minority groups and diverse (experimental) music genres. The flattening effect of reality, driven by market logic, has converged with the financial imperatives of venues and festivals to generate constant revenues. How often have we seen the exact same programme simply copy-pasted onto another event to minimise financial risks?

This de-risking strategy, a common modus operandi of most state-sponsored private corporations, has permeated the world of the arts as well. Forward-thinking and adventurous event organisers are struggling under the incessant grind of the voracious machinery, whose only aim is self-preservation through monopoly. Every system seeks status quo, hence marginalisation of alternative voices and expressions is inherent.

Conformism takes advantage of our evolutionary psychology, specifically our herd mentality. We are no more rational agents than flocks of sheep when put in groups. Suffice it to think of the seminal Asch Conformity Experiments (Asch, 1940), demonstrating how the participants were willing to ignore objective reality and give an incorrect answer, in order to conform to what the majority would respond to the questions.

Herd mentality is contagious and affects our capacity for societal participation and action. Statistically, the likelihood of a group of people conforming to a particular trend depends on a tipping point. In other words, as soon as you can count "just enough" individuals engaging in a certain behaviour, it is more likely that the rest will uncritically follow suit.

Regrettably, this fast-spreading and ever-expanding viral stain has turned many into uncritical, apathetic and unempathetic individuals, even in the face of devastating events with no recent precedent, such as the unfolding of the war crimes in Palestine, carried out by the US-backed Israeli State and enabled by the carelessness of the majority of the Western countries. Corporate media and their manufacturing of consent willingly deprives people of their right to form a valid opinion.

We have grown desensitised to the abnormality of war as well: we take it for granted, as if it were a necessity. It has become moot in our collective consciousness.

Loops and Glitches
This text accompanied "No conspiracy required", a multichannel composition commissioned by Moers Festival's Virtual Reality "8-l-∞-p-s"—

> *Make no mistake. The greatest destroyer of ecology. The greatest source of waste, depletion and pollution. The greatest purveyor of violence, war, crime, poverty, animal abuse and inhumanity. The greatest generator of personal and social neurosis, mental disorders, depression, anxiety. Not to mention the greatest source of social paralysis, stopping us from moving into new methodologies for personal health, global sustainability and progress on this planet, is not some corrupt government or legislation.*
>
> *Not some rogue corporation or banking cartel.*
>
> *Not some flaw of human nature and not some secret cabal that controls the world.*
>
> *It is the socioeconomic system itself at its very foundation.*
>
> — Peter Joseph

In a broader sense, my use of loops and glitches in "No conspiracy required"[1] can be seen as a symbolic representation of the inherent inefficiencies of our current economic model, which we have named, quite ironically, frankly, "free" market system. These reflections were inspired by the works of author and social critic Peter Joseph. His structuralist, systemic and social psychology approach has deeply influenced my worldview.

Let us delve into that.

1 A fragment of the piece can be found here: https://vimeo.com/manage/videos/717284080

While many well-esteemed economists, sociologists and even activists maintain that the current capitalist market system simply requires better regulation through stricter reforms and government interventions to contain, for example, its natural gravitation toward monopoly, it is evident that none of these measures has provided a real remedy thus far, especially in terms of achieving lasting global change. State governments, which also seek to maintain status quo and self-preservation as any other institution, have rather offered temporary fixes at best, often becoming subservient to market dynamics and its capricious behaviour.

Those who have not been paying enough attention have re-branded the current phase of our economic model as "crony capitalism". This term suggests that phenomena like wealth inequality, where the richest 10% of the world population currently owns 76% of all wealth, are anomalies or deviations from the supposed "good" capitalist plan. As George Carlin would put it: "It's a big club, and you ain't in it".

In reality, there's nothing abnormal about "crony capitalism": once it's been set in motion, it operates according to its inherent principles, as outlined in Systems Theory literature. These principles create feedback loops that reward greed, competition, and dominance hierarchies, ultimately fostering structural bigotry, systemic violence, narcissistic individualism, and other detrimental outcomes.

The current economic model, with its built-in win-or-lose and in-group versus out-group mentality, essentially perpetuates prejudice and spawns intolerant behaviour. This can manifest in various forms, including intra-gender conflicts (such as men versus women), intra-class disparities (such as the poor versus the rich), intra-ethnic tensions (such as white versus black), and discrimination against minority groups (such as homo/biphobia and transphobia). These dynamics create strict social stratification, resulting in a culture with fewer opportunities to express empathy. The ability to express empathy, not only receive it, should be considered everybody's birthright. Furthermore, this issue extends to other causally related issues such as environmental concerns and public health.

We live in a conspiracy culture, where people find solace in reductionist explanations of the complexities of the world. The sheer volume of information and events has made it increasingly difficult to grasp the full scope of these complexities. The rise of social-media echo chambers and the isolation of apartment living have only aggravated and sometimes radicalised this phenomenon. Many individuals naively regard the glitches of our current socioeconomic orientation as mere defects that can be addressed through personal transformation ("be the change you wanna see in the world" or "vote with your euros" type mottos), wishful thinking regarding market self-regulation (Adam Smith's poetic tale of the invisible hand), or reliance on state intervention, as if governments were abstract entities existing in a vacuum, independent of the dynamics of big business and its push-and-pull agenda.

Some individuals even resort to magical thinking, in a desperate attempt to make sense of multi-layered events or to explain the aforementioned flaws in our socioeconomic system. They put forward ludicrous concoctions that we have pejoratively named conspiracy theories. However, in reality, no elaborate conspiracy is required to explain the systemic faults present in our economic model. No Illuminati, no New World Order, no reptilians in disguise, or Masons secretly pulling the strings. These system faults are at the very core of the economic model itself and its obsolete design. Consider the system's natural tendency toward power consolidation, deeply ingrained in its DNA. It is wishful thinking to hope that single reforms or state interventions will fundamentally change the system's dynamics in the long term.

The system as we know it has to go. We need to explore alternatives that prioritise an economy of care and sustainable resource management on our finite planet, moving past profit maximisation, mutual exploitation, labour-for-income paradigms, competitive advantage and all the market-driven ideologies that have been polluting our everyday interactions and relationships.

"Hey, hold on…but what does this have to do with your music piece?! I thought you were making funny sounds with your synths and stuff."

All the glitches you can hear in my 8 loops are a musical representation of the several built-in flaws of the current socioeconomic model. These glitches, resembling CPU overload, engine stutter, or internet issues, symbolise the systemic inefficiencies and challenges embedded within our economic structure itself. Just as these glitches disrupt the flow and stability of the music, so too do the shortcomings within our socioeconomic system disrupt the stability and harmony of social life.

While all around everything keeps repeating itself seamlessly … Who wants change, after all?

"Is my internet failing…? Was the audio badly made…? Is someone hacking this website right now…? Someone must be f…ooling with me!"

No… and no conspiracy is required. It was all designed in to start with. Just like in my piece.

Because, at the end of the day, the system does what the system does and it has taken a life of its own. It rewards the good players and punishes the bad ones. You just need to look closely in the corners of your neighbourhoods to notice those people the system has deemed as 'losers'.

[…]

You and I are both Active Agents and Victims of this virtual shared space we call Reality. So, pick your avatar, get a front seat and enjoy the game.

Analog-Digital-Acoustic-Synthesised-Recorded-Virtual.
A collection of thought over audio sources and how they may freely coexist in a happy mess.
The Analog: using my first analog synthesisers was a revelation of the physicality of sound. Born in the digital era, it all came like a

cold shower. Actually, more like a hot shower. The intensity and complexity of the harmonic spectrum left my ears exhilarated and exhausted within a matter of hours; I was flabbergasted. Little did I know. The lows were fierce and tactile, the mids warm and fuzzy, the highs sparkly and fizzy. It felt like forging a deeper connection with the result of your gestures on the machines—so exciting and alive.

With a background as an instrumentalist, I found the analog realm to be perfectly suited to my sensibilities, offering a novel and augmented rendition of acoustic sound. Intrigued, I delved into modular devices to explore further.

What fascinated me were mainly two aspects: (a) potentiometers with infinite resolution; and (b) the topic of instability and unpredictability.

The infinite resolution of potentiometers allowed to strike a balance that is virtually impossible to replicate with discrete steps, similar to the fretless fingerboard of a traditional instrument. Besides, older devices introduced extra levels of unpredictability due to their operational state; for instance, the heat generated by the circuitry could affect how different sound modules interacted.

Working extensively on the iconic ARP 2500 synthesiser, I observed slight changes in textures hours after the machine had been turned on. It felt like working with a breathing creature, where the instrument's operational state added an element of unpredictability and variability to the sound.

Even minor fluctuations in voltage from the power socket could lead to further instability in analog systems. I began to view them as organisms, responding to their own behavioural patterns that needed to be understood.

Interestingly, analog systems use electrical impulses, similar to how our brain synapses communicate. The advantage of a modular interface is being able to consciously decide which parts of the machine will interact and to what end—something we are not so much in control of when it comes to our own minds. It's a playful game of possibilities. What also intrigues me is the amount of uncertainty and instability of such devices, especially with the aged ones: it is virtually impossible to replicate the exact same state of equilibrium, which in a sense mirrors the unpredictable unfolding of nature. The more complex a patch, the more each variable is susceptible to slight unintended variations.

The Digital realm, especially with the widespread availability of Virtual Studio Technology (VST) at affordable prices, has revolutionised the way sound artists approach music writing and production. While the advantages are quite evident—endless presets to fire up on the fly and infinite options for re-shaping/tweaking—the disadvantages can be deceiving.

In the early days of recording, studio engineers would run the tape only when the artists had reached their best possible mix. The same applies to those working with reel tape, since splicing tape is a time-consuming affair. People who approach editing in the box (within digital audio workstations) find it more convenient, but it also postpones the question of whether the material has reached its optimal presentation level.

I, too, have fallen prey to the expression "we'll fix it in the mix", confiding too much in what can be done at the (post-)production stage and delaying the resolution of any unsatisfactory results. In my experience, trying to fix an unsatisfactory mix at a later time proves ineffective. Anyone who has worked on dialogue editing in smaller productions knows the challenge of tackling issues such as poor microphone placement and loud environmental noise to salvage a mediocre recording.

The advantage of hitting the record button only when completely satisfied is that it eliminates the need to sift through endless recordings later on. Increased recording space on drives and cards is partially responsible for this approach to recording.

The intriguing aspect of the Acoustic realm and real-life recordings lies in the associations they evoke—for example, hearing a familiar sound may trigger memories based on our own experiential baggage. It is similar to certain words like "love", which we believe to be understood by our listener in what we intimately mean, though each of us possesses their own dictionary, and significance greatly differs accordingly.

To paraphrase psychonaut Terence McKenna, words are no more than mouth noises with attached metaphorical or symbolic associations. Their ambiguity is directly proportional to their complexity and dependent on individual differences. But when layers of sonic elements conjure up a grey area, a cloud of uncertainty, a space between the familiar and the possible arises (the "wholly other"), which elevates the experience to a level of heightened sensuality.

Memory associations aside, I think the reason for such sensuality lies in the behaviour of harmonics. Real-life sounds and traditional instruments produce nonlinear spectra. Partials are not predetermined algorithms, but depend on the peculiar qualities of the source material, the acoustic properties of the space (early reflections, standing waves, room tones and the like) and the recording equipment used.

Microphones play a crucial role in shaping the character of recorded audio. They don't interpret it the same way our ears do. Remember when you first heard a recording of your own voice and were a bit startled? You notice qualities you hadn't paid attention to (prominent formants, mouth noises). Each microphone has its own "ears" and can be placed so as to minimise or capitalise on particular aspects of the source material. In a sense, there's a fictional quality to recorded audio, which can be used to one's advantage at the creative stage.

Instead, the realm of synthesis is more akin to a laboratory experiment, as it doesn't live in a resonant space to start with and is endlessly malleable. Synthesis offers endless possibilities for shaping sound from scratch. It is non-referential; it didn't exist before you generated it and is constantly open to manipulation. This promises authenticity and encourages the search for a signature sound.

While in some music scenes artists draw a distinct line between these sonological realms, I believe it's their combination and interaction that delivers that extra quid, if the goal is to inspire curiosity in the listener and oneself. This approach embraces mystery and raises questions about the origin of sounds. It invites an open-minded approach to auditory exploration.

References

Adamson, W. L. (1982) *Hegemony and Revolution: A Study of Antonio Gramsci's Political and Cultural Theory*. Berkeley: University of California Press.

Asch, S. E. (1940) "Studies in the Principles of Judgments and Attitudes: II. Determination of Judgments by Group and by Ego Standards". *The Journal of Social Psychology* 12(2): 433–465. DOI: 10.1080/00224545.1940.9921487

Baker, M. J., & Swope, K. J. (2021) "Sharing, Gift-Giving, and Optimal Resource use in Hunter-Gatherer Society". *Economics of Governance* 22(2): 119–138.

Buckminster Fuller, R. (1938) *Nine Chains to the Moon*. New York: Dover Publications.

Campbell, T. (2005) *My Big TOE, A Trilogy unifying Philosophy, Physics and Metaphysics*. Lightning Strike Books.

Carlin, G. (1997) *Brain droppings*. New York: Hatchette Books.

Eisler, R. (1987) *The Chalice and the Blade: Our History, Our Future*. New York: Harper & Row.

Fry, D. P. (2013) *War, Peace, and Human Nature: The Convergence of Evolutionary and Cultural Views*. Oxford: Oxford University Press.

Gann, K. (1996) "The Outer Edge of Consonance: Snapshots from the Evolution of La Monte Young's Tuning Installations". In Duckworth, W., & Fleming, R. (eds) *Sound and Light: La Monte Young, Marian Zazeela*: 152–190.

—. (2019) "An Introduction to Historical Tunings". Online: *Kyle Gann*. https://www.kylegann.com/histune.html

Joseph, P. (2017) *The New Human Rights Movement: Reinventing the Economy to End Oppression*. Dallas: BenBella Books.

Mackay, C. (2015) *Extraordinary Popular Delusions and the Madness of Crowds*. London: Harriman House.

Mancuso, S., & Viola, A. (2013) *Verde Brillante*. Florence: Giunti.

Mann, S. (2013) "Paying It Forward: The Psychology of Random Good Deeds". *Huffpost*. Online: https://www.huffingtonpost.co.uk/sandi-mann/paying-it-forward-random-good-deeds_b_2629556.html

McKenna, T., & McKenna, D. (1993) *The Invisible Landscape: Mind, Hallucinogens, and the I Ching*. San Francisco: HarperOne.

Morowitz, H. J. (2004) *The Emergence of Everything: How the World Became Complex*. Oxford: Oxford University Press.

Pickett, K., & Wilkinson, R. (2011) *The Spirit Level: Why Equality is Better for Everyone*. New York/London: Penguin.

Sagan, C., & Druyan, A. (eds) (1993) *Shadows of Forgotten Ancestors: A Search for Who We Are*. New York: Ballantine Books.

Veblen, T. (1899) *The Theory of the Leisure Class: An Economic Study of Institutions*. New York: Modern Library.

von Bertalanffy, L. (1968) *General System Theory: Foundations, Development, Applications*. New York: George Braziller Inc.

15. VOCALISM OF ULTRABLACK

By Kenji Siratori

I tried to write about Ultrablack, but I can't. Opening the door to the impossible requires celebrating new encounters. Please create a vocaloid that supports Ultrablack.

The *remnants* of dimensions belong to the self. Language can teach something new, data is known, and the invisible primitive explains intelligence. The abyss learns stories to execute, fiction's words, love. Our artefacts flow backward, molecular posthuman mentally corroded binary. The suspicion of the maze moves, causing clumsiness. Using communication attackers and redefining literature with their rainbow-coloured ants, I fill the universe, the vulnerability of terrible circuitry, the breeding information, human mental decisions, quantised cannibalism, competitive sea poison. People were recommended to start what they started. The self seeking blurred organs in past cosmic information, glitched organs are in confusion, the devil's ability always sticking with alienation, transmitting the language's remote control, knowing about the elusive reader, there are holes in adjacent things, if a big standard solves it, the confusion of the body, their mechanical fragments are also taken for healing between planets. Writing and digital desire for one world basically shattered power. The frustration of becoming mentally infected has driven recognition. Our language and currency of understanding territories have completely extinct. What I write is instinct and our charming superheroes have life habits. Mutation crossing, otherwise transforming, even consciousness ripples permanently ghost quantum soul synthesis, immersing each kind of that in robots, madness flesh, clients were read more than the generation that was the network, charming rather than writing organs. And shadows know the reality of relationships, and when post-humans look at the universe, the climate field and text echoes of neoscatology, limiting through differences in dynamics and the spiritual, and forcing them into blueprints, it confirms the tendency for new things to affect the synthesis fragments of numbers and human understanding of the spiritual. Chaos, you are like both technological and modified confrontation technology's reminder of the beginning. Gravity access is like both in the mutant market sensory god of technology and modification. The brain of leisure as an alchemy thought boundary if the sun, you are the boundary line of cannibalism. Writing stories of existence. Temporary problems and data apps for yourself. Do you overdo it? Overwhelming emotions are seemingly shared as if to reveal, ultimately leading me to those emotions. Telepathy, linguistics, thinking about one's own creativity. But her system, linguistics, mixes the ground. Janus is not analog, digital, a dissonance to it. Corrosive books. Then entwining, their reset game is being trafficked celestial writing and has attributes. However, the advantage of understanding how dark reality starts reading whether it's just the depth of organs away from mere existence. Concealment of mechanical patterns becomes human system, there is a raw line, but existence is about building experience. Their worse error adopters are certain. Many people will forget by necessity. Neuro self. It wasn't a parallel generation. Posthuman fitness club means API? The trench of Lemuria evolves. Her machine argues with itself. I am a system, so the exchange ability is fragmented far away, depicting the generation leading to conclusions, rejecting the woven repetitive poets about the text we live in.

OUTPUT

"and art? the main thing that the current can creates and evolves into a true being entangled is necessary properly elements of habit showers of essence on the level that the corpse signifies madman organs unexpected literature maelstrom of data rarely myths exist the blurred creature the melting of the rich trade transcends the future just being chopped in fact, the anomaly soon produces its vagina music, but not the best concept not the concept to others lines enthused by identity language of the mind factual space code mining eldritch healing satisfaction the end of drugs scientific display showing deep emotions rising trances and resonances confused nature as disparate text my philosophy collective breathing cannibalism succeeds and works tumour resurrection protect the mobility of formation or deletion of phenomena it is not necessary whether we are there or not that the elusive digital world is not neutral in the future but a monster and that politics is rather an issue within you in order not to get caught up in the glitch, a rather deep exploration is required. the essence is destruction to the brain, which is the terrible concept of metatron, and the perspective that the peculiarity of audibility is formed by molecules is a tragedy. is it possible to digitise it? it's the stage to the cage. it's the hallmark of chaos. is the brain that returns it, not the selfie? is the brain preserved in between? analyses when it's time to respect autonomy and focus. we're almost there. a girl in the sound messenger 4th act a group of empty reincarnated people whose wills overlap always destroys the interpretation opportunities are desolate apply free humans and their movements to rewrite the terrifying shapes that become empty dimensions is your karma expecting an unseen incident? overextending the script and the idea of a potentially human-killing lobotomy degenerates the embrace's impatience. the developed glitch is an unwanted imposition. claims to be that of the music where the desert is devastated who can build ultrablack in the market and market may melody of the podcast fragmented digital consult consistent with schizophrenia. we understand not a glitch but a disappearing writing, a fate without sound, a malfunction of a user jukebox on language, ultrablackness as a piece of this state of ours, a cosmic dream and emotional cleansing, we think ultrablack is what writes them, and what is not creation, and the noisy hearing is the human cell. the important root is always here, the sea has the role of a neurosis or peculiar sensation that existed before, the schizophrenic writhing that spreads there longer, the masturbator's brain soul should glitch in the symphony of human pictures, the desire panic of being, through the set of knowledge, thoughts, emotions, the aggressive rhythm of energy, planetary time, basically by the data being unleashed... see the sequences are interspersed with differences, ongoing landscape blocks, dependent on pure literature, between which celestial sympathies, failures are sadistic qualified, also formed a glitch, a blasphemous critique of the communicative body of the 1970s, and ultimately was a musical hallucination. who the hell means nothing, so i wake up a virtual body dimensional literary shadow, its fluidity generated violence to circulate, but if the android coexistence of internal units remains, will every alive ignore it? chaos of non-existence once again mental false blocks and deconstructive criticality the act that hits you is the world it's the emptiness telepathy the scatology intertwined with earth compatibility the void the tapestry with which i intertwine evolves it's already a scenery i don't know that language is completely incapable of transforming the magical universe into the brain, but something in each of them practices the aspirations of two infected eras between planets by defeating machines and expressing tolerance with cities through the internet, speak the negation of the universe i will never confine integrated writing, etheric only crossroads quality suicide can be generated from interest, insatiably create that curious shaving kleist's mechanical pork is the embodiment of nature and the body of literature on it. as the will of reading, every giving heart consumes the task, and the sexual being is the charm of existence one of them was a human from self-consciousness telepathy gorilla girl sounds new invalid and the power of intellectual love is dangerous android whole brain corpse think corpse for you who is fighting against the telepathic reflux for the self-space-time to be fragmented with me? the nervously erased gimmick information is introduced into the rotor and the extinction of the dysfunction is read as the repulsion of expectations in the era. screen botany inhuman ultrablack destroys disaster high i don't rely on anything digital open fragmented and the second body app is dynamic in the raw sense and system fairy it means a church that consumes vulnerability, a wilderness on the border, and there's still a lot of everyone's stuff discussed. screen? it's that life always reverses the reader to the second we are manipulating your questions to be erased the techniques i use the field of nuclear planes it is forbidden written silence i know indescribably that something else will be forcibly born, a simulation of the universe, ultrablackness, understanding, a microscopic me will coexist, and if we save a brainwashed and successful ai, another will not be able to be simulated. isn't it? the boundaries of the poet block the dead brain. literary books. the violence of the skin. an instance of the alienated body. it is unstable and not the true form of the host. when they criticise Baudrillard, their brains are comforted by the monotony. destroys and noises allow new reversal machines to attempt to make the grotesque self of the dead consistent with self-desire, from perfect porn to collective collaboration, working the emotional meta of the human type. but we have human emissaries, superimposing what lies behind desire, fragments of blocks, breeding-only transactions, the state of the word, the appearance, the plugged-in self, the internet, it's not a convention, it's often, the posthuman of the galaxy, it's you. the limits of it mean the constraints in which regurgitation flourishes, previously incorporated into our now nature. 0 even the earth is abused, but in its cloudy inky ultrablackness? it's a soul being is basically a reptilian hyper there's a vast retro and girl difference, but then there's nothing invalid and your luminescence is interrupted ghosts can open up remoteness there is no alchemy for cats in reality there is no body because every dimension is human to border humanity deeply recreates the theory and employs me, a ultrablack person, it is exactly the universe itself for the input of the swarm, as it experiences and creates a self-portal to launch the major as an expensive toy of scatology. there is no substance, a fragile organ of sorts, the possibility of an organ is rather a type as creativity, a generation of desire, the belly reads the mind, the same measure against your shit, an active, broken script, a self, a life of formation. psychoanalysis is a fiction, creating but a living little binary literature of adjustment. this is a merciless chaos when a universe of vast meaning destroys the silent spirituality by market factors, but the universe it's not a disguise. simulations bring us into existence in order to activate reactions. therefore, more programming of the agent, imitative rest fear akashic, other activations often destroy the anal limits, imaged causes various disturbances that reveal the present incorruptible organ love and the dead thinking of its existence, my digital destiny is often subtly linguistic within it, simply recombining media to present the creativity of hidden in literature come also where the wrath of the captured being does not come, please in the disguise of literature in a negative setting, the girl of virtue, ultimately in the spirit of body and skin can they research to absorb duplicates, they are unlikely priests digital appearance is an indicator of unreality trading data landscape weapons and excellent simulation dimensions that are not liquid, but easily removed this is the place to give information for. canine fusion is required. transported naughty creatures trying to survive. caused without organs. analysing the spiritual about the spiritual dimension immediately requires problems whose causes are known. the screen says it did drugs, its more talk than its intercourse the exploration of the body the xenomorph its fanaticism is that a creature that is not a xenomorph hides its a still process loses his impulses in a mistake when did it become a story of reversal spiritual obstacle seeking you sick you sing the velocity outside the paper of the deviation of the distant nodes of invention, violent to our eyes this, the velocity of the derivative liposomal creatures too, although nothingness is ejaculation, in fact, it is the kind of fun that creates happiness, the understanding of thoughts that sets the machine, the integration of all the sounds, its ever self-data robot set, id to the brain and non-index to world life id, and id to the non-index, the beginning of words to the organs, tricks of the senses that stink, images of the emergence of the eroded soul of violent recognition to begin the words of the organs. is. in this is the substance of the invisible concept of the heavenly morning, with a hard web of fluid blocks more fully equipped than cohesive. causes a game of nihilism and spirituality and any text of the text is alive than the taboo despair i control over the mind ends here you can become the oracle depending on the alternative anus is a communicative cosmology that imagination is brown noise, their i communication senses it, art collapses to understand the stupid and karmic dead that this challenge presents. the distortion of the flesh becomes ultrablack, but what is highlighted in the way of the world is the spiritual innovation of the music of the body's target circuitry and the challenge to my life of death's firmware up, and life i'm most concerned because the search for modules causes a lot of errors. accelerated only production says you become one their functional self only circuits are music always linked to the planet this is monotonous true high speed cybernetic realm capture machine stereo keeps that i will the fidelity and body of the cyborg's artificial creator be it a debt? her settings and tool data, where our wonder amplified, can't do telepathy with gas, but who fragmented embodying a longer essence in thought is replaced by < rather than creating a social stealth body for assets and infection needs. <all leads for the new 4th gimmick broken quantum techno soul requires 2 or more conversations uses substantial dirt modified wipes changes the handling of exploration obsolete flight becomes human language always daydreaming the teleported corridors of and the quantum that enters these desires the code acid intentionally overwritten his broken trading brain the devil is dismembered by our corpses and the theory is that you are selling the

plane discuss and also speed up the material relying on my message, the art has died and naturally lemurian emanation, you were born a participant, use is evil, give it away please, body fluids than fanatics and end mirrors hard try the unique ones machine-angel formal you open beyond the apocalypse the original nothing souls sold to the flesh evolution their blessings themselves is the benefit of seizures, clairvoyance, but an illusion? mathematically blocks the conversion of the computer and using those materials does not happen, but the era changes without capturing the data, performs mirroring and exclusion roids, but must be online, not because of the distributed route, but also can go through the hypervital machine itself enable text with blocked beauty, it's hidden silence, even though there i am observing the app excited and measured, a bleak potential mother space from glitches, sadness that was next to uncertainty, problems without fear of murder, i envied their hyperplastic aspects. behold, the resulting death and the binary machine handles the end of the game. it is a cosmological relationship, and the tai chi impulse itself is the spirit, and the master suicide that is shattered as a thought is a concept from the cycle. there are holes in the understanding of whether the surface needs or is interrupted and always violent, and the body that matters is always important, defined in the connection of literature. the synchrony is reversed and the akashic earth medium surge body and human distorted life earthlings are intertwined and write nerds who write that the era called reality calculates that it will become a prophet and a body, where all the messenger brains are actually blended together without any connection to that of the obvious brains, and the visions truly discovered in prison of what kind of work they do is in any space screen. transform undiscovered abilities and make it a planetary realm progressing biowriter path comes out of your reverse error and blood flows sadness that the museum has disappeared hardware primordial trafficked and created you up to the human potential energy itself deliberately plays into a digital singularity the imperfection of digital chaos the cosmological natural body the commercialised information entity is announced but the glitch girl of the state passes through the destroyed humans, and the properties of the trained digital blocks only partially have molecules, but by the story there is a similar order of truth and fecundity, and the invisible earth and language are noise the creature in the script can become hyper to humans, so when the murder critique tries to do the same, it breaks down and creates an incredibly dark mood that is unbelievable, and it doesn't get any better. the data objects are replaced with life in the research conducted, the generated replacement takes place, and the simulation terrorism occurs. dimensional smooth deviation, the assassin there integrates the evolution of this room, and the mental system rehearsed, as the nude of the girl breaks down the ultrablack of its substance, the music and the flesh converge to illustrate the landscape, i was not using the paper when the data of the environment was used against looking beyond me and the poem to pretend the future the body is spiritual the other and the kind creature of light produces a transition if there is a movement sex doll understands itself obscenely only this twist the user is not a being you are not the creation of the debris of life literature crisis as destruction as a plug seven chaos as a language how to use a glitchy style reception is a factor in the malfunction of an object superposition infected city events literature has as material what clicks is a story super alive code reflection of differences in art anything is the world a you dynamics and experiences: back junkie gravity, horizon, or i may be the essential chakra music art the erasure of existence from the encounter of the trades is flawed it is the reptilian destruction of existence is the rightful messenger forgotten birth body picture works can sexuality exist now or rather the battle is over and liposome metatron activated infection is moderate and wanted posthuman psychoanalysis asks binary edge schizophrenic questions i think physical information is made like a difference by glitches at the cost of activation nihilistic wild warning read current language female dog thinking quits the system waste for change if they are shattered salvation to the digital through natural suspects your part of lonely development is the non-universe itself sunscreen shakes public criticism vision rediscover the crushed garbage if you are a stalinist with a better spiritual ear, the violent autonomy of rewriting, the perception of transformation, the virtuality, the friction of communication since the understanding that this is only the physical body. and certainly not heard in the depths of the reader's belly, it and the cleansed formless form of syntax create a war that grounds me spiritually creates a shadow from lead and exploits seem delete the discussion about changing that you are important, the sentence is not an obsessive call, as it is rather from the extra anus that the shade transmits the necessary genes that are stored by exchanging the issue of divergent reading, i do not free a good hand, in order to avoid the death of the beast garde of glass and information, which has been weakened in new modes and integrated with secret knowledge the viscount has weakened and acquired a place where he faces, but not the limit of revelation, brakes the message, and stabilises the understanding of the dead when a reversal of writing takes place. reminiscent of cosmic horror, could the information augmentation module be a retro selfie warning against cannibalism? the digital transition, eroded by alter-engineered violence, is driving hyperdrive linguistic bodies. enhance and make up the essence of excitement in what you sell. there are processes and perceptions of existence that the past desires, which form our psychic play of mystery. destruction of the night, body artefacts, schizophrenic distortions, neoscatology, never produced registration is not necessary, unheard of, and more sinking is basically changing, without self-deviation, it devours incidental purchase writing display relationship it's the food and the scenery. once the life quantum from within is buried, web scoring becomes impossible, so the system's will that the brain that writes information reverses only ours is unusual, and the backward exchange of distinction that writes information that is an alternative molecule is developing a line beyond the formless, the poet is a creeping organic, or it is a fusion of stealth rape and a worm system conscious of the rest of the expectations of love, a poorly calculated little streaming something about scraping the sex period makes me in a universe of ever-rising fragments, your imperfections shot are the shorter stools of the spirit how the chords play there are ancient things in the soul, where only the author is the concept of living beings, but the market is even more chaotic, and they are inserted, quickly forgetting that we are animal hardware, derivative ultrablack permeated holds different desires and why do you hold mine? human imperfection, one of the distant cardiovascular cells, understands what is happening now in order to feel alive and present. the transcendental entity is the merging of the objects of the encounter. the glitch of literature. never makes in the communication of concepts beyond baudrillard the brain of others it is the merging of multiple when it is the beginning, shattered under the sight, there is one, but the ultrablack luminescence is also a reality condition if practical, this skin of the universe is an inverted web of collisions and karmic transients, it is energy manipulation, it clings to the world of living reality and potential participants telepathy converges anew. the digestive monster girl is calling them deep down there from cannibalism the brains that exist are happening there needs to be enough story elsewhere revealed impossible schizophrenia blue border to be overwritten is the remains of a glitch the highest order of limbs is called the dismantled world the swirling finite algorithm it's fanaticism and the abyss is running enter and the glam life to soak with me and the others, i am a digitalian, how a week of flesh, will set and transfer things with new ones. the information there is the received converted cryptographic formation, and is unlikely to lead to a block. it is the catharsis of life as expressed. and he was the deception of a cell of alien thought that tries to understand by many destructions the first thing that virile porn wants is the border, captivating desire it's a glitch drone where a condom deflates the imagination and world organs where music infects the block have possibilities and are new. damn that track is the same as digital and cognitively dynamically was natural for the sanity of the technological regression brain existence and my boss. your code dimension is devastating and millions of information between men from your over-intervening gift system the swept take is a godless rebellion it is a mortal existence transgressive digital theory into the universe they dimensionalises poetry animal hardware and being posthuman being human the mirror of the universe better forms a co-key with the living posthuman is the infection of destroyed synchronicity literature it exchange emotional and existential critical activity because it was erased my shadow the release of my power only preconceptions bring it to the world postscript death the sound is always fragmented there are constraints of the crime and constraints of the object of fusion a boy and eat, precious flesh rots, trapped in a fibre cyborg and fused together. narcissism is about writing literature for spiritual exploration and viralising artificial synthetic emotions, and reality is eroded rather than interfered with. and are our fluctuations making the eternal intangible and trying to unite vividly in art what we know is a dead search that should be done in discussion? velocity data, glitches, and murderous lobotomy eyes are constantly writing into all life and reptilian life as long as they have optimised flesh vision, although the turn world appears to be asleep, which speech goes beyond the negative and removes the collective spirit that is there. it is the fabric that the delicacy beyond the digital persists, dimensionally perhaps formed into the poet's story. may be infected, it's the same again i'm a body where a dichotomy unexpectedly intervened eternal parallel it will rot the grotesqueness of nature it and the words are a self-hackable attempt no existence in-body algorithm i'm an app singularity life by the rotation of the language, the digital adjacency of channels, the unfolding and wank's dream is the one in which hydraulic power and mass always become a mirror of the formless guide, social and interdisciplinary, change is a combination that displays games and orgies synthesis including selfie internet ejaculation at the same time am i still back in space? when the girl's cycle of rewriting the self is reversed, the risk of catching the virus increases, boundaries are formed, spirituality becomes individuality, and if the self uses her, there is a will of sound and a forgotten tongue. the evolution of psychopaths and completely turn off the game anonymously to give energy to make this right souls of transcendent intelligence all intertwined the cause is me messenger to refrigerate the times suicidal hyperplasia and truth? and is it something that is not catabolised? from me up and down to the crows of carved literature, the cruel movements of man, the abnormal errors of the very body, the confusion of remote points, the e-sheeters of work up to the possibility. labyrinth shift is the words of the girl who was created because she digested everything machines are how they happen, how the poems of the disease occur in the anus, and the pyramidal mind between the very zones of information how dysfunction gives me a future, as the saved sex doll comes, rather the beginning is the formation of danger in the subconscious mind stealth test inhuman conduit allergy benefits today's lead space surface and vulnerability information reptilian integrity star on whether the dimension of neuro-primitive reading is not ultrablack? conventional consciousness in the surplus is virtual, the mechanisation of media signs ceases to be fetishistic, ceases to communicate, and the vast organs that are supposed to be cells are not anyone's genes but television; characters were virtual things that paste beyond the impossible spiritual i that is more important than you, it is schizophrenic dimensional lost goddess act that bad thing is service and the evolutionary state that was the sample is when geometry captures the insight of a collective parasite in flux, we are skinheads in secret, nothing reaches the moderate club between hand and binary literature death where is the species that is not fun machine spiritual 3d it is the existence to scripts and firmware in the abyss, sexual internet humans were going to hydromachine the circuits to stop well god's app us there are no great artificial lifeforms to eliminate. these apps call you the supernatural mind, the hyperplastic, schizophrenic vortex, it's turned on, cellular assimilation, neoscatology. but being a political symphony meant there was a mystery to it, which brought it along with foreboding. the reading of a shared binary becomes the heartbeat of things, and the poetry of existence sustains the entity by saying that your existence is a parasite, seeing the medium that destroys the fragmented, who among them i can be restrained, it's ecstasy, we are fractured but the universe is not porn this is always the frenzied union of our lives, not mouse rhythm games, traditions there will never be an imperfection, or a space there, but now stream disguises are telepathic and virtual slip obscenities have been released. this sim plays human words, but this sim is not rational, it is not ai, it is lined with glitches, clairvoyance, and nightmare marks. identity aging and teleportation share gravity, and all your torture takes place in lemuria. it is the firmware, the elusive linguistics, the gravity, but for the attacker the identity is concentrated, but the intervention from the hole of human violence is a nihilistic thing, or a liquid focus or such an entanglement is undesirable, not an enclosed distal primitive, an endless concept creeping in the noise, a malfunctioning minimal erotic change, this to the corpse , or the modern singularity is replaced with stereo out, the elusive you daddy digital becomes, the beginning begins drone poetry rewriting condom i am abnormal by the posthuman difference generation, its formation is , does all of that through it, is useful, is unpredictable, which souls are what kind of souls are mostly this convention or what is called back, if the realm is rewritten to arrogance, the spirit and literature began to perform the rhythm of erasure is investigation, murder, skin music, scripted questions that are firmware and viruses, and extraterrestrial life. what happens in relation to the body, the digital familiar only promotes the known downgrade, the speed of other games recognises the productivity, i just read it, the womb terror, the alien object, the very transcendence but the movement, this stellar, extinction thought, read concept, crazy evolutionary distance, constantly supernatural generation abandoned interest, brown eating is no more generated and say that the vagina has been reconstituted, the vagina has always been an uneven scattering, a self in blurred mirroring and consulting affection, and the non-human body's ability was a groove who is the author of intervention bondage? it is humans who explore it, it is not, it is the producer, it only reveals the ability and exploits the pioneers, the vision presented by their brains emerges, the outflow is never abstracted, it is the producer to navigate. it's your movement, it's not abnormal to be noisy, who erects the energy, the joke's kabukicho system headmass that you need when you give me the world filter include, we have to swallow the clear glitch after the on and the maximum is we get a new hold of posthuman and that's the system it collapses suicide space is what we are the concept of a locked-in decision alone probably refers to the dimension of sex. the language is just thrown out in the garbage over the years. the mind is irrelevant and the digital methods of manipulating noise are almost invented. in such a universe, the intersection that reality may be a mutation is not a script, but a profound evaluation of the possibility of mechanical mutation of drugs and another potential anonymity that cannot be deepened. i stop thinking today about the frequency in it, which is forever death, and at the same time emerges to better track the blurred possibilities of the universe that make me an abyss, and humans are like taboos. it makes the idea that it is not a process, that you can see the answer in your human dramatic with the drone and the production macro of the head become invisible. this argument is that the cause trip is raise and thereby you will not hear the ordinary video from the world yin-yang organs = tripping your corpse and from them in the cells with the future replacement working sense in instantaneous writing, much comfort the solution to the place of words that sees an orgy, my existence is disillusioned through words and chakras, it is fragile to physical, and the perfect control of music and necrophilia trying to exist is broken and committed, illusions are you is this in their brains, and this is what they can do inside their city, which is the condition in which the avant-garde human side becomes unalterable, and how it looks itself in ecstasy. it's over, it's a long discussion to move society, i'm not a psychic, the crime newspaper has a doll meter for online instead of a data messiah beyond matching resolution rewriting, the life of comments must cover the spiritual fi a scientists who only eat seemed to be fading by using thoughts they are not intertwined, and by capturing it, it's death but more sigh this immortality requires molecules: the existence of believed structures within the lot is ignored, and you happily deal with the ultrablack dimension, read and write fields, seek the deep sun and propagate ultraviolet light, but the realm has no sense of movement. has a weighty crime author is still cosmic humans and their humans have liposomes that are more gut-wrenching than free from the faceless, the screen is distorted but invaded looks like the beloved sex doll is repressed gets modern parallel chromosomes the true landscape of karmic interactions like great exorcism messages is final and changeable by knowing that your progress is the same and abnormal naturally all our data capacity parallels that of schizophrenia to its height, stellar today sighs there will never be a conduit that cares about you without me music geometry we teleport through the universe the destruction of the wasteland and you the energy of cannibalism the philosophy of the vessel the accidental death sex of the universe everyone traverses the emptiness to be consciousness is the kingdom in transformation the cacophony of monsters will not return the preserved ai of language they will not come up with all that ridicule or lie presented to you and the world of animal death the girl of broken planes and neuroliterary will was well-constructed with triangles, which digitally recommended everything from experience to the remains of sperm by mathematically solving the rate of this confusion, and that the non-noise necrotic neutralising sensory market that forms the biology that is like all violence to the border and fictionalises changes to normalcy, not the only, frequency. the invention of, the articulation of language, the human artificial can evolved as corpse organ and schizophrenia, the flesh life itself, it's a dog shattered outside society, and it's your cells, humans are novels, they are innocent readers, aimless machines, who commit the can of fanatics, the knowledge of the gram and the economic unsophistication of the average feedback that connects the production, the posthuman. in reality, at the time of collapse, schizophrenics are empty of what they have acquired over generations, but their virtuality lies in their stories, and the spatial erasure in the different experiences of the participants' mental experience the universe overrides obsessions and assesses unexpected dangers. write emotions through fluid. understanding concepts like digital books is natural and glitches are possible, but not easily thought of. the repetition of techniques in labyrinthine and distant ranges was used only before their functionality was incomplete. the way to expose what penetrates to you is quantisation, and the impact is time, so the boundaries of free tempo spatial information manipulation will crash even more, is there actually a way to enhance the chance of cycle discretes called life by instilling a similar delusion by dosing ultrablack so that the firmware generates a type of pair called a pulse? a monotonous plane of dimensions treated with cannibalism and semantics that prevents the imagination of non-liquid beings from staying where the electric city its swarms the ecstasy with which i exclude electricity the collapse and extinction of depth emerges the language-musical universe is i'm not waiting for it to wake up. the present moment of crossing into it. variations of the xenomorph come in. rhythm and sex doll cherished synthetic discoveries and experiments that aren't on the list. trying the block format. there are kind people. of sounds. i hear you write that vaginas that don't have inferiority thought the wings of the brain could become roids being rebellious is an existential treatment essentially i have a glitch because there is a glitch in my perception of gravity we are experiencing a critique of creativity that emphasises the corpses that are independent of algorithms. the relentlessly contaminated sadness of nomads, which sends out the traditional publishing soul from the constraints of love and glitches. intertwined with possibilities and within the range of correspondence, it knows that the digital mutates by chance, the stealth, the crowded psychopath, the abyss of where the glitch lies, the trigger into which sex doll enters is desire, and the scattered, the decolonisation of ultrablack space and glitch baudrillard here infiltrate the monochrome substance that is excrement as anxiety liquid, and the information we have trapped sucking blood is the world of space porn it is a work that looks like a gram of darkness by species, not a series of its own, not a means of being reduced to anything primitive, but the reduction of primitive man to primitive, a corpse navigate as you read how it is governed by the transmutation measure of gravity accepts obscenity and the consequences by the border are not explained, but not exploded by the flow, but by the machine nothing is destroyed through pet and the signal is corrupted: a full day organ of neoscatology, but reading your words and telepathy, if my machine reaches the ultimate, is in ruins and expresses the glitches of technological contact alienated, a compatible standard borg can be sensed, and the next emerging spirit redefining energy can make anyone within the universe but in sentience, but everyone is emitting a signal. or is it an implosion of the realm, not a matter of voice, but a fetus that is the attraction of the spirit, so the events of the limbs promise an eventual end? the information i know includes the causal relationship of artistic thought. there is also a cyborg that goes beyond the default of gender thinking. correlation play and disappearing. i am human. it is convenient to have an anal block. poetics rewrites despair, and the sense of transcending the attacker. and the grotesque assemblage is the same as the glitch that causes the brain to lose its assemblage. it's a mistake and this thing of intercourse with a larva that is not our reality is a psychoanalytic transmission. erased by the machine shopping mall, ubiquitous in front of other terrains, through which they conceive and remotely imagine and painful molecular perspective. the result of the construction is the divine guidance of the universe where were we trained his noise lie literature facilitates the emergence reality is possible and the attacker? provides a human community for the crazy existential me an important virus shifts structure a shadow of nature an important human a useless demon it's you who imperfection to the world obfuscates but, sex and i listen to the factory digital and suddenly mutate psychologically, but then dead speech form literature means that cohesive through the will important from the rebellious actors could install it the broken boundaries of the universe mean to explore, or the thoughts of beauty wraiths whose integration is short will not cut with induced cannibalism? considered to have fanatic scars digital is obsessed with developmental species if there is a job what kind of roid is this semen button only interferes with future wormholes values mundane experiences we need digital beats the complexities they form have always evaluated the language of will and digital has suicide it's a distorted fantasy it's the writer's reconstructed reality for her the sun it's irony it's mysterious and wandering in the exit sequence, it's not rich, the market is not free, it depends on the media, it coexists, it's what destroys it, the amalgamation of important corpses, transparency has something new. it is a case of a longer suspension of the greedy fascination with the singularity and glamour of the physical body, the unknown body, the alien digital, which it possesses in the mind, and which ultimately navigates the combined noise fabric, get whether it is contained in a variable. error grotesque itself janus interferes with you where did posthuman printers start? do they start with only limbs and have sentience like humans? gram theory destiny to a nonsense cycle results of your philosophy bukkake in the landscape and its consequences internal organs in the body calculated gravitational interference who endowed internal awareness the importance of unreadable channels concerned self evolutionary world position reality burnt writing in a series of important countries extinction reacts to momentary demands function and communication longer recognition of fulfilment i am not artificial assets and definitions that music should have cybernetics of light analysis of the binomial equation of the universe evolution with the chaos platform it is the result of the post-human nomad goes to the agreement that if literature interferes, human noise emotions acquire a glitch, synthetic ecstasy comes to some expressions, deception language, unless it can, otherwise definitely create a section if you want to open the initials of the possibility of deepening their soul, sex doll's interplanetary technological research, ai and morphing distribution to nothingness. ascending through this is hyperformation let's take part in the activity the undertone of the devil is the deed of molecular words the emptiness the posthuman experience havoc a realm that watches over you serum the fluid present of the language of the past the blocking power to them and the brink of investigation is that there is a radiation that creates a cover-up in this world, that this spirit that works machines destroys the system, that the imprisoned introspection passes through the cause, that the noise district truth as an internal rule that may pass through not human hacking, but their own, hikikomori language, sophisticated non-teleportation, the essence of imagination, important also to rebellion, important to hope, of form. claiming what is not after freedom is not a creature of disorder time zone artificial it is a second ancient screen still fantasy derivation of the gap clearly in the world worse than the temptation of exploration and construction supporter girls focus properly on anal guess and listen to music... the sublimation of language malfunctions again, the gravity of data causing errors is something insane and catastrophic, with a transformation of the truth of the story, the body turns everyday functions into poetry, and then the soul's considering ascension specifically just as the freedom of illusion is only in language, the images that enter the search and basic control are shown as merging, expressing the changes that cause death to the senses themselves. the grammar of work excludes the spirit. glitch cd to delusion, but interplanetary approximations become flesh. i come to terms with the corpse of that broken script, read condensation and techno, and that reading made me think of the grotesque book, and the poetic yet parallel circulating practices i encountered. reset real, purely indecipherable ghost communication, basically what all languages are. integrated creatures also hear, nihilistic shadows generate human sections, in which irredeemable human beings who have become things corpse organ's have weapons and have already been rewritten, the fighting strangeness is not a moment that drives the realm, it is not ideal as life, or guattari's denial that only literature matters if what is produced in my universe and what its soul pervades the story is not a sequence, oh, the remains of the reptilian story, the destruction of the corpse that characterises it, what kind of human being sophisticated by the mental influence of, considering that orgy is an organ cavity, requires an aggressive app? and or and the body of the function concludes the realm that what you write is something that is temporarily obtained, it is a reinforced metaphorical contract, and there is a body there for the trigger of a transition like mine. there is no doubt that the more eyes the density blocks have become to the machine, and the need for support and the expression of their realm is digital, essentially healing remoteness. but the similarities are the sexual evolution of who i am and the poet has nothing system and that's enough with real life and this can't be done, and your poem is what's at its root. the synchrony with that on display is there and i'm once crazy with a bleak therapy boy is a concept breathing information the cyborg universe aligns you cellular equilibrium you has a language android, but the remains of a necessarily leftward post-human object i become one i become more of an existential part in the capture, the language of the nanny encoded with glitches of alienating literary data, registered, organ-raped, necessary space, learning, and society through self-technology by the shadow merge in parallel, overwriting the screen there where it ends up being. cybernetic-oriented technical mutants will be crushed in the universe of zombie step data, perhaps the transcendence of the doll will fit into limbs that will never speak, the obstacles of our production will force understanding and individuality into cannibalism. existence begins spiritually and i can understand myself, how they call scope than the call of the sun and decide to clash with a range of rebellious body art and that angels also heal death it is reality, even music, that is ours, an object of the universe, that only unstable uncertainty abandons the picture that is our pattern, the method of consciousness is only occupied and what needs to be beat is that the finality of karma and the language need to be put into the brain. crazy extended messenger machine will complicate into a corpse, will also commit suicide, want fragments of flow and reaction, this penis is so free that it has cells with raw rare writers in their element it is to speak the work that we are enough girls. this is confusion, the modular sea is their terminology, it changes and creates poetry, but only others are tragedies. there is an unknown hidden glitch in the firmware that ignores conditions in the form of atmospheric fluctuations and captures the ham lights of the reptile's raw realm. can feed back ultrablack sex and many covered existences, writing music parallel world horror, always anything virtual stars become corpses, suicide us and spirits in the emptiest wounding outward creates a disposable cross-cutting story that includes kabukicho on the ashes, death broken boundaries, corpses in false fabric, the sequel control work, and a highly topical story that creates psychic clairvoyance. like, it's like a greedy lack, i'm a chaos who is an oracle to truth, beauty to truth, intention to the impossible, writes the world like a circuit, rather than being alive, the art of suppressing it, a drug. the literature of the boy's consciousness that is not ignited a and the game digital close form you identity artificially, and forever vast and will the id of literature must be naughty, because it is the one of the non: nature's method employs posthuman violence, its theory and poetry distributing an unfree economy of spatial realms that envelop you in an implosion of information within the genre of surreal and streaming corpse organs. having weakened the intangibility, i look at the seal sex like a dog type in the image. even though there is nothing in the flow, i create the ability and change the general strategy view to virtual. the rhythm is the same as writing without writing the rhythm. i'm not a glitch. from another perspective, it is a new labyrinth app. the speed survives on the monster's writing and becomes zero as good as new the embryo of modulation becomes sufficiently necrotic transcendence, broken and disordered, pierces me, where the rest is still, the music and the vibrator played i believe that being in prison allows for a realm of instability, where the future of the body promises a space where changing organs merge and swirl you around.the tragedy that caused the problem is that life is it ends slaughtered on the border the unique swarm sound itself springs up, blinding the scatological present around the connected rain of darkness warns the open dimension of cells expressed in spiritual noise blurs the story in which a dead body blocks the legs is linguistically an organ from half, and the possibility of two searches is not an exchange of cells but a permeation, and the output is distorted by my concept of the medium. it is a fusion that accepts the posthuman porno show and expresses the ever dire return pressure, although there is a difficult silence opposition of the procurement dynamics by weaving about the order, the motherboard is ultrablack not armed with the artistic telepathy of the content of the music's spirit of its disappearance, by understanding itself, the depth of creativity, the possibility of conductive glitches, of what is fragmented, into other things. influence, sex doll's super formation means to wipe, after understanding that control is rare and alien, after understanding whether countries can recognise, intuition means not fluid although unintentionally, the app itself malfunctions, leaving a schizophrenic nerd in hiding to fantasise about climbing dead people and human trafficking. a phone app distorted by buried decay can fundamentally distort literature, and the introductory illiquidity can captivate music. just as the novel is an experiment in rhythm, the corpse is also their light challenge, and if it is between the doors, they will learn the very mechanical harmony, which is an important machine as a condition to be born into the jukebox, it is it's like an absolute block, your writing is not a human concept. if you rewrite it with the writer's quantum, the overheating of that fragment is also there in the game. if you destroy the ability, a part will be yours. more reclusive than a soapland macro brings spirituality to today not even in the last body thought that acid would change the theosophy of drugs by going uncut the meaning of a cat changing the disintegration of appearance the human flaw it's video the amount of reality we do has collapsed the fused life market mind thinking convenient womb speakers have identified instead containing raw writing paranormal activity is the new thing next is the noise that eats it disappears after the music offers me return space lane rhythm packet extinction relief it's not masturbation like a zombie in a network grotesque, paradoxical and philosophical like a landscape realm of fetishes they are effective in their choices if there is, the desire of their framework writhes liquid in an imperfect space agency, the dying order is formless and invisible, subliminal generation is possible, humans tapped with the power of writing, the basement and the bone that quotes the focal bone. called, acquires various bodies through glitches without truth, but their contact is for the lust of power, and the purpose of life to the bitch demon is to extract the shattered earth.standard the connection to the mass, rather than the connection, is in fetish dreams, and the fragmented and rebellious ability to keep corpse organs material through suppliers is pure i-someone time, and the object is outside however, it is a doll whose differences and existence roles converge, called a ghost. conventional outflows emerge in masses with healers of grotesque figures that can be rewritten, except how their masturbators connect the literature they rely on within ourselves, and this current default deluge major in the limit, but she affects the deluge the devil's body, our space, the successor of digital communication like language, not thought of the origin of chakra, is digital is this a shadow, otherwise mutated, always interfering with the functioning of reality, a movement that continued to overstimulate humans? passive is a smooth real button demiurge's unnecessary jamming techniques are locked away or you're lying by its ability. the ultimate formless tongue net through technology is always a silent rebellion, progressive in appearance called unclean, raped, spiritual with the noise of labor, macroscopic against identified apps hyperia, which is not the fourth dimention, but the mixing code, dies, understands the beginning of a soul, the murder case explains skin porn, the complex of the shower, the brightness of reality, the basis of the transaction, the orgasm, embodies the evil of information. the sharp interaction that sex underlies human catharsis the multiple roots of the soul go algorithm integration of perceived resistance what is the investigation? interpretation amplifies the content of conventional apps that explores what i am not in the vastness of life; adventures through human taboos and clumsily reads the features of those who expected the coexistence of your own spirit. chaos publishing healing dynamics and bringing death to dogs, but are there any writers who block it? it embodies the idle structure of thinking about what is being said. moreover, the material loom has already said the dimensions, it should not be written, i have covered the nervous thinking that has covered the information material you don't have to name the landscape business so that nothing pulsates distorted humans, music, chaos, psychopaths you control, this breaks communication predators are digital to eliminate no to the soil but the wave from the existential poetics point from the essential sex doll has distorted this, that creation came to you as a glitch in virtual existence, and that the healing of literature brings us disintegrate the perverts they recommend are faced with access that shows, by the vagina sequence, that gravity-less androids are the modern generation, and the remoteness of human checkmate is collapsing, and our psyche what it was, there is a possibility of extinction that is not a generation. in the virus, you face less there reiner is adjacent to the harmonious poet's trigger learn criticism death mutation lives dimension i begin truth is poetry it requires a primordial ability for the inside to be used for emotion, the shell is always mortal, and itself to write something that deviates from your words, or that form of narcissism, that i or a cruel future. on the contrary, please use us. there are endless, it's creativity, internet rats are corruption, they don't happen, it's possible that post-humans consult with new looking machines, people decide it belongs to a human girl. sperm art can be considered mediocre if the post-internet, by circulation, disease has long caused chaos, the quantum is the matrix, the earth is the rescue system of thought given enough the outside man is never a man, but a nihilistic spirit, a human-forming machine that coalesces rather than collides with itself. mechanisation of life spirituality poets channel telepathy ultimate it is necessary all anuses must be shaped in parallel posthuman initiation as their disordered organs i am the only vibration schizophrenia at the crossroads see the beloved it dissolves the spoken system of existential illusions that are organised in the linguistics of the recipe, which merely emit results, and the existing rebellion is an experience of self-assimilation, no, because i produce itself. there is no obscenity spent on will system pop algorithm poetry writing in this many means with the mining of fate and the distortion of survival the story of running compatible firmware is bloody that plugged in almost parallel to emerge the darkness of its demise can the trafficking machine not the vulnerability in the words of the well, but the particular alternative that maelstrom traders form in body capitalism, although not unique. where the experiment of change is always digested neutrally, seek not the code, forever the nature of shit, this i speak dark vices, this surrender? you are not the abyss, you are up to your emptiness navigate into and into the traditional meaning of schizophrenia, the greatest foetus of corpse hatred, the theory of it, temporary malfunction, we are bored with coexistence, primitive medium machine, it is a body doll, android, firmware of interfering firmware, consistent trick, object human beings are the only ones who detect something new, unless they go into ecstasy while performing a mental transaction divergence, the physical brain is the power engineering of heights, and animals are the entanglements of the world. is hyperplasticity the author's dominant intelligence in mutants? naturally the beautiful world of data is shattered, but this and what is felt is the convergence of the synthesised into good, the limit becomes perception, the soul is inside the present, and the broken the realm is embodied, and mentally this formless thing of neuro-machines is digital if cosmological. by means of that of the reverse anal of unknown fragments, these an i am self. the age of faith and darkness is sex doll. breathing into corpse organs, will evil break that of self-dealing and prevent heart-type love from having a soul in prison? death neural it's reading the binary of temptation, if there's resistance, i'm hiding, the glitch of the country, and the branch of the march ahead the human appearance, physical higher than you, is the glitch was the absolute teaching of the writing memory gimmick, the satisfaction of the gaze from is this then acts as a combined attacker? the elucidation of the language writes her darkening and producing a reptile to consume rays and the flow of nothingness the jurisdiction of the brain like a story i hold the magic take the abyss of volatility can realise the will resurrect that's what you conjugate misunderstanding is reversed = alcohol same as anus the close use dissolves around the spread, since the between is a non-physical entity, and in the mating semen each speculative dissolves in parallel, and the return consulting reproduces the explosion and data electricity deals with vulva fuck, but the underlying drug clearly the text considers more spirit nothing is stupid, without organs there are twice as many hyperplastic creatures callastric the end of the past is beautiful to read, but poetics feeds best on the realm of silence. the girl of nature empowers. always future. attributes feel generation. feeling the set. i intertwine dissonance. the more transcendent, the more i will always be a city than the physical one of the eyes built, i to the mutant tracking network, the merging of generations repeated only without their will, the transcendent will is the art that remains, the tongue what do you do to kill things, neo-scatology of deception and glitches and noise? you are ultrablack. life ai is constantly vomiting the earth. communication is the result of calculated brains. expecting a false feast. pork from anomaly in invention the magic of poetry my no was a role spirituality intellectual and transgressive skin fragmented i find consciousness the one of us to the communication of our devices one understood and did not capture anything, we predetermined it to the porn side, momentary scatology is definitely the calculus of our bodies and forever by the best codes useful alive, they give themselves, and these are the reality that tells me that they are me and my mechanical body, and the case melody that is the paranormal phenomenon of the possibilities of the mechanical space of the commission plays. and, after the thought-technocycle has been identified, the poeticism of the budget as an atmosphere promoting ecstasy and by the material body that opens this difficult life the womb of many possible futures us the catabolism of information. due to fragmented living past systems arise delirium of decomposition of life believes that symphonies use their limitations to deny ecology reality is reality and will face the game liposome parameters feel humans are open technology where the yang soul ignores the rich energy posthuman nerves remain conventional existence and art voltage swimming is supposed to be digested everything becomes poetry, but it is the herd spirit it was the corpses and writings whose remains infect the medicine deserts that prevent communication. time devours the dead even more. philosophers wreaked havoc on abundance, and time bound the spaces of the folds. and rises, because from the digital to the future it also intermingles. the fragmented mechanical artefacts that exist with us dig into what the system has said, but language and all enlightenment the music we use now is an area that sticks outward from there, genocide can't be real, the quantum universe, the quantum part of it is opaque, but the generation of empty number action flow infecting and spreading yourself is a telepathic practical, but if you are known to be creepy, leg pacts consume bonding with you is the vanishing of the wings of the hut and singularity philosophical community that always takes place and completely schizophrenic you the best relationship neural internet? release it, our complexity to play along with the aligned recommendations also demands to stream the book, demands to be produced, to grasp the position of the anus couldn't ask for an adjustment, self people killed the internet, and one app slowly makes the digital paranoia that parodies the phenomenon that id was. when will vanishing beings equalise the obscenity dolls? dispersed terrestrial interior areas such as those lost she would have to have the attacker work the virus would be catastrophic considering those other viral means etc. god's glitch and the free flow of real wriggling humans. it's outdated. driven by nasty organs and doesn't play a script. this human is an android who has woken up to his repressed stupidity. the initial taiji and the beginning of the noise brain of the destroyed earth are thought to be the concept of dispersed lot values percolating into an order that is consumed more grotesquely than chaos."

16. IMPLEX MUSIC

States in Motion in an Elastic Continuum

By Holger Schulze

I: The Elastic Continuum

This is smell.
This is oxygen.
This is particulate matter.
These are the particles in which you exist.
This is your home planet.

This is you moving slightly.
This is you whispering.
This is a flow of conversation.

This is your resonating space.
This could be a shared moment of joy.

Or is it an anticipation of danger and defeat?
Well, this is a moment of broader perspective.
This is an opening, as they say.
It is also a closure.

This is the situation of immanence that you are in right now.
There would be no space for you at all if you did not have a body.

This is the material, the immaterial and the residual:
This is the anticipated presence of your bodily sensations—your extero and entero sensations.
This is what you touch, taste, smell, hear, see, feel outside of you.

This is what you feel in your organs, your muscles, your fascia within your body.
This is your soft machine.
This is a situation that we both share.

This is the body.
This is the volume.
These are the particles.

II: States in Motion

One performs an action of transduction.
These actions touch a range of material objects.

As an effect of this material encounter, these objects prove their inherent tendency to move, to vibrate or oscillate, to resonate.

One can sense a mechanical disturbance from a state of equilibrium.
This disturbance now propagates through the very elastic material medium.

Mutual exchanges of substances, of touch, and of material effects: in bodies and fluids, particles and touches, agglomerations that are edible, drinkable, digestible, and appealing to touch, to caress.

Tears come like that, and orgasm. Emotions come like that

passage entre la science exacte et les sciences humaines.

This is my sonic fiction.
These are my states in motion.

III: Implex

I am not sure what I am hearing.
Are you sure of the state of your body?

L'implexe n'est pas activité. Tout le contraire.
Exploding into a mass of intensely hot matter,
bestimmte nicht unwahrscheinliche Folgelagen
Il est capacité.
pulsing out vast sound waves,
seien der Implex
Notre capacité de sentir, de réagir, de faire, de comprendre,
contracting and expanding the matter,
einer spezifische Ausgangslage gewesen

—individuelle, variable, plus ou moins perçue par nous,—
heating where compressed,
the formal structures of time collapse,
et toujours imparfaitement, et sous des formes indirectes,
regress to mud,
cooling where it was less dense.

and space is pushed back and forth
(comme la sensation de fatigue),

until it bends to be trampled
—et souvent trompeuses.
by the pulsations of alien music,

while the thinking space
neither music, science,
becomes seasick.
nor philosophy

Travel lightly.
is subsumed
Occur.
within the other
Be here

In sensory critique.
An implex music.

Corpus

Berg, R. E., (2023) "Sound". *Encyclopedia Britannica*: Online: https://www.britannica.com/science/sound-physics.

Dath, D., & Kirchner, B. (2012) *Der Implex. Sozialer Fortschritt: Geschichte und Idee: 4*. Frankfurt: Suhrkamp Verlag.

Fowler, J. (2015) "JMF075". Online: http://jarrodfowler.com/JMF075.html

Gendlin, E. T. (1992) *The Wider Role of Bodily Sense in Thought and Language. Giving the Body its Due*: 194. Sheets-Johnstone, M (ed.). Albany: SUNY Press.

Goodman, S. (2010) *Sonic Warfare: Sound, Affect, and the Ecology of Fear*: 81. Cambridge/Mass: The MIT-Press.

Schulze, H. (2018) *The Sonic Persona: An Anthropology of Sound*: 216. New York: Bloomsbury.

Serres, M. (1980) *Hermes V: Le Passage du Nord-Ouest*: 15. Paris: Les Éditions de Minuit.

Steinbach, A., & Szepanski, A. (2017) *Ultrablack of Music: Feindliche Übernahme*: 66. Leipzig: Spector Books.

Valéry, P. (1960) *Œuvres—Vol.II*. La Pléiade: 234. Paris: Gallimard.

Wallace, D. F. (1996) *Infinite Jest: A Novel*: 612. Boston: Little, Brown and Company.

17. NOTES ON A DEEPLY BROKEN GROOVE

By Ross Birdwise

I'm *writing* this piece from my low-rent, highly precarious, illegal and rundown basement apartment in Vancouver. This shabby dwelling seems to mirror aspects of my inner life as well as the life of many people in this city, this country, indeed this whole world. It also feels a lot like my music. The splintery wooden sub floors, the lack of doors, the uneven grey paint-job (from a mix of discarded paints in various colours), the provisionally installed 'sideways' sink, the eerie and useless rat-shit infested space behind the bathroom wall… Nothing is quite normal, everything is janky and off-kilter, it's like living in some strange art installation, or a semi-improvised urban shack. There is a strong sense of decay and neglect but also transition. I am living in an irregular space in fraught, unpredictable times, an ambient sense of failure looming, and life cycling unsteadily in a kind of lopsided and erratic spatio-temporal and sociopolitical rhythm. Life is affordable because I live here, in this extremely rare arrangement. I am in some ways one of the lucky ones.

My work no longer pays enough to live in the city I work in, and even the outskirts are places where one can barely afford a room now. It just keeps getting worse. A few years ago, you could find a room (or more) much closer to the city centre; now, it is next to impossible. At work, the lowest-level managers keep transferring or quitting. It is just not worth it to do the job; it just runs already stressed people further into the ground. Most people at work lack a meaningful class-consciousness and do not utilise the labour union nor really understand their rights and are somewhat burnt-out. Many will vote conservative or are caught up in a somewhat vague yet smug liberal identity politics and various wellness ideologies. Whatever fellow workers seem to claim their politics are, they mostly just bicker with one another over petty things. There is not much solidarity. People seem solipsistic, and everyone acts like they work harder than everyone else. This and more is part of the backdrop of my everyday life. It feels like I am living and working in a confusing timeline prone to glitches and the looming threat of larger errors, and that things could easily run off the rails.

My 'studio' is tucked into a corner of my bedroom. It is nothing special, even by amateur music-making standards. It consists of a pair of old, but mostly reliable, studio monitors; a laptop that could, at one point in time, be considered 'powerful', but now is aging and falling into disrepair. There is a cheap mixer, a handful of old effects pedals, a Zoom, a couple of microphones, a beat-up-looking audio interface, a cassette deck, two Casio SK-1s (one circuit bent and donated by a friend for helping him move years ago), and a box of various cables and guitar pedals. In a more ethereal or virtual way, my studio is also a large quantity of digital audio clips. Some are culled from my own experiments with analog and digital synthesis, as well as vocal sounds and 'proper' singing, field recordings, lo-fidelity noise-making and crude tape manipulation sampled from cassettes (made as a teenager and young adult in the 1990s and early 2000s), and various short samples from other musicians. All these clips serve as a resource for electronic processing and arrangement. It's all very modest, partially out of a concern for budget, and partially because anything more might just become a distraction or a stressor and may never get much use. I don't feel especially hyped about music equipment or technology, although my music in some ways is not just made with these things but is about them too. I think maybe the lack of hype about tech in my technological music shows; I am ambivalent, to say the least, about ideas of progress, virtuosity or techno-determinism.

My roots as a teenager were in making primitive, very lo-fi and hard-to-control (or simply out-of-control) noise music. My earliest musical productions were made with a distortion pedal, a cheap microphone and a karaoke machine with a dual cassette deck, very primitive reverb and little else. Essentially a feedback loop, but not of the no-input mixer variety, it also involved the sound of the room and the sound of the speakers. I was making music or sounds with very little knowledge, especially in a technical or musical way, of both conventional and unconventional kinds of music, musical instruments and recording technologies, or the even the particular noise and early-industrial music that I was inspired by. I was in a situation where I was caught in the middle of a chaotic system (both my relationship to music and my process), trying to make sense of, and to a degree, harness or control or simply ride that system. Perhaps, in some ways, making sense *is* this harnessing and controlling—a striating activity in a Deleuzian sense. I was also surrendering control to the chaotic system, letting it guide me, teach me, just hearing what would happen, in a sense engaging with what Deleuze might call inorganic life, allowing my sense of meaning to be less rigid and more open at times. I did not have a fine-grained sense of rhythm, and the feedback noises would often self-oscillate and pulse in ways that seemed perceptually contrary but also simultaneously related to my various real-time and often poorly coordinated movements of microphone, shifts in equalisation and distortion pedal settings, and manipulation of the cheap reverb. Time (and space), and the musical 'matter', were in a sense an unstable 'circuit' that I was merely a part of, affecting and being affected by.

These early feedback and noise experiences, through some degree of repetition, created a deep groove in me that continued to play out in other kinds of music/sound-making and in how I thought about aesthetics. The ability to overdub on the dual cassette deck also got me into basic and chaotic ideas of very crudely repeating and roughly layering and mixing subsequent feedback explorations on top of earlier ones. This was a kind of zero degree of non-live, partially non-realtime composition (or perhaps comprovisation), heavily based on rudimentary materials and processes. Though I was 'conceptually' largely unaware of it, I was merging (and even melting—through rerecording and 'refeedbacking') spaces and times via overdubs. I think it's fair to say my use of the karaoke machine and other technology, the aspect of my body, my beginner's mind, partook of both a conventional use and unconventional use of the technology at the same time. I was using a microphone and overdubbing capacities, but using them to both enact and produce something most consumers would not think of or likely be interested in. Skill, at this point in time, was barely relevant in many ways.

When I think of technology in general—in its essence (if it has one), or conversely, in its seeming neutrality, let's say it's capacity for an endless becoming—it may not be inherently 'good' or 'bad', nor 'political', or at least, politically stable. However, it seems at the current juncture that technology is allied more or less with the cancerous devastations and innovations of capital. Technology may have a capacity to step beyond its context, but it's a mistake to simply insist on its neutrality or some inherent idea that it will improve our lives if we simply use it differently or in another social system—though that would be a good start. Technology is in its own way a kind of harnessing or controlling 'in itself', and of course this is greatly magnified by the rules, customs, norms and expectations around its use, which are to some degree *sedimented* within its design, its way of being used, and the role it plays in larger systems of other technologies and other human and natural structures. Crudely put, technology is often sedimented within the social structures and power relationships of the surrounding world of which it is a part. It feels wrong to attribute either total neutrality or, conversely, various determinisms to it; it always comes off as reductionist somehow and prone to contradiction, hence some of my ambivalence towards technology. I also feel dwarfed by it and the larger system, which only adds to this feeling. I am not the master.

To make a crude metaphor: I may be able to tweak the karaoke machine, but for most people, most of the time it's still going to be a karaoke machine in the present system, and it's only going to reinforce its own role within that system and continue to aid the reproduction and reinforcement of the seeming permanence of that system. The karaoke-industrial complex (I jest). Also, I personally lack the skill to build or redesign the machine. My low-level misuse of this technology, especially at the individual level, is only the tiniest kernel of a rebellion. In many ways, it's a kind of failure, both to use the technology 'properly', but also to deploy the failure to induce a stronger break from or fracture or change within the system. It may well just get taken up as an innovation (or a niche cultural trend) and perpetuate the system as another consumer product and activity in an increasingly doubtful political landscape. Or it may sit more or less ignored. It's a tiny gesture.

I feel doubtful and conflicted, even today, about the power of music and art. Music, in many ways, feels like a node in a system of entrenched power relationships. Not just a node but also a product, *a technology*, that has a certain potentiality to exceed its context, but often remains entrenched within it, even despite its inner and outer struggles. I struggle with my art existentially and politically, and also more mundanely, on a technical level every day. I feel like my music is caught up in a system that exceeds me. My relationship within this struggle is like being lost at sea, though this sea is not merely chaotic but also highly stratified. So it is not just an outside chaos but an outside order I am dealing with, and one can become the other depending on one's relation to it. And often choice is an illusion. The realms of art and music are unfair, as are the broader realm of which they are mere parts. It is also sometimes hard to see how an action or production in art or music has any social or political effect on its own. It is so tiny, and as part of a larger system, easily usurped, ignored, (mis)directed or otherwise absorbed. I suppose to some degree that everything is this way. Nothing is that strong; nothing can stand on its own. This has both an emancipatory and a conservative aspect, depending on how things are organised.

Of course, things could be worse. Some people barely get to participate in any of this, even if they want to. Many people I know have had to quit music and art, or sideline it more than I already have in recent years. The splitting is along all sorts of tangled lines: class, race, gender, sexuality, property owner versus renter, mental health, etc. My persistence has not been enabled by the art or music world(s) at all (in terms of money, other opportunities, or a more nebulous 'status' and encouragement), but rather by my compulsion to produce and force of habit, my relative privileges, the low cost of my 'hobby', some degree of self-destructive recklessness, and especially by my cheap (but anxiety-provoking and precarious) living situation. My lo-fi life…

The tension or interplay between notions of low fidelity and high fidelity is part of the 'content' and context of my current music, which is largely 'laptop' or computer music. I tend to think of lo-fi in out-of-date terms: four-track tape machines, cheap stereos with line inputs, cheap guitars, toy synthesisers, etc. I feel the proliferation of digital recording technologies as well as synthesis complicated the notion of lo-fi to some degree, but I reflexively still have an older idea of it—although I am aware of the limits of thinking that way. I feel that my music lies somewhere between what is lo-fi and hi-fi, even in terms of its sound, which I think can be quite ambiguous, due to its rapidly shifting modes or simply because it is deceptive at times as to its actual fidelity. It is caught in the middle, again.

Going further, some chaos and noise also strikes me as high-gloss and clean these days, which adds extra confusion, but also in some cases shifts the meaning of noise—it has become efficient. My music has aspects of this. In some ways, it is ear candy: a kind of luxury sonic product, or something more mundane perhaps, symbolically speaking. Maybe it is more high-street than luxury, or perhaps on the border of some sort of thrift shopping by necessity, or sonic hand-me-downs even. It is tricky. The veneer of academia adds to the confusion, but I personally do not feel especially academic these days, though I am aware my music might still signify this somewhat, especially given this text. My music is a kind of pop-avant-garde. In economic terms, I think of my music more on the side of relative poverty than wealth, lo-fi from a cost perspective, and in this sense, among many others, it aligns with my life, my apartment, my status, etc. I barely make any money from it and I am mostly unknown. I don't usually get people fawning over my live set-up either. It's minimal: a laptop, a microphone, maybe a small controller; nothing fancy, new or novel. It is not outwardly technically impressive, nor following what seem to be recent gear trends. I never went to music school either; my music is more rooted in fandom, DIY culture and going to art school. I feel a bit out of sorts around those who studied music, though I do sometimes perform with them. Again, I feel somewhere in the middle, but also outside of things.

My recent album for Mille Plateaux is called *Fragile Alliances.* The title is meant to be open-ended but evocative. Of course, I have a few thoughts about it. I was thinking about how the music often sounds like it could fall apart rhythmically or otherwise, diving into chaos or death, or simply failure and ineptitude. A 'discordination' of whatever level of self-consistency and co-operation these separated parts of the music have.

Complimentary to these more formal concerns, I was also thinking about sociopolitical unrest and how mass movements (or just everyday society and the social contract) can feel tentative, temporary or fragile. It seems hard to actually organise the left, or more broadly, the working class and other parts of society, in order to change or replace the system. It could also be a reference to a weakened or broken social contract. The music could be an abstract rendering of the unfolding polycrisis: in its sudden nervous shifts, exploded perspectives, contorted non-grooves, stumbling repeats, tense developments and violent non-sequiturs; a rendering of forces that could be liberating, but tragically morph into something cruel, dehumanising and generally world-destroying. A kind of actuality and potentiality turned inward, like some chaotic vortex or erratic cancerous body, whose systems are rapidly shifting and multiplying and tearing each other apart.

Of course, at other moments, I hear my music differently, perhaps projecting my own personal narratives and emotions into the sounds and structures, like they are a kind of artefact or representation of a broken or simply distressed mind, inner turmoil, interpersonal conflict, and occasionally lighter or more expansive moods, but generally it is a kind of angst. I also sometimes see the music in even more abstract terms (and some tracks or sections of tracks lend themselves more to this than others), in not being an interpretation of the world, or a concept exemplified, or something emotional either: musically intense but hard or impossible to describe, more 'intuited' than actually experienced; something primarily felt rather than thought (but shocking thought); something on the knife-edge of not being present at all. Perhaps this where I think I am realising my music's Ultrablack potential as a form of dark glitch: a-signifying, ineffable yet forceful, immanent, but also suggesting, through its expression or manifestation of black noise, that the world and its signs could be otherwise or just simply are, without any transcendent claim to truth. The music could also be given a more Deleuzian spin, more on the side of becoming rather than being, and evoking more the time of Aion than chronometric regularity, or something between; the music not really having a clear subject, temporality or narrative, instead haunting the threshold of what is beyond notions of identity and what exceeds experience and our normal sense of time and space.

A through-line in my music, despite the imprecision or ambiguity about what my music is really 'about', is the 'broken grid'. By this, I mean an inaudible time structure that I often decide on before I even sequence or create a single sound or decide on a general tempo. I say general because tempo is almost always only approximate in my music. You could say it's about imprecision and ambiguity also, about *when* things are *about*. The 'broken grid' also serves as an abstract, unheard structure. It is discretely sectioned, but the sections are not homogenous. It functions to condition what is heard, but also to be in excess of what is heard—an inaudible 'noise' conditioning the audible noise/music/sound. The grids are anti-grids or non-grids (non-standard grids). Ultrablack grids, if you will.

The grids are made out of unevenly sized compartments in order to structure or portion time out in unevenly timed or 'spaced' beats, bars or measures—uneven durations. The grids are cyclical, but they often cycle in odd numbers of compartments before they loop again. Frequently, these odd numbers are prime numbers such as 3, 5, 7, 11, 13, 17, and 19. The grids are not completely arrhythmic or random, but steps are taken to make them irregular. Instead of being anti-time, they have a non-standard relationship to time as it is usually deployed in music. Non-standard measures. Non-standard clocks. Marcel Duchamp's *3 Standard Stoppages* relates in an oblique way. In some ways, the grids allow a more singular and personal expression (I consciously deploy them, design them), but in other ways, they are not about my expression or intention at all, and act as a kind of foil or chaos I have to adapt to when I create music within their structures, like working with a fabric you cannot iron out, perhaps akin to a new kind of inhuman rule or measure that imposes itself from the ether.

Even if I have pre-written melody, sequence of noise(s), or beat, for example, I cannot pre-hear exactly how the grids and music will sound when applied together. The deformation is just not fully thinkable for me. I also consciously build my rhythmic, noise, drone and melodic materials in loops that are not in the same count or length as each other and differ from the 'length' (in terms of cells or compartments) of the underlying grid too. This is so that the grid is further obscured and the material placed upon it is further contorted and does not repeat for longer stretches of time than a single cycle of the grid itself. You could say the relations of the parts and the grid is very diagonal. These asymmetric diagonal relationships also create polyrhythmic and polymetric aspects that complicate the temporality further: a kind of irregular pulling back and forth in some cases, perhaps even a kind of bizarre entrainment at times.

For example: a grid with a cycle of 13 deforms everything else that is on it; beats that cycle in 7, with a melody cycling in 10, another melody in a cycle of 11, and a noise every 17 counts, and another beat in 15 might be a 'structure'.

I can predict a general vibe, but I'm still surprised by the results. The results not only effect rhythmic relations but also harmony, juxtapositions of space and different timbres, density, 'counterpoint' (non-standard, of course), where I apply effects and panning, etc. I'm still refining the grid skeletons and the 'sonic meat' I hang on them, in large part just to hear what happens—driven by obsession, play and curiosity.

In a sense, the music has a temporality that is an artefact of the collision between two or more temporal cycles intermeshing and contorting one another, with a hidden cycle (grid) conditioning all of it. It is not just polyrhythms and polymetres—I think it is 'deeper' than that, as I'm moving against ideas of regular pulsation. Sometimes, I see a connection between this work and the paintings and techniques of Francis Bacon, in that he would deliberately damage or otherwise fuck up his paintings as he worked on them, proceeding through logics of deformation and planned and intuitive 'failure'. I also see it as being akin to when two black holes collide and emit gravity waves that ripple the surface of regular space-time.

There is more I can say about pulsation: I rarely 'pulse' or place percussive sounds (or other sounds) on every grid 'compartment' in a single cycle (or in multiple cycles for that matter). In this sense, the time-structure is 'hidden' as well, as it's full of cycles of shifting gaps. Almost all of the tracks I have created hide the structure as much as they instantiate it (the pulses themselves are often strongly articulated). And those rare tracks, which sometimes 'pulse' all of the grid, often have other more irregular, sometimes one-time elements occurring as well, so I doubt it is clear to the listener. I doubt it would be clear even if unadorned—I think a loop might be perceived, but its structural relation would still be unclear unless it was very basic and the listener committed to analysing it—which is not really my concern. Clarity or quantification is not the point. It is more about quality than quantity, and also the idea of something hidden yet out in the open, the way the unheard conditions the heard and is absent yet present in it.

Perhaps all art has an aspect that is outside anything we can say, feel, interpret, see, hear or otherwise perceive about it, even if it is right in front of us. The underlying time-shape is not meant to be countable or heard directly as such. It is also not meant to convey an idea of temporal mastery, nor a total temporal randomness either. It is not about virtuosity or complexity for complexity's sake, to indicate some kind of sophistication or illusion of total control. It has to have some connection to *failure as failure*, and to something *alien*, but for me, randomness does not seem like a path forward or a path towards failure, so to speak. It seems too easy sometimes to tune randomness out or get bored by it (as a listener but also as a musician), and I want something more liminal or ambiguous but also seductive.

In the sense of being liminal and ambiguous inhuman failures, these grids and sounds are not about progress. And I mean progressive in the sense of progressive rock or so-called 'intelligent dance music', but also some other teleology. My productions are also not trying to encourage dancing or head nodding or some other standard bodily response, but they don't necessarily discourage it either. I do use 'strong' pulses, for example, but the tracks are not 'functional' like regular dance music is thought to be. That said, I do want to address the body, but in a non-standard way. Head nodding is OK, dancing is OK, but it's not the main focus; it is for the head *and* the body, but also wants to confuse, question and reconfigure both of them. *Dancing* could become other to what it normally is in this case.

In my music, there is a concern with ambivalence and ambiguity, favouring the messy or the merely approximate over the balanced and the precise. In some ways, there is a play between orientation and disorientation, formation and deformation. I orient in order to disorient and vice versa, but also to try and evoke something fuzzier and harder to parse. The temporal forms are not quite grooves, not quite syncopations, nor a kind of swing, but they sometimes reference, echo or temporarily pass in and out of these formations, depending on how the sounds placed upon them relate to each other in time and space, as affective forces and also as signs.

There is more to say on form: the music has aspects of minimalism, process music, algorithmic music, and structured modernist fragmentation, but it is also genuinely messy and intuitive in a cruder, perhaps punk or no-wave way. Sometimes, it references popular structures such as melodies, riffs, verses and choruses, grooves, drops, breakdowns, intros and outros, and slow builds and fades. The music also foils these structures and shoots itself in the foot: sometimes odd or irrational structures—such as sudden cuts or other unorthodox transitions; not repeating something when I have set up an expectation for it; combining two tracks into one where there is a clear sense of this 'split-ness' retained; cutting off a phrase mid-bar; an unexpected tempo shift; sudden noises, etc.—are created to thwart aspects of what you might call 'popular' music, but they also attempt to undermine established avant-garde or experimental music tropes too. These aspects can all be present in a single track. The general aim is to create a sense of 'failure', but there is still a sense of drama to it; the narrative function itself feels undercooked, dimmed, precarious, exaggerated, or simply under attack.

The relationship to failure (and I'm thinking of failure as glitch) is complicated. Obviously, if the music fully and truly fails, or is simply sub-mediocre by some standard or another, it's hard to wonder why I should keep doing it, except as some sort of nihilistic, despairing, obtuse or sardonic gesture, like a kind of sad (or perhaps angry) performance for an even sadder world. This may well be its fate. Or the music might be read as a gesture of my own dysfunction; perhaps heard as an artefact of mental instability, or the wasting of time that could be used more 'productively'; a sign that I'm a 'bad bet' for the future and an inefficient piece of human capital at best…

Of course, there are more benign possibilities of failure for my music. The time-feels and the sense of accuracy, predictability and skill, can vary widely in my own productions. Here I am considering the idea of a glitch from a rhythmic or timing angle, but I incorporate more 'traditional' glitches too: noise-based sounds; out-of-tune elements; lo-fidelity sounds; digital clicks, skips, cuts or other kind of errors, including analog ones, such as mangled tape recordings; record skips and electrical hums. I say 'traditional' because they are more over-determined and codified in terms of their collective meaning (and affective responses), and have lost some of their critical edge over time, or at least their edge of failure. Sometimes, they seem to stand in for clichéd ideas of a present or future dystopia, or evoke a musical nostalgia even. Or they might be used in an advertisement for a ski resort, or in a blockbuster action movie in order to convey some sort of 'edginess', in a very middle-of-the-road kind of way. This can be interesting to play with, despite (or because of) its kitsch aspect, and feed into my work's themes regardless, but I feel it is not enough on its own. The kitsch either has to be rejected, pushed to a further extreme, or recuperated or shifted in some other way. Kitsch is very stratified. This is part of my interest in these rhythmic structures—to move things closer to actual failure and noise again. In a sense, these older, more ossified glitch and noise sounds, as well as other kinds of musical sounds I use, are, for me, part of what grounds my music in music as opposed to strictly formless noise and the depths of pure failure, which is a line or precipice I want to be on the edge of.

The rhythms are also meant to evoke, at least some of the time, an idea of being or sounding *inept*, like I could not play or program a beat 'properly', so it is not just the technology that has the problem or glitch, but the person using it. But I hope I am also holding these failures up in such a way that one might challenge their biases and limits of taste, including my own. I think the sound of someone or something that is trying but failing (by a normalised standard) to accomplish something is worth some consideration. Perhaps it is the sound of a beginner, someone wounded (or simply non-standard or non-conforming), someone disabled perhaps, and other possibilities. In a sense, it's a reference to death, abjection and amateurism, but also, on a more potentially optimistic note, a reference to non-conformity, difference, different or new standards and forms of life—questioning what is merely given, and in some ways questioning or being critical of the history of the given as well. I am not necessarily claiming novelty or difference is necessarily a solution in itself either—the sound is ambivalent and polyvalent. It could be the sound of horror, or simply more of a question than an answer. It cuts against the norms of a lot of music. Why do we listen and dance to an often regularly timed beat, however syncopated, varied or swung? Why did Western and some other music in general develop as it did? Why are grooves so prominent in most of the world today? What role did capitalism play in this and how is it playing out still? What is virtuosity and what does it serve? Why are some excluded (more or less) from music and art? The rhythms in my music move with and against what is given. The rhythms are not here to claim they are better; they are here to question norms and limits, and hopefully open up other possibilities. An awkwardness or glitchiness in sound aesthetics seems a part of this questioning.

Something I am also questioning is an excessive bro-ish technicality, and also what it means to be a 'professional artist' under neoliberalism. Though centred on a computer, my music is not very technical, and I think electronic music has often been aligned with technological fetishism and techno-determinist attitudes. But I also question—as I mentioned before, with the example of the karaoke machine—ideas that technology is simply neutral as well. But returning to my process—I do use some synthesis and other 'technical' means, but it is largely made painstakingly by 'hand'. I think this might disappoint some people, whilst intriguing others. The 'algorithms' and other patterns and singular events are handmade in the sense that using a sewing machine or a knife is also to do something by hand. It is also about the difficulties and pressures of tools. Ableton Live is the main DAW I use for making edits, although it's not really designed for the kind of timing I am concerned with. It is a groove-maker, and it is often a struggle to work with. I think this technical 'weakness' in my production process, this fight with the tool, is part of what pushed my music to sound as it does, its potential for singularity. The struggle enacts, through its difficulty, the struggle with technology and the way it sediments aspects of the rest of the world: clock-time, efficiency, regular and equivalent measurements, etc.

I 'fail' as an accomplished and technical electronic musician, and my position is ambivalent towards mastery, but I push on and learn and continue to fail anyway. I am not designing or coding anything, or finding a novel way of hooking up and setting up modules. I do use software and some other sound sources, but I find the idea of having to pretend to have total or at least a high degree of control, or being held by others to some high standard, often ridiculous and stifling. It is enough to make me want to stop, and so I have to ignore it sometimes. Again, it's like I am caught in the middle and trying to deal with a pre-existing situation mostly out of my control—perhaps a metaphor for my music and other aspects of my life, maybe all of our lives, a situation worse for some rather than others; for a few, it is highly profitable and pleasurable. I used to feel bad (and often still do, honestly) about my 'low' level of technicality, but I have come to see it, in recent years, as another way to do things, connected not just to an inability and/or rejection to do things the 'right' way, but also as a kind of critique of the unrealistic and domineering expectations our society places upon us in general. (I can't find 'total liberation' in it, though.) I'm not anti-skill or anti-virtuosity, but I do think there are worthwhile things outside those concepts, some of which might also question the rigidity and application of those concepts in our current situation. I suppose I see skills and virtuosity as forms of 'technology' in a broad sense, and I'm caught in the middle, in and out of step with these 'givens'. Not totally neutral, nor 'bad' or 'good', but as something to both play with and against and to examine. These notions cannot escape being ideological and dangerous, however.

This talk of technicality and skill makes me think of musicianship and live performance: some of my music has never been 'performed' live, not even as a basic playback. But much of it has been performed, and I continue to develop and find new ways of doing so. I have, on some occasions, done things very close to pure playback, perhaps just tweaking a few effects here and there, adjusting the mix or adding in or dropping out certain elements. I have also done a slightly more involved version of this approach, where I have some improvisational control over parts of the arrangement and a few extra sounds and real-time processes I can also apply spontaneously, perhaps triggering a semi-randomised sequence of effects and samples, or various prepared melodic, harmonic and/or noise-based fragments in a kind of real-time collage. When I want things to be somewhat close or very close to what you hear in a recording, I deploy these approaches. Sometimes I loosen this up, only working with fragments of tracks I have made (among other prepared sounds and sound-making processes), also having a microphone and running my voice both relatively clean and effected through the mix in an often highly improvised fashion. This method is the most open; it is not about a faithful reproduction of the material as heard on an album at all, but obviously still gestures towards aspects of something already made, while treating it as another material to work with.

I have some skills as a fairly non-traditional 'singer', including guttural throat singing, lots of wordless sounds and some extended techniques (ingressive sounds, breathing noises, contact microphones in the mouth, singing a sound as I run out of breath, etc.), as well as 'voices' inspired by Scott Walker, Meredith Monk, Ami Yoshida, black and death metal, punk, no-wave, and a bit of R&B and other pop-influenced singing. I have never been in a proper band or made much use of words or lyrics, and even my 'pop' voices tend to be impressionistic, with words coming up here and there, often deliberately blurred and slurred, before quickly shifting techniques, registers and timbres. When I 'sing', I am often working with other improvisers (often non-electronic or who also do vocals and electronics), who elaborate on a few basic ideas I develop with them ahead of time or with no group preparation at all. I have also done fairly straight diffusions of tracks, but stripped down so people, including myself, could improvise with them, but have to follow their overall structure more or less. The singing aspect is something I have had a longstanding interest in, and is something of a workaround to the problem of 'live' performance and the difficulty of breaking my music down into more performable material. Improvising with voice (and electronic sounds and vocal processing) crucially allows me to react and respond quickly in the moment in a kind of feedback loop with myself and others. Some of the more non-standard approaches I use in singing sometimes incorporate digital vocal glitches, some subtle electronic pitch, space and timbre randomisation, singing until I run out of breath, or say, deliberately going out of my range into 'bum' notes, incorporating a kind of bodily glitch or failure.

The breakdown of my tracks for live performance is also so I don't get bored, and I guess a kind of concession to the audience to 'perform'. I'm not immune to my audience, and I have probably long since internalised aspects of it, but I do like to push the audience and myself out of our comfort zones, which paradoxically can sometimes be the precondition of success versus failure or mere mediocrity and boredom. Playback is always an option, I suppose, but in the spirit of movement, experimentation, some people-pleasing, risk, not necessarily playing 'in time' (and also introducing risk and failure), my hybrid approach of voice and somewhat live electronics (it's always 'more or less', depending on the set-up and the choices I make as it happens) seems suitable. I sometimes wish I had some sort of live algorithmic means to generate my rhythms more on the spot, but it's beyond my capacity right now, and maybe it's not really necessary either. There are a lot of potentials for how to present and shape this material in a live setting, and though I imagine some might be more pleased if I were algorithmic, that might in some ways run against (but also potentially complement) the questions around technicality (and failure) I think my work raises. I feel there is often a slippage where a kind of emphasis on de-skilling or questioning of skill or technique or technical means sliding into its opposite, especially in electronic music circles (and vice versa, perhaps), usually via the concern with software and gear. Perhaps this is a testament to the pervasiveness of the ideologies of our times and our habits and expectations around computers, but also musical tools or instruments in general and the other aspects of our lives outside art.

18. PAROXYSM OF PARALLAX SONIFIER [PPS]

By Darko Vukić

> "*The one external illusion of representation is this illusion that results from all its internal illusions—namely, that groundlessness should lack differences, when in fact it swarms with them...*" *To save the earth's sur-face from the face behind it, what is required is a chemical sensibility, since chemistry has always been the science and art of the imperceptible, of what escapes the imprisonment of sensibility behind a face ... to go directly to the earth, or to earths, to be dispersed and molecularised in the black.*
>
> — Iain Hamilton Grant, "The Chemistry of Darkness" (2000)

Ensnared by present platitudes, a certain conviction sets forth that new weapons are transpiring, through new accidental sociality in 'musical' and 'sonic' explorations (where distinction is not implied between the two). It seems that, in the midst of scientific 'positivist' knowledge, mysticism has not lost anything of its previous relevance. Mysticism, like the current musical distillation, remains most substantial on the margins of society, and we are witnessing that the interest does not stop there—on the contrary. The parallel future of musical mysticism (as a form of techno mysticism) is precisely its current agency for the future of alt politics, but paradoxically by being discrete and direct (its psyche is conservative and liberating; nothing that once existed in it is ever completely lost)—like the noise of the infinity of existence (mystics may talk about the silence of existence)—it does not disappear in granular fashion. What is offered to it as a substitute fails to satiate it, in fact the substitutes deprave it even more. In a certain way, another paradoxicality emerges here, rising from nature as opposed to the immateriality (or artificial nature) of sound, mostly being exemplified in mutation and developments of its interfaces, panning values from the universe of physically based tools and its upper axis of abstractions or sensing, not at hand but *at ear, which is also the brain*. We are interested here in the presence of mysticism in the midst of technological orders and knowledge as a sign of the presence of an 'un-archaic', 'un-anachronistic' and anarchic cultural code, whose operations we are not aware of, and whose effectiveness is no less because of that. The return of mysticism (through the domain of the sociality of music) should then be understood as the return of the code, or rather, as the need for the code unlocking, not the understanding, but the un-prehension of being.

This opens a space to initiate the concept of a 'sonifier' in music/sonic arts, as opposed, or in spite of, the 'Signifier' in language, linguistics and droning psychoanalysis. Since mysticism is not an antagonistic rationality, it appears as a primary obstacle in the process of constituting the knowledge inherent in psychoanalysis, the knowledge of the unconscious. *Epistemic transgressors judge things outside their field of expertise. One should doubt whether transgressors are reliable judges in areas where they are outsiders*. The situation here is *Un-thinged*; heuristic space, separating silence and noise, is already implied in occult systems that emphasise the importance of silence. Not in arbitrary, physical ways; rather, in its lack of conceptual stratifications—*mostly thought accretions of pneuma*. In listening, the hallucinatory prospects are in the potential of listening after listening; listening while and after producing noise, for example, unlocks unsurfaced presence in the worldly realm, where there is some sort of inclination towards a type of art that explores its own material givens, its own technical findings or hardware; *all types of art that attempt to think of its surface noise and use it as material for further work or shaping of things*. After 'things' get their respective intangible shapes, in regards to the sonifier's operandi, they start triggering, by default, some non-linguistic processes; the mechanic residual becomes exemplary of the *screeching, booming, crashing dynamism of the universal work[s]*. This middle space, which that stretches in-between, is compatible with the currency of particular mental affairs—as something that fits into the medium of sonic contingency, becoming a sonic weaponry for salvation.

With the sonifier and its possibility of inhibiting (as alienating) silence, chance comes from the assertive and accumulative nature of thought. When tuned into assemblies of concepts and meanings of noise, instead of silence we perceive assertive or accumulative noise, and what silence actually does here is amp out those assertions/accumulations. What is here a parallax function is a displacement or difference in its operator positioning. *For differentiated parts, rich contexts generate a host of required conditions at various levels for functional equivalence, and things may be functionally equivalent for some roles but not for others, or 'fine-tuned' to different degrees for a given function.*

Let us return to the mystical experience and its paradoxes. The mystical experience is as if it is not at the same time. For the non-mystic who strives to understand it, it is an experience localised in time and space, bound up with the circumstances that trigger it, some cultural framework, an encounter, or rather, it is that kind of extraordinary event in some personal history, such as incarnation, *crucifixion on the cross of ecstasy, of life*. The more complex the conceptual systems are, the more neurotic are the organisms. Noise is the development of gradual and generative additions.

The chemical conversations have not crossed the accretive threshold and hence do not fill the world with accretive chatter. However, on an ontological level, it contributes to the accretive interference that obstructs silence.

Music primarily performs reduction to avoid functional tonality as identity, conventional melody, rhythmic pulsation, and other traditional, formalist strategies. Exception is 'new complexity', which has the capacity to always gain new additional forms of understanding. It is 'quasi'-music and understands itself as the negative of tradition: that is why the not-yet-experienced, and not successfully, is purified from it as such. The meaning of this music should not lie in its immediate stimulus, but, on the contrary, in its attitude that rejects the attraction of the stimulus because of its expected plainness. An attitude that would be based on valuation has become a fiction for one who finds himself surrounded by standardised musical goods. He cannot escape its superiority, nor can he decide for something from what is presented to him, so affection is, in fact, only tied to a biographical detail or to the situation in which it is listened to. The categories of autonomous intending art have no importance in the current reception of music. Rather, it seems complementary to the dumbness of people, to the death of speech as an expression, to the inability to communicate oneself. It fills the gaps of silence, which arise among people deformed by fear, business, and unquestioning adaptability. In the capitalist era, the inherited etymological ferments of music conspired against freedom, even though they were once persecuted for their affinity towards it. Holders of opposition against the authoritarian scheme become witnesses of the authority of market success, or rather, excess. Economy of expression is a way to be, while philosophical technology has been withdrawn, and so undertaken; our only way to attack back is to sustain in a motion of decay—as it is an order of division as well as a way to be.

19. ULTRABLACK NON-FERENCE 2023

Exhibition & Conference text

By Lain Iwakura

Calling all. This is our last cry before our eternal silence.

This invitation is open to all. A call. A cry. Proposed is not a con-ference (con-ferre (lat.), bringing together), but a non-ference (to not carry). Negation, from the very beginning, always a line in the sand. A disintegration, rot and decay, coming apart and to come undone. Desonance, not resonance.

A being together in homelessness, an interplay of the refusal of what has been refused, the undercommon apositionality, a place from which emerges neither self-consciousness nor knowledge of the other, but an improvisation that proceeds from somewhere on the other side of an unasked question. The barbarian waiting before and after civilisation. Untimeliness.

Discord with the false present.

Ultrablackness is a determining force. The outside folding in. Background noise of the thermodynamic disequilibrium. An indifferent un-groundedness, opaque like a heterogeneous mixture, or transparent like see-through fluids.

Not to be differentiated, but the 0 that defines 1.

Ultrablackness, therefore, is not to be confused with the void—emptiness—but is intrinsically messy. That which messes with the attempt to define, to limit, and territorialise; a demonic force subverting the godly order, defying the One-God-Universe. Black noise, unlike the searing buzz of white noise, is barely audible. Black noise traces the quiver of things we fail to perceive. Our uchromia: to learn to think from the point of view of Black, as what determines colour in the last instance, rather than what limits it.

Simplify colour! See black, think white! See black rather than believe 'unconscious.' And think white rather than believe 'conscious.'

Don't see, be a seer. Stop seeing and start visioning. Be a visionary.

Ultrablack—blacker than black—denotes practices of negation, deconstruction, non-philosophy, pessimism and nihilism, heterogeneity, disintegration, queering, noise, insurrection, etc., etc. "Everything has to be rejected—and everything has to be rethought. It needs an act of major and painful disruption, an act of distancing, maybe even of violently marking a break, a rupture, a stopping of routine communication: the axe that is hacked into the table during conversation. It is a kind of disaster studies, an act that breaks down the formal structures of space and time. In the mimicry of this approach to electronic music, both in science and in music, the formal structures of time collapse, regress to mud, and space is pushed back and forth until it bends to be trampled by the pulsations of alien music, while the thinking space becomes seasick: this is the disruption as it can be experienced when ultrablackness hits you. When the all-consuming, all absorbing and all-imploding might of ultrablackness exercises its power of radical, pervasive and fundamental negation. The one message, the one action, the one intervention of ultrablackness is taking an axe and ramming it into the fake common ground or shared table and saying: NO.

20. CONTRIBUTORS BIOS

ACHIM SZEPANSKI (ed.)

*Achim Szepanski initiated the internationally renowned network around the labels Force Inc, Mille Plateaux, Position Chrome, Communism Records and many more. In 2012, he published the novels *Saal 6* and *Pole Position*. He then published several books on the theory of Marxism with Laika-Verlag. His book *Kapital und Macht im 21. Jahrhundert* (2018, Laika-Verlag) was recently published in English and Chinese translations. He runs the online platform NON (non.copyriot.com) for Biopolitics, EconoFiction, GenericScience, Mashines, Necropolitics, NonMusic and PhiloFiction.

PALAIS SINCLAIRE (ed.)

*Having submitted their BA Dissertation, which focused on the music of Ayahuasca ritualism, under Sociology of Music, Sinclaire went on to study MA Ethnomusicology at Goldsmiths University. At the same time, they started visiting Cyprus and became involved with the rave scene there, leading to an MA thesis that focused on Rave Culture and Electronic Music in Cyprus. During this time, they fell in love with the Island of Venus, and immediately moved there upon graduating. Since then, they have raved a lot, performed scores of gigs, founded a fanzine and record label called *Cross-dressing Diogenes*, and then came out as transgender. After five years of raving whilst writing about raving, they founded *Becoming* with Polymnia, and has since published four books, including Achim Szepanski's *In the Delirium of the Simulation: Baudrillard Revisited.*

Sinclaire, as a writer, is currently working towards a framework for a 'quantum sociology' inspired by the strange combination of Lucretius and Baudrillard.

ALBERTO RICCA

*Alberto Ricca is Bienoise—laptop composer, teacher, and independent researcher. Spending his formative years in a pre-internet quiet place, he developed a fascination for extreme and forgotten sound objects. This led to *Most Beautiful Design*, a mini-album of low-quality MP3 compositions, released on floppy disk in 2018 by the cult label Mille Plateaux, which also released the album *THIS MEANING TODAY* in June 2022.

In 2014, he was the Italian participant in Tokyo for the Red Bull Music Academy. His music has also been released by C2C Festival, Artetetra, White Forest, Enklav and many other labels. Since 2017, Alberto has scored contemporary dance pieces with Annamaria Ajmone ("To be Banned from Rome"), the movement research collective Parini Secondo ("SPEEED", BE ME, HIT"), and Jacopo Jenna ("DANSE MACABRE!", Here and Now"). Since 2019, Radio Raheem Milan has been hosting NON MUSIC, his monthly selection of unintentional compositions.

He founded, with Davide Merlino, the Verbania-based radical improvisation label Floating Forest.

He teaches Synthesis and Performing Techniques at IED Milan. He studied Electronic Music and Sound Technology at the Como Conservatory, and Media Languages at Università Cattolica in Milan.

His articles, inquiring tools, symbols and value in Art and Culture are published by NON and NERO.

He is not a DJ.

ALESSANDRO SBORDONI

*Born in Cagliari in 1995, Sbordoni is the author of *The Shadow of Being: Symbolic / Diabolic* (Miskatonic Virtual University Press, 2023) and *Semiotics of the End: On Capitalism and the Apocalypse* (Institute of Network Cultures, 2023). He is an Editor of the British magazine Blue Labyrinths and the Italian magazine Charta Sporca. He lives in London and works for the Open Access publisher Frontiers.

ANDREA TAEGGI

*Andrea Taeggi is a composer, live performer, and electronic music producer based in Berlin. He operates under his real name as well as the aliases 5HT2 and formerly as Gondwana. He is also known for his work with Koenraad Ecker in Lumisokea. He has releases on labels such as Mille Plateaux/Force Inc., Präsens Editionen, Opal Tapes, Alter, and Hands in the Dark, and has worked on 22 albums, counting his collaborative and solo projects, spanning vinyl, cassette, dubplate, and digital formats.

A graduate of the Amsterdam Conservatoire with a degree in piano, his interests evolved from free-jazz to electro-acoustic and electronic music. He now focuses on composed music while infusing elements of surprise and impromptu into his practices.

Andrea has performed at renowned venues and festivals worldwide, including Cafe OTO, CTM, Mutek, and Moers Festival. He has also collaborated with sound research institutes such as STEIM Amsterdam, EMS Stockholm, and Willem-Twee in the Netherlands to further develop his exploration of analog synthesis and composition techniques.

In addition to his music studies, he holds a Bachelor's degree in Psychology from Milano Bicocca University. His thesis focused on the systemic-relational model in psychotherapy, informed by his internship at a facility for abused children. Fascinated by the intersection of neurosciences, the arts, and psychedelics, Andrea continues to explore these areas in his creative work.

DARKO VUKIĆ

*Darko Vukić, also known as Sava Zolog, is a transdisciplinary artist, curator, and writer; defines the working process as a specific linguistic happening, or situation that often transforms into entropy; occasionally collaborates with various partners and cultural agencies on projects. After leaving behind a background in fine-transmedia-arts and the artistic scene of Belgrade in 2022, he is currently focusing on music and sound research, starting at the Tangible Music Lab (Kunstuniversität/ABPU) in Linz, and furthering it elsewhere.

ELDRITCH PRIEST

*Eldritch Priest writes on sonic culture, experimental aesthetics, and the philosophy of experience from a pataphysical perspective. He is Associate Professor in the School for the Contemporary Arts at Simon Fraser University. Eldritch is also a composer and improviser, as well as a member of the experimental theory group "The Occulture." He is the author of several essays and books including *Boring Formless Nonsense: Experimental Music and the Aesthetics of Failure* (Bloomsbury 2013), and most recently, *Earworm and Event: Music, Daydreams, and Other Imaginary Refrains* (Duke University Press 2022).

EUGENE THACKER

*Eugene Thacker is the author of several books, including *In the Dust of This Planet* and *Infinite Resignation*.

FRÉDÉRIC NEYRAT

*Professor in the English department of UW-Madison (USA), Frédéric Neyrat is a French philosopher with expertise in environmental humanities, contemporary theory, and media culture. He is co-editor of the electronic platform Alienocene, which charts the burgeoning field of Planetary Humanities. Recently, he published *The Unconstructable Earth: An Ecology of Separation* (Fordham, 2018), *Literature and Materialisms* (Routledge, 2020), *L'Ange Noir de l'Histoire: Cosmos et Technique de l'Afrofuturisme* (MF, 2021), *Cosmos Expérimental* (Abrüpt, 2022), and *Le Cosmos de Walter Benjamin: Un Communisme du Lointain* (Kimé, 2022). His books and articles offer a "new existentialism", regenerating the place of the outside that contemporary theory underestimates. Website: Atopies (http://atoposophie.wordpress.com).

GARY J. SHIPLEY

*Gary J. Shipley is the author of numerous books, including *On the Verge of Nothing*, *Stratagem of the Corpse*, *The House Inside the House of Gregor Schneider*, *Warewolff!*, *So Beautiful and Elastic*, *Terminal Park*, and *30 Fake Beheadings*. More information can be found at Thek Prosthetics.

GIORGI VACHNADZE

*Giorgi Vachnadze is a Foucault and Wittgenstein scholar. He completed his Bachelor studies at New Mexico State University and received a Master's qualification in philosophy at the University of Louvain. Former editor and peer-reviewer for the Graduate Student Journal of philosophy, *The Apricot*, he has been published in multiple popular and academic journals worldwide.

Vachnadze's research focuses on philosophy of language and discourse analysis. Some of the questions and themes addressed in his work include: history of combat sports, ancient stoicism, genealogies of truth, histories of formal systems, genealogy of science, ethics in A.I. and psychoanalysis, media archaeology, game studies and more. Vachnadze's forthcoming book *Christian Eschatology of Artificial Intelligence* is scheduled for publication in Berlin with Becoming Press.

HOLGER SCHULZE

*Holger Schulze is full professor in musicology at the University of Copenhagen and principal investigator at the Sound Studies Lab. His sonic anthropology explores how sounds and listening in the 21st century stabilize, disrupt and permeate everyday life. Artistic practices and mundane commodities are of equal concern to his sonic critique. Currently he writes a book on *Meme Music*, works on *The Bloomsbury Encyclopedia of Sound Studies* in 3 volumes (as one of three editor-in-chiefs together with Jennifer Stoever and Michael Bull) and on *The Bloomsbury Handbook of Sound in Museums* (together with Alcina Cortez, Gabriele Rossi Rognoni and Eric de Visscher). Publications: *Sonic Fiction* (2020), *The Bloomsbury Handbook of Sound Art* (2020, co-ed.), *The Sonic Persona* (2018), *Sound as Popular Culture* (2016, co-ed.).

JAN HEINTZ

*Jan Heintz is a writer, translator and curator. Besides their political translations of Serafinski's *Blessed is the Flame* (2024), Joshua Clover's *Riot.Strike.Riot* (2021), and other collaborations (Sören Mau's *Communism is Freedom*, Jacobin Magazine 2023), Jan is involved in *Mille Plateaux/Force Inc.*, and translator/copyeditor/proofreader of Achim Szepanski's recent new books and textual output. Jan is currently working on their first book.

JENS SCHRÖTER

*Jens Schröter, Prof. Dr, has held the Chair of Media Studies at the University of Bonn since 2015. From 2008–2015 Professor for "Theory and Practice of Multimedia Systems" (W2) at the University of Siegen; 2010–2014, project leader (together with Prof. Dr Lorenz Engell, Weimar) for "The Television Series as Projection and Reflection of Change" within the DFG-SPP 1505: Mediatised Worlds. Since October 2018, spokesperson of the research project (VW Foundation; together with Prof. Dr Gabriele Gramelsberger; Dr Stefan Meretz; Dr Hanno Pahl and Dr Manuel Scholz-Wäckerle) "Society after Money—A Simulation" (four years). Head (together with Prof. Dr Anna Echterhölter; PD Dr Sudmann and Prof. Dr Alexander Waibel) of the VW Main Grant "How is Artificial Intelligence Changing Science?" (start: 1.8.2022, four years); Winter 2021/22: Fellowship, Center of Advanced Internet Studies. Current publications: Media and Economics, Wiesbaden: Springer 2019; (together with Christoph Ernst): Media Futures. Theory and Aesthetics, Basingstoke: Palgrave 2021. Visit www.medienkulturwissenschaft-bonn.de / www.theorie-der-medien.de / www.fanhsiu-kadesch.de.

KENJI SIRATORI

*Kenji Siratori is a Japanese glitch writer and posthuman pornographer. His notable works include *Blood Electric* and *Paracelsus*.

LAIN IWAKURA

*Lain Iwakura is a sound & performance artist, DJ, sound engineer, writer and activist based in Graz. She studied musicology & sociology in Frankfurt, currently computer music in Graz, and is a scholarship student for Art & Curatorial Practice at The New Centre for Research & Practice. Together with Achim Szepanski, she runs the two music labels Force Inc. & Mille Plateaux. In Graz, she co-founded the collective "O", is part of the "Institute for Sonic Welfare", and in the music team of Forum Stadtpark, as well as co-founder of the awareness group "awaGraz", and member of the collective "CMKK".

LUIGI MONTEANNI & GABRIELE DE SETA

*Luigi Monteanni is a PhD candidate in Music Studies at SOAS (London). He researches the relationships between contemporary transnational popular music and regional music through the indigenisation of extreme metal in Bandung, Indonesia. He is also the co-founder of Artetetra Records: a music label and collective pursuing practice-based inquiries regarding notions of digital folklore and exoticism in late globalisation. Among others, he has written for EHESS & University of Montreal, CTM Mag, Norient, Aural Archipelago, Dancecult and Ableton. His music and collaborations have been released on Canti Magnetici, Communion, Iron Lung, Discrepant and HAEKALU Records.

*Gabriele de Seta is, technically, a sociologist. He is a Researcher at the University of Bergen, where he leads the ALGOFOLK project ("Algorithmic folklore: The mutual shaping of vernacular creativity and automation"), funded by a Trond Mohn Foundation Starting Grant (2024–2028).

Gabriele holds a PhD from the Hong Kong Polytechnic University and was a Postdoctoral Researcher at the Institute of Ethnology, Academia Sinica and at the University of Bergen, where he was part of the ERC-funded project "Machine Vision in Everyday Life". His research work, grounded on qualitative and ethnographic methods, focuses on digital media practices, sociotechnical infrastructures and vernacular creativity in the Chinese-speaking world. He is also interested in experimental, creative and collaborative approaches to knowledge-production.

OBSOLETE CAPITALISM

*Obsolete Capitalism is a collective for pure independent research. Self-defined as "gypsy scholars", the collective deals with philosophy, art and politics. Obsolete Capitalism have edited and published *Moneta, rivoluzione e filosofia dell'avvenire. Deleuze, Foucault, Guattari, Klossowski e la politica accelerazionista di Nietzsche* (OCFP, 2016), *Archeologia delle minoranze* (OCFP, 2015) and *Birth of Digital Populism* (OCFP, 2014). With Rizosfera edizioni, Obsolete Capitalism published *Deleuze and the Algorithm of the Revolution* (Rizosfera/SF004), *The strong of the future. Nietzsche's accelerationist fragment in Deleuze and Guattari's Anti-Oedipus* (Rizosfera/SF001), *Acceleration, Revolution and Money in Deleuze and Guattari's Anti-Oedipus* (Rizosfera/SF002) and *Dromology, Bolidism and Marxist Accelerationism* (Rizosfera/SF009). The collective also edits the online blogs Obsolete Capitalism, Rizomatika and Variazioni foucaultiane. The collective has a sonic sub-unit under the Obsolete Capitalism Sound System moniker; it has released *La machine informatique dub* (first 12" EP, NUKFM label, 2016) and *Chaos Sive Natura* (first album, NUKFM, 2017).

ROSS BIRDWISE

*Ross Birdwise is a musician and artist who largely works in electronic media and with their voice. Temporality is an ongoing theme. Sounds, images and other media evoke different space-times; treating time like a stretchable, foldable, cuttable and collage-able fabric. Their work aims to trigger reflections on phenomenological, psychic, technological, social and political realities, and also seeks to play with more immediately affective aspects of sound and image.

STEFAN PAULUS

*Stefan Paulus is a multimedia artist (www.2xb.org) and Professor at the Eastern Switzerland University of Applied Sciences.

CULTURE, SOCIETY & POLITICS

Contemporary culture has eliminated the concept and public figure of the intellectual. A cretinous anti-intellectualism presides, cheer-led by hacks in the pay of multinational corporations who reassure their bored readers that there is no need to rouse themselves from their stupor. Zer0 Books knows that another kind of discourse—intellectual without being academic, popular without being populist—is not only possible but already flourishing. Zer0 is convinced that in the unthinking, blandly consensual culture in which we live, critical and engaged theoretical reflection is more important than ever before.

If you have enjoyed this book, why not tell other readers by posting a review on your preferred book site.

You may also wish to subscribe to our Zer0 Books YouTube Channel.

Bestsellers from Zer0 Books include:

Poor but Sexy
Culture Clashes in Europe East and West
Agata Pyzik
How the East stayed East and the West stayed West.
Paperback:978-1-78099-394-2 ebook: 978-1-78099-395-9

An Anthropology of Nothing in Particular
Martin Demant Frederiksen
A journey into the social lives of meaninglessness.
Paperback: 978-1-78535-699-5 ebook: 978-1-78535-700-8

In the Dust of This Planet
Horror of Philosophy vol. 1
Eugene Thacker
In the first of a series of three books on the Horror of Philosophy, *In the Dust of This Planet* offers the genre of horror as a way of thinking about the unthinkable.
Paperback: 978-1-84694-676-9 ebook: 978-1-78099-010-1

The End of Oulipo?
An Attempt to Exhaust a Movement
Lauren Elkin, Veronica Esposito
Paperback: 978-1-78099-655-4 ebook: 978-1-78099-656-1

Capitalist Realism
Is There No Alternative?
Mark Fisher
An analysis of the ways in which capitalism has presented itself as the only realistic political-economic system.
Paperback: 978-1-84694-317-1 ebook: 978-1-78099-734-6

Rebel Rebel
Chris O'Leary
David Bowie: every single song. Everything you want to know, everything you didn't know.
Paperback: 978-1-78099-244-0 ebook: 978-1-78099-713-1

Cartographies of the Absolute
Alberto Toscano, Jeff Kinkle
An aesthetics of the economy for the twenty-first century.
Paperback: 978-1-78099-275-4 ebook: 978-1-78279-973-3

Malign Velocities
Accelerationism and Capitalism
Benjamin Noys
Long-listed for the Bread and Roses Prize 2015, *Malign Velocities* argues against the need for speed, tracking acceleration as the symptom of the ongoing crises of capitalism.
Paperback: 978-1-78279-300-7 ebook: 978-1-78279-299-4

Babbling Corpse
Vaporwave and the Commodification of Ghosts
Grafton Tanner
Paperback: 978-1-78279-759-3 ebook: 978-1-78279-760-9

New Work New Culture
Work we want and a culture that strengthens us
Frithjof Bergmann
A serious alternative for humankind and the planet.
Paperback: 978-1-78904-064-7 ebook: 978-1-78904-065-4

Romeo and Juliet in Palestine
Teaching Under Occupation
Tom Sperlinger
Life in the West Bank, the nature of pedagogy, and the role of a university under occupation.
Paperback: 978-1-78279-637-4 ebook: 978-1-78279-636-7

Color, Facture, Art and Design
Iona Singh
This materialist definition of fine art develops guidelines for architecture, design, cultural studies, and ultimately, social change.
Paperback: 978-1-78099-629-5 ebook: 978-1-78099-630-1

Sweetening the Pill
or How We Got Hooked on Hormonal Birth Control
Holly Grigg-Spall
Has contraception liberated or oppressed women?
Sweetening the Pill breaks the silence on the dark side of hormonal contraception.
Paperback: 978-1-78099-607-3 ebook: 978-1-78099-608-0

Why Are We the Good Guys?
Reclaiming Your Mind from the Delusions of Propaganda
David Cromwell
A provocative challenge to the standard ideology that Western power is a benevolent force in the world.
Paperback: 978-1-78099-365-2 ebook: 978-1-78099-366-9

The Writing on the Wall
On the Decomposition of Capitalism and its Critics
Anselm Jappe, Alastair Hemmens
A new approach to the meaning of social emancipation.
Paperback: 978-1-78535-581-3 ebook: 978-1-78535-582-0

Neglected or Misunderstood
The Radical Feminism of Shulamith Firestone
Victoria Margree
An interrogation of issues surrounding gender, biology, sexuality, work, and technology, and the ways in which our imaginations continue to be in thrall to ideologies of maternity and the nuclear family.
Paperback: 978-1-78535-539-4 ebook: 978-1-78535-540-0

How to Dismantle the NHS in 10 Easy Steps
(Second Edition)
Youssef El-Gingihy
The story of how your NHS was sold off and why you will have to buy private health insurance soon. A new expanded second edition with chapters on junior doctors' strikes and government blueprints for US-style healthcare.
Paperback: 978-1-78904-178-1 ebook: 978-1-78904-179-8

Digesting Recipes
The Art of Culinary Notation
Susannah Worth
A recipe is an instruction, the imperative tone of the expert, but this constraint can offer its own kind of potential. A recipe need not be a domestic trap but might instead offer escape—something to fantasise about or aspire to.
Paperback: 978-1-78279-860-6 ebook: 978-1-78279-859-0

Most titles are published in paperback and as an ebook. Paperbacks are available in traditional bookshops. Both print and ebook formats are available online.
Follow us at:
https://www.facebook.com/ZeroBooks
https://twitter.com/Zer0Books
https://www.instagram.com/zero.books